Building for Life

ISLAND PRESS is a trademark of The Center for Resource Economics.

Library of Congress Cataloging-in-Publication data.
Kellert, Stephen R.
  Building for life : designing and understanding the human-nature connection / Stephen R. Kellert.
      p. cm.
  Includes bibliographical references and index.
  ISBN 1-55963-721-8 (pbk. : alk. paper)—ISBN 1-55963-673-4 (cloth : alk. paper)
  1. Nature—Psychological aspects. 2. Architecture—Environmental aspects. I. Title.
BF353.5.N37K45 2005
155.9'1—dc22

                                                    2005017200

British Cataloguing-in-Publication data available.
Printed on recycled, acid-free paper ♲
Design by Brian Barth
Manufactured in the United States of America
10 9 8 7 6 5 4 3 2 1

Building for Life

Designing and Understanding the Human-Nature Connection

Stephen R. Kellert

ISLANDPRESS

Washington • Covelo • London

Contents

Acknowledgments

Any book that attempts to tackle a subject as vast and little understood as the human relationship to nature inevitably benefits from the knowledge and assistance of many others who have helped over the years. I deeply appreciate having received all this wisdom and goodwill, which I can only briefly and superficially acknowledge here. Moreover, I will inadvertently neglect to cite many who have assisted me, and I apologize to them in advance.

On the connection between humans and the natural environment, I owe a special thanks to Gaboury Benoit, Bob Pyle, Peter Kahn, David Orr, the late Elizabeth Lawrence, Tom Mumbray, Chris Myers, the late Paul Shepard, Terrill Shorb and Yvette Schnoeker-Shorb, Gus Speth, and Edward O. Wilson as well as many past or present students, particularly Nicole Ardoin, Tori Derr, Syma Ebbin, Kevin Eddings, Tim Farnham, Iona Hawken, Laly Lichtenfeld, Jai Mehta, Bob Powell, Sorrayut Ratanapojnard, Terry Terhaar, Christy Vollbracht, and Rich Wallace.

I also owe considerable thanks to many who have expanded my understanding of the theory and practice of sustainable—or what I prefer to call restorative environmental design. Some of these persons include Jim Axley, Bill Browning, Randy Croxton, Judith Heerwagen,

Grant Hildebrand, Steve Kieran, Rafael Pelli, Jonathan Rose, Don Watson, and many current or previous students, including Javier González-Campaña, Marty Mador, Terrence Miller, and Ben Shepherd. I am particularly indebted to Marty Mador, who helped me complete the final draft.

As always, I owe a special thanks to many at Island Press for their extremely valuable editing assistance, which certainly resulted in a far better book than originally submitted—most particularly Jeff Hardwick and Heather Boyer as well as James Nuzum, Barbara Dean, and Dan Sayre.

Finally, I very much appreciate those kind enough to allow me to use their illustrations, including Stefan Behnisch, Kent Bloomer, Bill Browning, Walter Cahn, Randy Croxton, Javier González-Campaña, Sir Norman Foster, Alexandra Halsey, Grant Hildebrand, Sir Michael Hopkins, Cilla Kellert, Frances Kuo, William McDonough, Steven Peck, Cesar Pelli, Alan Short, Mike Taylor, and John Todd.

Introduction

Interaction with nature is critically important to human well-being and development, but sadly has become compromised and diminished in modern times. Through deliberate design, this connection can be repaired and restored. Unfortunately, contemporary society has become confused about the role of the natural environment in people's physical and mental lives. Many believe that the progress of civilization depends on subjugating and converting, if not conquering, the natural world. Indeed, many see this progression as the essence of civilization.[1]

Why should they presume this to be so? First, most people recognize that the production of huge food surpluses by a tiny fraction of the population permits others to obtain their basic needs at relatively low cost and to exercise an extraordinary degree of mobility. Producing such surpluses has until now relied on the wholesale conversion of natural habitats into vast monocultures used to grow a small number of crops or raise a few species of livestock at massive industrial scales. Second, modern society has made a range of manufactured products available far beyond what even the richest would have thought possible a millennium ago. The variety of goods available at a typical mall today dwarfs what the most privileged nobility would have experienced in the past. This contemporary level of consumption has depended until now on massively extracting, fabricating from, and then disposing of huge quantities of natural resources. Third, most people today anticipate relatively good health and long lives, which they attribute primarily to the miracles of modern medicine, whose "conquest of disease" has largely relied on suppressing other life forms through championing antiseptic conditions.

All these trends of subjugating and eliminating wild nature have, at least until recently, been supported by the conventional design and development of the human-built, principally urban environment. It is sobering to realize that only two centuries ago, Great Britain was the first nation to have a majority of its population residing in an urban area, now arguably the most common feature of modern life.[2] Today, some two-thirds of the developed world lives within the shadow of a metropolitan area. And the greatest migration in human history is happening now, as hundreds of millions of people migrate from the countryside to the cities in China, India, and elsewhere.

Urbanization has historically relied on converting natural diversity into largely homogenous landscapes of impervious surface, consuming enormous amounts of resources and materials, and generating huge quantities of waste and pollutants. Consequently, the modern urban environment now consumes some 40 percent of energy resources, 30 percent of natural resources, and 25 percent of freshwater resources while generating one-third of air and water pollutants and 25 percent of solid wastes.[3] This prevailing paradigm of urban development is neither necessary nor sustainable and constitutes more a design deficiency than an intrinsic and inevitable flaw of modern life. Still, these tendencies have collectively encouraged many to believe that the benefits of contemporary society depend on massively exploiting, if not conquering, the natural world. For many, progress and civilization have been equated with humanity's distance from and subjugation of nature.

Nonetheless, most people continue to intuit that the health and diversity of the environment are fundamentally related to their own physical, mental, and even spiritual well-being.[4] Most sense that the natural world is far more connected to the quality of their lives than is revealed through the narrow metrics of material production and modern economics. In poll after poll in the United States and in other countries, the majority of respondents cite the environment as important.[5] The stubborn belief persists that the natural environment is profoundly related to people's physical, psychological, and moral well-being, an assumption that is reflected in many of our preferences, cultural creations, and constructions. Our connection to nature figures into the materials we choose, the decorations we employ, the recreational choices we make, the places we live, and the stories we tell. Nature continues to dominate the forms, patterns, and language of everyday life, despite the impression that, in a narrow technical sense, the natural world often seems neither necessary nor germane to the functioning of a modern urban society.

Despite the evident connections, contemporary society still fails to recognize and defend the importance of healthy and diverse natural systems to sustaining the quality of people's lives, especially in urban areas. Perhaps we have taken for granted what has always been readily available, like a fish failing to recognize the virtues of its water realm. The presence of the natural world has been an unquestioned constant for much of human history, generally noticed only as an adversary or appreciated only when no longer accessible. We have only recently encountered nearly ubiquitous environmental damage and a feeling of alienation from nature produced by huge human populations, consumption, urbanization, resource depletion, waste generation, pollution, and chemical contamination.[6] Only during the past fifty years has the scale of our excesses fundamentally altered the earth's atmospheric chemistry, causing the widespread loss of biological diversity and even threatening the future of human existence.

Thus, we confront two warring premises in contemporary society regarding our relationship with the natural world. On the one hand is the widespread belief that the successes of the modern world depend on controlling and converting nature. On the other hand rests the persistent impression that human physical, mental, and even spiritual well-being relies on experiencing healthy and diverse natural systems. This book explores and defends the latter view, that nature—even in our modern urban society—remains an indispensable, irreplaceable basis for human fulfillment. It examines how degrading healthy connections to the natural world impoverishes our material and moral capacity. Finally, it addresses how through deliberate design we may restore the basis for a more compatible and even harmonious relationship with nature.

The focus is thus on three major issues. First, empirical evidence from diverse sources is marshaled to support the contention that experiencing natural process and diversity is critical to human material and mental well-being. Second, childhood is considered as the time when experiencing nature is most essential to human physical and mental maturation, even for a species capable of lifelong learning. Unfortunately, for both children and adults an impoverished natural environment has become widely common, especially in urban areas. Thus, the book's final section considers how a new paradigm of designed development can help reestablish the beneficial experience of nature in the modern built environment.

Underlying much of this examination of humans and nature is the concept of biophilia.[7] *Biophilia* refers to humans' inherent affinity for the natural world, which is revealed in nine

basic environmental values (discussed in chapter two). Developing these nine values can foster physical capacity, material comfort, intellectual development, emotional maturation, creative ability, moral conviction, and spiritual meaning. The inherent inclination to attach value
to nature, however, is a "weak" genetic tendency whose full and functional development
depends on sufficient experience, learning, and cultural support.

The adaptive interaction of culture and nature is vital at any point in a person's life. But,
because this interdependence is biologically based, it is logical to assume that the most critical period in this formative development is likely childhood.[8] Young people need to engage
the natural world repeatedly and in multiple ways to mature effectively. Yet, for many children as well as for adults, modern society has produced an increasingly compromised and
degraded natural environment that offers far fewer opportunities to experience satisfying
contact with nature as an integral part of ordinary life.[9] The many symptoms of this declining condition include extensive air and water pollution, fragmented landscapes, widespread
loss of natural habitats, destruction of biological diversity, climate change, and resource depletion. These trends have resulted in threats not only to human physical and material security
but also to nature's role as an essential medium for people's emotional, intellectual, and moral
development.

These deficiencies of modern life can be ameliorated through adopting an innovative
approach to the design and development of the human built environment. This new paradigm,
called *restorative environmental design,* focuses on how we can avoid excessively consuming energy,
resources, and materials; generating massive amounts of waste and pollutants; and separating
and alienating people from the natural world. As intimated earlier, the current environmental
crisis is considered a design failure rather than an unavoidable aspect of modern life. Both the
knowledge and the technology exist to better reconcile and even harmonize the natural and
human environments. However, meeting this enormous challenge will require two conditions.
First, we must minimize and mitigate the adverse environmental effects of modern construction
and development. Second, and just as important, we must design the built environment to provide sufficient and satisfying contact between people and nature.

In recent years, alternative design and development approaches—commonly referred to
as "sustainable" or "green" design—have emerged that focus on minimizing the adverse effects
of the built environment on nature and on human health. The label "restorative environmental
design" is used here instead of "green design" because the former underscores the need to
also reestablish positive connections between nature and humanity in the built environment.
The damage caused to natural systems and human health by modern construction can be min-

imized and mitigated through many strategies, including pursuing energy efficiency, using renewable energy, reducing resource consumption, reusing and recycling products and materials, lessening waste and pollution, employing nontoxic substances and materials, protecting indoor environmental quality, and avoiding habitat destruction and loss of biodiversity. This overall objective is called *low environmental impact design,* a necessary but by itself insufficient basis for true sustainable design and development. Although essential and challenging, low environmental impact design ignores the equally important need to restore beneficial contact between people and nature in the built environment. Unfortunately, low environmental impact design has become the primary approach of sustainable design and development today.

The additional objective of fostering satisfying contact between people and nature in the built environment is called positive environmental impact, or "biophilic," design. *Biophilic design* includes two basic dimensions: organic (or naturalistic) design and vernacular (or place-based) design. *Organic design* involves the use of shapes and forms in buildings and landscapes that directly, indirectly, or symbolically elicit people's inherent affinity for the natural environment. This effect can be achieved through the use of natural lighting, ventilation, and materials; the presence of water and vegetation; decoration and ornamentation that mimics natural forms and processes; and other means. *Vernacular design* refers to buildings and landscapes that foster an attachment to place by connecting culture, history, and ecology within a geographic context.

Thus, restorative environmental design incorporates the complementary goals of minimizing harm and damage to natural systems and human health as well as enriching the human body, mind, and spirit by fostering positive experiences of nature in the built environment. As we shall see, each of the major design emphases associated with restorative environmental design—low environmental impact design and the two aspects of biophilic design, organic and vernacular design—is an outgrowth of three theories (described in chapter three) that explain how natural systems affect human physical and mental well-being. Specifically, (1) low environmental impact design sustains various ecosystem services on which human existence relies, (2) organic design fosters various benefits people derive from their tendency to value nature (biophilia), and (3) vernacular design enables a satisfying connection to the places where people live, also a necessary condition of human well-being.

The final chapter summarizes and integrates the various scientific, theoretical, and practical considerations of this book by addressing the ethics of sustainable development. It examines how the connection between human and natural systems—particularly this connection's importance during the childhood years and the challenge of restoring beneficial connections between the natural and human built environments through deliberate design—is fundamentally an issue of values and, ultimately, of ethics. It confronts such basic considerations as how we think we fit into the natural world and how the relationship between nature and humanity reflects our basic conceptions of what is good, right, fulfilling, and just.

Most "utilitarian" approaches to these ethical questions emphasize how protecting nature sustains people's physical and material existence. Yet many view this ethical point of view as too narrow, advocating instead that we protect and sustain the natural environment for its intrinsic importance, independent of its material benefit to people. Positing that both of these ethical approaches are flawed and insufficient, this book instead advances a greatly expanded utilitarian ethic of sustainability that promotes the health and integrity of natural systems not only for their physical and material rewards but also because they advance equally important human emotional, intellectual, and spiritual needs. This ethic of sustainability embraces a vastly expanded understanding of human self-interest that reaches far beyond the cramped confines of economic materialism or the unrealistic idealism of nature's value independent of human welfare. This broad utilitarian ethic recognizes and affirms how the natural world serves as an indispensable basis for what it means to be not only physically and materially secure but also emotionally and intellectually whole, endowed with a sense of love and beauty, and reverent of creation.

The book addresses many complicated aspects of the connection between nature and humanity throughout the human life cycle and how we may design, develop, and sustain this relationship. These considerations raise complex matters of science, theory, policy, practice, and philosophy and inevitably confront many unknowns. However, we can learn and communicate only so much through the limited language and discourse of empirical science and rational management. In such circumstances, we can also rely on a measure of speculation and subjectivity when considering such complicated issues. Thus, this book closes by invoking another well-established tradition used to foster understanding, one that depends more on intuition and introspection: the narrative, or storytelling, tradition. Specifically, this book concludes with a narrative epilogue, using storytelling to achieve a richer, fuller comprehension of a more compatible—even harmonious—connection between nature and humanity. The stories confront the same issues addressed in the earlier, more scientific and management-oriented chapters, but this time in a personal, subjective fashion.

The narrative epilogue includes five related stories, which follow a hypothetical person through varying stages of his life, from middle childhood to late adolescence to early adulthood to middle age to a final narrative involving his children and his children's children. The first story, which begins in 1955, portrays the world of a six-year-old boy. This is a time rich in exploration, discovery, creativity, and imagination as well as contest and confrontation. The boy's world consists of family, friends, neighbors, and the familiar critters of nearby nature. This is also a time of challenge and loss for the boy, a period when his relation to nature becomes a source of enduring value and security.

The second story occurs in the early 1970s, a time of late adolescence marked by struggle and turmoil. The context is suburban, a housing development in a rapidly expanding town where roads are designed to accommodate traffic rather than pedestrians and where shopping malls are replacing local establishments. Pockets of richly textured nature nonetheless remain, places where an adolescent can encounter remnants of wonder and inspiration. The narrative's focus is this rapidly changing social and environmental milieu and the child's shift from adolescence to a more autonomous adulthood.

The third story occurs in 1985 during early adulthood, a time of economic and social aspiration and striving. The location shifts to a large West Coast city and a modern Japanese metropolis, both places of intense activity and ambition. Human invention and technology predominate, the natural world having receded to distant vistas and cultivated landscapes. The fourth story occurs in 2004 at a time of middle age in a midsize old industrial city in the eastern United States. The man has achieved comfort and security, but at the cost of compromise and disappointment. An unusual opportunity arises to restore both the natural and the human landscape through a risky business venture, offering a chance for personal and environmental redemption. The epilogue's final story jumps generations ahead to 2030 and then to 2055, a time of continuing uncertainty but also of an emerging new covenant of compatible relation between the natural and human built environments.

This book thus engages many complicated, challenging issues through both rational examination and narrative reflection. At times, the conclusions appear sobering, bordering on pessimistic. Still, the overall outlook is fundamentally optimistic, confident in the human capacity to envision and create a world of a compatible, and even harmonious, relationship with nature. Despite our enormous capacity for consumption and development, humans are not viewed as a kind of "weed" species that inevitably impoverishes the natural environment. Instead, people are seen as capable of existing in sustainable relation to nature, even of enriching the natural world's productivity and health. This choice reflects the extraordinary free will of our species, a double-edged sword that can result in life-affirming creativity or self-destructive behavior.

Both theory and evidence are advanced to support the view that human physical, mental, and spiritual well-being remains dependent on the quality of our healthy interaction with the natural environment. Modern society has clearly diminished and compromised this possibility. Yet the understanding and technology needed to restore positive ties between nature and humanity exist and are ever expanding. Nobel prize–winning biologist René Dubos labeled this potential that of "wooing of the earth." He suggested:

> Wooing of the earth suggests that the relationship between humankind and nature should be one of respect and love rather than domination. Among people the outcome of this wooing can be rich, satisfying, and lastingly successful only if both partners are modified by their association so as to become better adapted to each other. . . . With our knowledge and a sense of responsibility for the welfare of humankind and the earth, we can create new environments that are ecologically sound, aesthetically satisfying, economically rewarding, and favorable to the continued growth of civilization. But the wooing of the earth will have a lastingly successful outcome only if we create conditions in which both humankind and the earth retain the essence of their wildness. The symbiosis between these two different but complementary expressions of wildness will constantly engender unexpected values and new hopes, in an endless process of evolutionary creation.[10]

The objective of restorative environmental design depends on wooing the earth in a deliberate, knowing, and gentle fashion. Doing this will be immensely difficult given the current extremes of human consumption, population, technology, urbanization, waste, pollution, and environmental destruction. Can people ever know enough to fabricate effective solutions to complex large-scale problems? Perhaps we would do better to pursue a more modest, restricted, gradual process of resolving the problems of nature and humanity. Unfortunately, the enormity and pace of the contemporary human onslaught on natural systems dictate otherwise, leaving us little choice but to respond ambitiously. The uncertainty of the outcome represents the particular morality play of our age.

2

Science and Theory of Connecting Human and Natural Systems

W hat do we know about the relationship between natural systems and human physical and mental well-being? The truth is, not much. Various wide-ranging studies of the human experience of nature have provided only fragmented, inconsistent information rather than definitive answers.[1] By contrast, the ways disturbed and degraded natural systems negatively affect human health and productivity, as well as how human activity damages the condition of the natural environment, have been much more widely studied. Little systematic, empirical investigation of the more positive human-nature interactions has occurred, particularly of how the experience of nature fosters human physical and mental well-being, and even how beneficial human actions can actually enhance the functioning of natural systems (see Figure 1).

This chapter explores the positive dimensions of human-nature interaction, reviewing evidence of how the experience of the nonhuman environment can enhance human physical and mental productivity and satisfaction. We focus here on ongoing contact with nature, something that could be called "ordinary" in the dictionary sense of "routine, usual, or commonly encountered."[2] Our primary focus is how the experience of nature as a normal aspect of people's everyday lives at home, work, or play, or in their neighborhoods and communities, affects their basic health and well-being.

Studying the Relationship between Human and Natural Systems

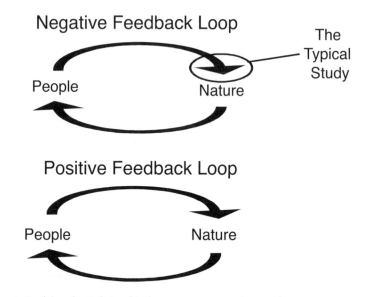

Figure 1. Studying the Relationship between Human and Natural Systems

When we think of ordinary nature, we envision a potted plant, a backyard garden, a lawn, a nearby park, local wildlife, or even ways we decorate our homes or construct our workplaces. Does this include domesticated creatures and habitats, or nature experienced in largely controlled or contrived ways—for example, a cultivated garden, a caged bird, a pet dog, a landscape painting, a television program? Yes, if this contact with nature, even though experienced in indirect and sometimes symbolic ways, occurs in our routine, everyday lives. All such experiences of the nonhuman world relate if they occur regularly and affect human well-being. What about contact with relatively undisturbed natural systems or even wilderness settings? Again, yes, as long as this contact affects people's ongoing lives. Thus, this chapter will also examine how immersion in relatively pristine settings can affect people's ordinary existence, especially among youth.

We will also consider very different kinds of contact with nature, such as symbolic, representational, and vicarious interactions with the natural world. This contact could include reading books with a nature focus, seeing the natural world on film and television, or viewing nature's simulated, metaphorical expression in decoration and art or through language, story, and myth. All of these activities reflect humans' relation to the natural world as long as they exist in the context of people's ordinary lives and affect their feeling, intellect, and behavior.

These aspects of the human experience of the natural world raise the question of what we mean by "nature," a complicated issue considered here only briefly. Environmental psychologist Joachim Wohlwill defined nature as that "vast domain of organic and inorganic matter that is not a product of human activity or intervention."[3] Though certainly valid, this definition is too narrow from the perspective of this book, which also concerns itself with how experiences of the nonhuman world that are the deliberate product of human construction and creation (e.g., domesticated animals or symbolic representations in the built environment) affect human well-being. Thus, we will consider human contact with nature to be any form of direct, indirect, or symbolic expression of the nonhuman world that is integral to people's lives, be it a local marsh, a nearby river, a city park, a manicured lawn, a houseplant, a landscape painting, a television program, or a wilderness area—all of which and more can affect people's everyday perspectives.

This examination of human relationships to the natural world occurs along two broad dimensions. First, people vary in their degree of closeness to nature, ranging from—at one end of the axis—highly familiar settings and domesticated animals, such as pet animals and backyard gardens, to—at the other extreme—wilderness-dependent wildlife and pristine environments, with the middle ground occupied by, for example, captive zoo creatures or a nearby municipal park. Second, people experience varying kinds of contact with the nonhuman world, ranging from direct and indirect contact to symbolic or vicarious encounters. Direct contact involves the experience of relatively self-sustaining natural features and processes—for example, walking in a forest ravine, swimming or fishing in a free-flowing stream, or hiking and camping in a desert area or on a mountaintop. Indirect contact involves interactions with elements of nature that require ongoing human input, intervention, and control, such as tending a potted plant, a manicured lawn, or a fish aquarium. Symbolic or vicarious contact does not involve actual physical experience of the natural world but, rather, the metaphorical, symbolic, or vicarious encounter of nature, such as the simulation or mimicking of natural forms in buildings and constructed landscapes, depictions of animals and environments in photographs and paintings, fictional and nonfictional portrayals of creatures and habitats in story and myth, and the use of floral patterns in decorative or ornamental objects.

This chapter examines how all of these forms of contact with the natural world can affect human well-being and development. The basic contention is that the functioning and maturation of the human body, mind, and spirit depend on the quality of people's ongoing experience of nature. Because we evolved in a biological rather than an artificial or machine-dominated world, we have always relied on—and continue to rely on—repeated experience of nature to achieve our physical and mental health and productivity.[4] Some related findings considered here include the following:

- How living in or near open space and protected areas can enhance human functioning and well-being, especially when compared to situations with little or no access to such natural settings
- How the experience of nature can affect human health and healing, including recovery from illness
- How contact with nature can foster social ties and relationships
- How work settings with attributes such as natural lighting and natural ventilation can improve worker satisfaction, enhance performance, and reduce stress
- How contact with nature can enhance intellectual performance and problem solving
- How neighborhoods and communities characterized by superior environmental quality foster positive environmental values and a higher quality of life (as well as the reverse)

We consider how contact with nature in parks, gardens, the workplace, health care facilities, and outdoor areas in relation to companion animals and in ordinary neighborhoods and communities can deeply affect human physical and mental well-being, satisfaction, and productivity. We also review the results of an ambitious study of how the health and integrity of natural systems affects human performance and quality of life in a variety of urban, suburban, and rural communities located within a single watershed. This wide range of inquiry will hopefully provide sufficient support for the hypothesized link between contact with nature and human physical and mental well-being.

The chapter will then conclude by examining three theories that help elucidate the interdependency of human well-being and the natural world. First, we explore the concept of ecosystem services, or how healthy natural systems provide people with essential goods and services that support their basic existence, even in our industrial and increasingly urban society. Second, we consider the theory of biophilia, or how people's inherent affinity for the natural world can confer a range of vital physical and mental benefits. Third, we examine how people who live in secure, familiar places are more likely to derive the benefits afforded by healthy ecosystem services and various biophilic values that tend to make their lives more satisfying and productive. Let us begin this exploration with an examination of how parks and gardens can affect human well-being.

Parks and Gardens

It has long been the stuff of legend and anecdote that parks and gardens exert a beneficial and even restorative and healing impact on people.[5] The many purported benefits of contact with gardens, open space, and park-like settings include rest, relaxation, contemplation, restoration from illness, and spiritual renewal.[6] This universal assumption is reflected in the ancient tradition of "sacred" groves and spaces, largely undisturbed areas often perceived as places where deities or "guardian spirits" reign and where people can experience physical, mental, and spiritual inspiration and renewal.[7] The scope of this assumption is suggested by the extensive expanses of sacred places found throughout the ancient world. For example, more than twice the land area of historic India was designated as sacred groves than all of the officially designated protected areas found in India today—and with arguably a greater degree of public appreciation and protection.

In Europe and the United States, establishing parks and protected areas was historically tied to the presumed physical, psychological, and spiritual benefits in pristine and urban areas.[8] This perception, for example, contributed strongly to the creation of the national parks system in the United States. In urban areas, designers, such as the pioneering landscape architect Frederick Law Olmsted (designer of New York's Central Park; see Illustration 1), argued that people's physical and mental health depended on regular contact with attractive natural scenery.[9] Olmsted suggested: "A man's eyes cannot be as much occupied as they are in large cities by artificial things . . . without a harmful effect, first on his mental and nervous system and ultimately on his entire constitutional organization. . . . The charm of natural scenery is an influence of the highest curative value."[10]

The association of parks with people's physical and mental well-being has, however, only recently been systematically explored. Although studies remain sparse, various investigations have documented diverse psychological and health-related benefits of people's contact with parks and open space, including relieved stress, increased peace of mind, enhanced coping, improved physical fitness, and greater creativity.[11] Much of this data is derived from social surveys, but some investigations have included physiological indicators of well-being, such as reduced blood pressure and improved muscle tension. Even passive viewing of attractive natural features has been found to reduce stress, increase relaxation, foster "emotional balance," and improve cognitive functioning (e.g., better concentration, attentiveness, and problem solving).[12] The results of these studies have been impressive and consistent. The physical, emotionally restorative, and even healing effects of nature have been especially observed in park-like settings and gardens with such highly preferred features as savanna-like meadows,

Illustration 1. Urban open spaces created in the late-nineteenth and early-twentieth centuries, such as New York City's Central Park, were often rationalized as places that enhanced people's physical and mental well-being.

large and mature trees with wide canopies, forest edges, brightly colored flowers and shrubs, and the presence of water (e.g., a clear pond or a fast-flowing stream). Summarizing some of these findings, social scientist Terry Hartig and colleagues concluded that contact with nature can help people "wind down, revive flagging spirits, stave off burnout, provide time for reflection and acceptance, [and] join with supportive others."[13]

One particularly revealing study, conducted by Hartig and his colleagues, examined the emotionally restorative and intellectually enhancing effects of park-like settings in urban areas.[14] This investigation included a sample of college students who were recruited to perform several intellectually difficult, attention-demanding, and mentally fatiguing tasks. Students were randomly chosen and assigned to one of three groups: one that took a forty-minute walk in an urban park, another that walked for forty minutes in an attractive urban area dominated by buildings and human activity, and a third that remained indoors seated in comfortable chairs while listening to music and reading for the same time period. After forty minutes, the members of each group completed a proofreading assignment. A survey administered following this experience revealed that the greatest gains in emotional restoration ("higher levels of positive and lower levels of negative affect"), as well as greater attentiveness and concentration, occurred among the students who walked in the park. By contrast, significantly lower levels of emotional and intellectual restoration occurred among the "urban activity" and "indoor activity" groups.

Several other studies have reported stress relief, emotional well-being, and intellectual functioning as common benefits of exposure to parks, open space, and natural settings in nonurban and especially in urban areas. Yet it would be oversimplifying to conclude that rest, relaxation, and restoration are the only positive effects of parks and open space. Like any experience of nature, the physical and mental effects depend on the kind of experience and activity involved. For many people, parks and the outdoors provide less the opportunity to relax than the chance to be stimulated or challenged, to express physical prowess, and to engage in competition.[15] Whether relaxation or stimulation, park-like settings foster a range of physical, emotional, intellectual, and spiritual rewards depending on the circumstances and the kind of person involved.

The appeal of parks and gardens has often been attributed to their aesthetic qualities. The experience of natural beauty has been correlated with relief from stress and other physical and mental benefits.[16] Aesthetic responses to nature have been viewed by some as a universal instinctual human tendency (as discussed later in this chapter). This genetic inclination has been tied to various adaptive benefits, including rest, relaxation, curiosity, creativity, an enhanced exploratory drive, a greater capacity for problem solving, and the recognition of symmetry and harmony. An aesthetic appreciation of nature has been associated with such environmental features as bright and flowering colors, long vistas, or the presence of water, all of which have, over evolutionary time, tended to enhance human sustenance and survival.

Environmental psychologists Rachel and Stephen Kaplan have suggested that the physical and mental benefits of parks, gardens, and open spaces stem from four observed characteristics of these settings: "coherence, complexity, mystery, and legibility."[17] Coherence is the human capacity to recognize and discern order and organization in nature; complexity, the ability to identify and respond to diversity and variability in the natural world. Both tendencies can be related to such functional advantages as critical thinking, problem solving, and creativity. Mystery is the ability to examine and investigate the complexities and uncertainties of nature, while legibility reflects the human capacity to orient and navigate natural settings. Both attributes encourage people's organizational, analytical, and imaginative capacities.

Outdoor Recreation

A related body of knowledge has examined the effects of outdoor recreational activities on people's physical and mental well-being. A wide range of activities can be classified as outdoor recreational, including hiking, camping, nature study, ecotourism, birdwatching, whale-watching, fishing, hunting, and more. The motivation to pursue these activities varies widely and includes competition, sport, scientific interest, exercise, nature interest, and aesthetics. These motivators vary by degree of commitment, the environmental setting where the activity occurs, the length of time involved, the extent of a person's expertise, and other factors that affect the meaning and impact of an outdoor recreational activity.

These outdoor experiences sometimes occur in extraordinary settings. Yet these unusual activities have significant, even profound, effects on people's emotional and intellectual well-being under more normal circumstances as well. For example, consider the impact of immersion in relatively undisturbed natural settings. Both anecdotal and a growing body of structured research suggest that this outdoor recreational activity can exert significant and even life-changing effects on participants, particularly late adolescents, when substantial challenge and adventure occur in the company of others.[18]

A review by outdoor recreational researcher Alan Ewert of a wide range of studies concluded that outdoor programs can result in significant physical, psychological, social, and educational benefits that sometimes affect participants for long periods of time in their ordinary lives. Major social-psychological effects described by Ewert include enhanced self-esteem, self-confidence, and personal effectiveness; improved coping skills; greater independence; and an increased willingness to take risks. Major gains in coping skills have included improved initiative, efficiency, personal responsibility, organizational ability, and the willingness to see tasks through to completion. Significant improvements in cognitive and intellectual performance have been enhanced critical thinking and problem-solving abilities, greater curiosity and creativity, and better performance at school or work. The physical challenges of these programs also commonly result in greater strength, fitness, stamina, endurance, and coordination as well as the acquisition of various outdoor skills (hiking, climbing, orienteering). Major cited changes in personal values have been greater peace of mind, a clearer "philosophy of life," and enhanced spiritual well-being. Finally, Ewert found the interpersonal and social gains of group-oriented programs to be improved cooperation, the ability to work in teams, avoidance of conflict, respect for others, leadership, and the capacity to make new friends.[19]

Similar results were observed in a large-scale study conducted by this author and colleagues of programs offered by three well-known outdoor organizations—Outward Bound, the National Outdoor Leadership School, and the Student Conservation Association.[20] This study, which involved more than eight hundred participants representing all socioeconomic strata, collected data through surveys, interviews, and direct observation. Two kinds of research were conducted: a retrospective study of those who had participated in only one organization's program over a roughly twenty-year period, and a longitudinal investigation of participants just before, immediately following, and six months after the programs. This research design allowed for assessing both long-term impacts and the more immediate effects of participation not influenced by recall or participants' varying willingness to be involved in the retrospective study. All of the programs occurred in relatively wilderness settings in the United States in the Rocky Mountains, the Pacific Northwest, the Southeast, or the Southwest.

Three-quarters of respondents reported that participating in the program had been among the most important and influential activities of their lives and had exerted major impacts on their personal, intellectual, and personal development. Moreover, these results occurred in both the retrospective and longitudinal studies and among all three organizations. Dramatic improvements were observed in self-confidence, self-esteem, and "self-concept." Most participants reported significant gains in independence, autonomy, optimism, peace of mind, and ability to cope with stress. Less pronounced but still striking improvements occurred in interpersonal skills, including being able to work with others, tolerating others, and meeting and working with new people. Substantial benefits were noted in such cognitive skills as problem solving, resourcefulness, seeing tasks through to completion, and making difficult, complex decisions. Statistically significant majorities reported a far greater appreciation, concern, and respect for, and spiritual connection with, the natural world.

Beyond the statistical findings, many participants provided qualitative responses regarding how their experience in the outdoors had affected their ordinary lives and outlooks. These observations poignantly reveal how contact with relatively pristine nature under unusual circumstances can exert substantial impacts on people's everyday lives and personal development. One teenager commented:

It was the best thing in my whole life. I won't ever forget it—really an opportunity to be independent and find myself. I am more content, compassionate, and self-aware than I have ever been. It affected the way I look at people, the way I feel about myself, the way I look at the natural world and in general the way I lead my life.

Another participant explained:

The experience while isolated and out of the realm of everyday life, is applicable to everything that I do. Because everything was such raw emotion and the outer events so simple, the personal challenges faced and overcome were within myself. Much of what I faced had to do with my own fears and weaknesses. Overcoming them changed me as a person. When I [now] face a more "complex" problem in the [normal] world, I need only to go back to see what solution I came to when it was just me against myself surrounded by simplicity and the answer becomes clearer. [Participation] allowed me to experience a connection with nature and simplicity and balance within that will be with me for the rest of my life. It brought to me the limitless[ness] of my potential and taught me to surrender to peacefulness.

Both statistical and qualitative evidence thus suggests that immersion in nature can exert life-changing effects on the lives of participants that persist long after participation. We now turn to the benefits and effects of a very different experience of the nonhuman world, the relationship with pets, or "companion animals."

Companion Animals

The somewhat unusual term companion animals is used here instead of the more common term pets because the former underscores most people's primary motivation for bringing these creatures into their lives. During historic times, domesticated animals largely served as sources of practical gain and were often referred to as "beasts of burden." In modern society, however, these creatures are far more likely to be regarded as friends and considered an integral part of the human household.[21] This degree of commitment varies greatly depending on the person and species involved. Dogs, cats, and sometimes horses tend to be the most valued and cherished, while less affection and commitment is shown toward birds, reptiles, fish, and even "companion" invertebrate creatures and plants that retain their essential "wildness."

Much research has examined the physical and emotional effects of contact with companion animals under both normal and distressed circumstances.[22] This research has generally found that companion animals foster substantial physical and mental benefits. Interacting with companion animals has been correlated with enhanced calm, peace of mind, and physical and mental restoration and healing. Companion animals have also been reported to increase social interaction by acting as "lubricants" that stimulate contact even among strangers.[23] Various studies reveal that bonding with companion animals can enhance a person's self-esteem, self-confidence, and self-image. Well-known veterinarian James Serpell concluded that people who have companion animals tend to be "more self-sufficient, . . . optimistic, and self-confident [in comparison to] non-owners."[24]

These benefits can be especially pronounced when people face stress and disorder. Various studies have documented the physical and psychological effects of contact with companion animals among persons suffering from mental impairment, isolation, and diverse physical maladies. These findings, however, are often derived from studies involving small samples and nonrigorous data collection procedures. Still, a large amount of consistent, impressive documentation supports the apparent therapeutic healing effects of companion animals on people suffering from various physical and mental illnesses. Some studies report major improvements in physical and emotional symptoms, more rapid healing, and faster recovery time among persons who have contact with companion animals. Impressive, pioneering research of the emotionally disturbed in particular has been conducted by, among others, psychologist Boris Levinson, psychiatrists Samuel Corson and Aaron Katcher, and veterinarian Alan Beck. These studies generally report that contact with dogs, cats, birds, and even fish can produce significant physical and mental improvement. These results are not universal, and negative findings occur occasionally, especially when the companion animals are inappropriately chosen, inadequately treated, or placed in situations marked by tension and hostility. Yet the overwhelming majority of studies report that the careful use of companion animals yields significant therapeutic gains, including stress relief, enhanced recovery from disorder, and greater physical and mental well-being.[25]

The work of the psychiatrist Aaron Katcher and his associates has especially highlighted the therapeutic effects of companion animals on sick and disabled persons. One carefully conducted study by Katcher, Friedmann, and Beck examined the effect of companion animals on persons recovering from heart attacks. Two groups of patients, who were demographically and symptomatically matched, were studied. One group received conventional treatment, while the experimental group was exposed to companion animals and then compared with the patients who did not receive such exposure. The researchers reported that the presence of companion animals significantly increased survival and recovery rates: "Mortality rates among people with pets [was] one-third that of patients without pets."[26]

A more recent study by Katcher and his colleagues examined boys suffering from attention deficit hyperactivity disorder (ADHD), a malady involving difficulty controlling emotional impulses, inadequate conflict management, and highly strained social relationships.[27] Boys suffering from ADHD were randomly assigned to two groups experiencing different kinds of contact with nature: (1) an outdoor challenge activity involving canoeing, water safety training, and rock climbing, and (2) an animal interaction activity consisting of interaction with and care of companion animals. The two groups swapped activities midway through the study. While researchers noted significant therapeutic gains for both activities, the more positive, significant, and lasting effects were observed for the animal-care experience. Contact with companion animals resulted in greater improvement of ADHD symptoms, better learning, and superior school performance when compared with the outdoor experience. The companion animal experience also produced greater speech gains, better nonverbal behavior, improved attentiveness, and an increased ability to control impulsive behavior. Moreover, these differences were still evident six months after the program ended. Katcher and his associates concluded that a positive, caring relationship with companion animals can relieve stress, foster social interaction, improve empathy, and contribute to task performance.

The results of these studies suggest that contact with companion animals can substantially enhance the ability to give and receive affection, improve self-confidence and self-esteem, engender a feeling of being needed, and promote emotional and physical healing. Summarizing the benefits of a relationship with companion animals, James Serpell concluded: "Pets don't just substitute for human relationships. They complement and augment them. They add a . . . unique dimension to human social life and, thereby, help to buffer [people] from the potentially numbing and debilitating effects of loneliness and social isolation."[28]

A far smaller number of studies, however, have documented negative effects stemming from an inordinate dependence on companion animals.[29] Some researchers report people using companion animals as human substitutes to compensate for inadequate relations with other people. Some companion animal owners have also used their animals, notably dogs, to vent hostility or aggression toward other people. However, these deficient uses of companion animal are relatively rare.

The diversity of negative as well as positive effects of companion animals should not be surprising given the extraordinary popularity of pets today. In the United States alone, the number of cats and dogs is said to exceed 100 million animals, not to mention the hundreds of millions of pet horses, birds, reptiles, and fish.[30] These enormous numbers suggest the importance of companion animals in many contemporary peoples' lives, and the presence of companion animals is likely a universal characteristic of human existence throughout history and across all cultures.[31] Thus, it is probably wiser to view companion animals less as substitutes for other people than as another form of potentially beneficial relationship between people and nature that complements and enhances the human experience.

Still, the sheer number and diversity of companion animals today is striking, especially considering the potentially high costs and difficult maintenance of these creatures in the urban household. What explains the widespread prevalence of companion animals in modern society? Perhaps they have become more important as we have shifted from an extended-family to a nuclear- and single-family oriented society. Increasing transience and mobility may also contribute to the emotional value of companion animals as friends and perceived family members. Diminishing contact with nature in an increasingly urban society may further motivate people to bring these nonhuman creatures into their lives.

Recovery from Stress and Disorder

In addition to interacting with companion animals, more general contact with nature has also been found to promote recovery from stress and disorder. Certain plants and habitats—gardens, seashores, hot springs, mountains, and deserts—have long been associated with stress-relieving and even curative effects. The presence of flowers and other aesthetically appealing vegetation has also been linked to calming, healing effects on the sick and disabled. Several scientific studies also report that the presence of plants in hospitals and the exposure of patients to "therapeutic gardens" can produce symptom-relieving benefits.[32] Some investigations have found that patients generally prefer vegetation in their hospital rooms, attesting to its comforting and healing effects. One investigation reported that contact with nature in hospital rooms, views of the outside, and exposure to gardens were among patients' most widely stated health care preferences.[33]

Several investigations have reported that the sight and sound and other sensory experience of nature can reduce stress and tension as well as foster recovery among patients suffering from clinically diagnosed disorders.[34] One impressive study conducted by environmental geographer and psychologist Roger Ulrich and his colleagues focused on patients recovering from gall bladder surgery.[35] The patients were matched demographically and, following surgery, were randomly assigned to one of two types of hospital recovery rooms: one with a window view of trees and vegetation, the other with a view of a brick wall. Patients with the outdoor views had significantly better recovery rates, more positive responses to treatment, and substantially less need for medication than those who saw only the brick wall. The researchers reported: "Patients with the nature window view had shorter post-surgical hospital stays, . . . fewer minor post-surgical complications, . . . and received far fewer negative evaluative comments in nurses' notes. . . . The wall view patients required far more injections of potent narcotic pain killers . . . while the nature group took more oral doses of weak pain drugs."[36]

Ulrich and his colleagues conducted a similar study in Sweden of 160 patients recovering from heart surgery. This time the patients were randomly assigned to three types of recovery rooms: the first with pictures on the wall of water and trees, the second with abstract wall art, and the third with only blank walls. The researchers observed significantly less anxiety and fewer demands for strong pain medication among the patients who had pictures of water and trees. By contrast, the highest stress levels occurred among the patients whose walls were decorated with abstract art. In another study of Swedish psychiatric patients, Ulrich and his colleagues again exposed patients to representational art, with one group viewing pictures of flowers and an appealing landscape while the other group saw abstract art. The patients with the nature art demonstrated more positive effects; the patients who viewed the abstract art showed more negative responses, and some normally nonaggressive patients even attacked and smashed the pictures.[37]

Most studies have found that contact with actual rather than representational nature has the most consistent and powerful therapeutic effects. Yet the Ulrich studies and other investigations established that pictures of nature also can produce symptomatic gain, including lower stress levels and more rapid healing. For example, a well-controlled study of persons facing surgery examined three groups of patients: one group exposed to "serene" depictions of nature, a second to highly active outdoor scenes (such as ocean surfing), and a third to no pictures. Significantly lower blood pressure levels were observed among patients who viewed the serene nature depictions.[38]

Another study conducted by Aaron Katcher and his colleagues examined patients facing major dental surgery. Three randomly selected groups included one group exposed to fish in an aquarium tank, a second group who observed pleasant pictures of nature, and a third group who faced a featureless wall. Nearly all patients revealed some degree of stress, but those patients exposed to the fish tank exhibited far lower levels of physical discomfort and "treatment aversive behaviors" (similar levels of stress reduction also were observed among patients who received therapies such as hypnosis).[39]

Work

The benefits of exposure to nature have also been demonstrated in the workplace. Most workplace contact with nature involves exposure to pictures and decorative art or to potted plants rather than direct experience of the natural environment. Still, the data are impressive and generally support the contention that contact with nature in the workplace fosters physical and mental well-being and can even enhance productivity.

Most early research on the effects of the natural environment on work performance focused on the negative problems stemming from climatically controlled buildings marked by extensive artificial lighting, inadequate natural ventilation, and furnishings, paints, wall coverings, and products that contained artificial "off-gassing" chemical substances.[40] Poor lighting and ventilation, high levels of pollutants, and the common presence of molds in these buildings were linked to various clinical symptoms, resulting in the identification of "sick building syndrome" and "building-related illness." Specific problems included respiratory and skin disorders, excessive fatigue, and various physical and psychological ailments that generally resulted in high absenteeism, poor morale, lower productivity, and clinically diagnosed disorders.

More recently, studies have begun to focus on the positive effects of exposure to nature in the workplace. A growing body of evidence has found that work settings with extensive natural lighting and natural ventilation, the presence of natural materials, and direct and representational contact with nature can result in greater physical and mental well-being, higher levels of worker satisfaction, and even increased productivity (Illustration 2).[41] A study of European office and factory workers, for example, found that the simple viewing of nature reduced job-related stress and improved emotional well-being. Another European investigation of workers in a windowless environment found fewer allergies among persons randomly given plants compared with those who did not have plants. A study of American office workers reported that those with a window view had less work-related frustration and better physical and mental health than those lacking outside views. Another investigation determined that employees with windows had substantially fewer physical symptoms that those who worked in the building's windowless core. Yet another study found that office workers with no windows were far more likely to decorate their workplaces with pictures of nature and with potted plants than those who had outside views of trees and open spaces.

One productivity study reported statistically fewer errors and more efficient performance on a computer task among workers assigned to offices with plants in comparison to those lacking vegetation. Another investigation found that workers with plants had lower blood pressure and better attention levels than those without plants. In a NASA study, employees given photographs and posters of nature had significantly higher levels of "cognitive tranquility" in comparison to those lacking visual depictions of the natural world. Several studies report that workers with natural ventilation and natural lighting demonstrate more focused attention and superior cognitive performance than those in artificially lit and ventilated settings. A prison investigation reported that inmates confined to cells with views of nature had fewer sick calls, headaches, and digestive problems compared with inmates lacking visual access to the outside.

Collectively, this research suggests that workers who have greater contact with nature—be it natural lighting, natural ventilation, natural materials, outdoor views, or pictorial depictions—generally have better physical, emotional, and intellectual well-being. These effects are also occasionally associated with economic gains. Improved natural lighting and

Illustration 2. Recent research suggests that natural lighting improves the health, morale, and productivity of office workers. The recently completed Genzyme headquarters in Cambridge, Massachusetts, designed by Behnisch and Behnisch, is distinguished by its unusual amount of natural lighting.

ventilation have been correlated with a 6 to 16 percent increase in worker productivity. Contact with nature has also been reported to result in substantially improved quality of work, reduction in errors, fewer manufacturing defects, lower absenteeism, and lower sickness rates, all of which frequently produce significant economic savings.

Few of the reported studies, however, have been rigorously conducted, and few involve large sample sizes. One major exception is research by psychologist Judith Heerwagen and her colleagues of office and factory workers at a major furniture manufacturing facility in central Michigan.[42] This carefully designed investigation examined workers prior to, immediately following, and six months after a move from manufacturing and office facilities with minimal environmental amenities to new facilities that included such "green" features as enhanced natural lighting, natural ventilation, the use of natural materials, improved energy efficiency, restored wetland and prairie environments, outdoor picnic areas, and walking trails. The new facility, designed by architect William McDonough and his associates for the office furniture company Herman Miller, appears in Illustration 3.

The researchers examined worker stress, motivation, satisfaction, health, performance, and emotional well-being. Most employees rated the new facilities as superior in lighting, air quality, "healthiness," and aesthetic appeal. Workers also responded positively to enhanced opportunities for outside contact with nature, improved views, and restored wetland and prairie habitats. These changes produced substantial improvements in work performance, with researchers reporting a 20 percent gain in worker productivity nine months after moving to the new facilities, as well as significant increases in job satisfaction, physical health, and relaxation. Workers were more likely to express such sentiments as "looking forward to work, being in good spirits at work, excited about work, and happier" in the new facilities. A minority of employees reported little change, and improvements were generally greater and lasted longer among office workers than among manufacturing workers. Some factory workers also reported greater fatigue at the end of the workday, although this change appeared to be more a consequence of higher work levels in the new manufacturing facility. Still, the results of this precise investigation reveal substantial improvements in physical and mental well-being and productivity among workers who had enhanced contact with nature in the workplace, which resulted in "better . . . work performance, job satisfaction, and . . . work spirit."

Homes, Neighborhoods, and Communities

The studies reviewed rarely consider the effects of contact with nature in people's homes, neighborhoods, and communities, and surprisingly little data is available on the subject. One

Illustration 3. The Herman Miller Company facility in central Michigan, designed by William McDonough and Partners, is notable for such sustainable design innovations as widespread natural lighting, natural ventilation, energy efficiency, and restored prairie and wetlands habitats.

particularly relevant set of findings emerged from studies of a residential community designed to lessen adverse effects of home construction on the natural environment as well as provide residents with increased contact with nature. Known as Village Homes and constructed in the mid-1980s, the housing development consisted of 220 modest-size homes (from six hundred to three thousand square feet) on a sixty-eight-acre site in Davis, California (Illustration 4).[43] The development, designed by Judith and Michael Corbett, retained a surprisingly large proportion of area in open space despite the high housing density, with about a quarter of the area dedicated to an agricultural "edible landscape," recreational open space, and a greenbelt. Houses were also separated by narrow, winding pedestrian and bike paths lined with flowers, shrubs, and trees; the paths in fact occupied more space than the vehicular roads. Designed narrower than usual, the streets were positioned behind the homes and along the periphery in highly vegetated areas. In place of sewers, drains, and underground pipes, the development obtained regulatory permission (after much difficulty) to construct aboveground vegetated channels (or "swales") to control stormwater, which followed the land-scape's natural contours. Sustainable design efforts included tight building construction, extensive insulation, solar orientation of the homes, solar water heaters, and plant shading and have resulted in roughly one-third to one-half of the energy use that would normally be required by a development this size.

Enhanced contact with the natural environment resulted from the extensive open space, pedestrian and bike paths, and widespread natural creeks and drainage channels. Agricultural areas fostered increased interaction with the outdoors among the development's residents. Closely situated homes, pedestrian paths, and common areas led to improved social relations. A study of Village Homes residents found that, on average, they knew "forty neighbors, compared with seventeen in the standard development, and had three or four close friends in the neighborhood, compared with one in the control group." A more subjective reflection of the enhanced sense of connection with both the natural and human environment occurred in the following comments from a former resident comparing his childhood at Village Homes with his life as an adult in a more conventional urban neighborhood:

> Growing up in Village Homes gave me a sense of freedom and safety that would be difficult to find in the usual urban neighborhood. The orchards, swimming pool, gardens, and greenbelts within Village Homes offered many stimulating, exciting, joyful places for me to play with friends. We could walk out our back doors into greenbelts full of all kinds of trees to climb with fruit to eat and gardens with vegetables to nibble on. Even when we were young, the network of green-belts allowed my friends and I to go anywhere in the community without facing the danger of crossing a street. Now that I am no longer living in Village Homes, I feel locked in by the fence in my backyard and the street in front of my house. I felt a loss of the freedom I had as a child.

Judith and Michael Corbett, developers of Village Homes, also attest to the aesthetic and recreational benefits of the natural drainage system, especially for the neighborhood children:

> Another feature that makes life in Village Homes seem closer to nature is the natural drainage system. Where [Michael] lived when he was six years old, there was a creek near his home. It was his favorite place to play. When he was twenty, he went back to find that spot, but it was gone. The streambed had been filled and leveled and the water diverted into a concrete pipe under a street. When it came time to design a neighborhood in which to live, one goal was to deal with runoff water as an asset for our children to enjoy.

Illustration 4. Village Homes, a residential development of more than two hundred homes on a sixty-acre site in Davis, California, designed by Michael and Judith Corbett, has achieved extraordinary environmental and social benefits.

Extensive pedestrian paths, open space, and agricultural areas enhance the development's connection to the natural and social environments. Houses are clustered into groups of generally eight residences, which face one another across vegetated pathways. The agricultural areas consist of fruit trees, berry bushes, grapevines, and vegetable gardens, which offer residents an unusual chance to interact productively with the landscape and more positively with one another and the outdoors. A major characteristic of Village Homes is its strong sense of community, which is encouraged by an active homeowners association, on-site school system, community center, and common playing fields. A greater sense of physical and mental well-being derived from increased contact among residents and with the natural environment has resulted in comparatively little housing turnover and significantly higher resale values. The developers report:

In the beginning, housing prices in Village Homes were comparable to prices elsewhere in Davis. However, at this writing, calculated by the square footage, Villages Homes is the most expensive place in Davis. . . . This is due less to the houses themselves—they were built at the modest end of the housing scale—and more to the neighborhood, which is seen as a very desirable place to live. The homes come on the market less frequently . . . and they sell twice as quickly.

A related study of two residential developments in Massachusetts also found a strong relationship between property values and the occurrence of open space.[44] The two housing developments were built around the same time with roughly similar, 1,600-square-foot homes and comparable housing densities. The major difference was that one development had homes sited on small individual lots and the remaining area devoted to open space (encompassing roughly half of the development), whereas the second development had larger individual housing lots but little common open space. When compared twenty years following construction, property values were significantly higher in the development with the much higher proportion of open space. The researchers reported: "In the mid-1970s, homes in both developments sold for about $26,600. After 20 years, both had appreciated significantly, but the average price of the [subdivision with little open space was] . . . $134,200, while the [price of the homes in the development with half in open space] was . . . $151,300."

Often, the positive effects of open space and greater contact with nature are assumed to be relevant mainly to people who can economically afford to appreciate such amenities. By contrast, it is sometimes asserted that the benefits of greater contact with nature are marginally relevant to socioeconomically impoverished people, particularly urban poor and minorities who are forced to cope with the more immediate, basic needs of survival and security. This assumption is contradicted, however, by the results of pioneering studies—conducted by psychologist Frances Kuo and her colleagues—of Chicago public housing developments whose residents were very poor minority persons.[45]

One study compared residents in two architecturally identical housing projects, with the only difference being the presence or absence of trees and grass in the projects (Illustration 5). Residents were also randomly assigned to the housing projects and had no control over the landscaping. The vegetation had been totally removed from one housing project primarily to simplify maintenance. The other project had some remaining vegetation, mainly sparsely situated trees, shrubs, and a covering of grass. The investigation found that residents in the vegetated housing project had significantly higher levels of physical and emotional well-being, greater capacity to cope with stress, better conflict management, and higher cognitive functioning. Specifically, the researchers reported: "Attentional performance [was] systematically higher in individuals living in greener surroundings; [and] management of major issues [was] systematically more effective for individuals . . . living in greener surroundings. . . . It is striking that the presence of a few trees and some grass outside a 16-story apartment building could have [such a] measurable effect on its inhabitants' functioning."[46]

In another study of different public housing residents, Kuo and her colleagues found major quality-of-life differences among residents distinguished by living in buildings surrounded by concrete and asphalt versus buildings with trees, grass, and flowers. They observed that residents of the buildings with vegetation had significantly stronger social ties, better interpersonal relations with neighbors and even strangers, a greater sense of safety and security, and a stronger feeling of community. Moreover, substantially less violence and crime occurred in the public housing project with vegetation compared with the one surrounded by only concrete and asphalt.[47]

Greater New Haven Watershed, or "Mastodon," Study
The studies considered thus far provide partial evidence that contact with nature enhances people's physical and mental well-being in their neighborhoods and communities. Most of these studies, however, had relatively small sample sizes, few numbers and types of communities examined, and a lack of data related to environmental quality and human quality of life. My colleagues and I addressed these limitations with an ambitious, large-scale study of diverse rural, suburban, and urban communities located within a single watershed. This investigation assessed the link between the health of natural systems and the physical and mental well-being of residents in several communities. Specifically, it examined eighteen neighborhoods or, more technically, "subwatersheds" (tributaries of one of three related river systems in an overall watershed) located in south-central Connecticut.* The watershed encompasses the drainage of three rivers that converge on New Haven harbor on the Long Island Sound. The size of the watershed is about 250 square miles (or 400 square kilometers) and includes 275 streams, part or all of seventeen towns, and a human population of about half a million people. The main urban center is New Haven, with 130,000 residents, and the overall watershed is roughly 13 percent urban, 24 percent suburban, 11 percent agricultural, and 41 percent forested. The eighteen subwatersheds or communities examined comprise roughly 28,000 acres and have a population of 78,000 people, who reside in a range of urban, suburban, and rural communities.

---

* Professor Gaboury Benoit, an environmental chemist, and I served as the project's principal investigators, assisted by Professor David Skelly, a landscape and aquatic ecologist; Professor Mark Ashton, a plant ecologist; Professor Paul Barten, a hydrologist; Professor Lynne Bennett, an economist; and Ms. Emly McDiarmid. The project was funded by the National Science Foundation, the U.S. Environmental Protection Agency, and the National Oceanographic and Atmospheric Administration through the Connecticut SeaGrant Program.

Illustration 5. (*top and bottom*) Two nearly identical Chicago public housing units were compared, with one unit having vegetation and the other lacking it. Residents of the vegetated unit had significantly higher levels of physical and emotional well-being, better coping capacity, and superior conflict management.

Several criteria guided the choice of the eighteen subwatersheds. First, we needed communities with a range of environmental conditions, from relatively high quality to environmentally stressed. Second, we wanted areas of varying population densities that included urban, suburban, and rural neighborhoods. Third, we needed a mix of the first two criteria to determine how variations in environmental quality influenced environmental values and quality of life, as well as the reverse. Thus, in addition to the more typical conditions of relatively good environmental quality in sparsely populated areas and of disturbed natural areas in urban settings, we included rural communities with relatively poor environmental conditions as well as urban neighborhoods with comparatively healthy natural systems so we could examine the relationship of human and natural systems independent of population density. Finally, we included only "first order" subwatersheds or neighborhoods—meaning they had streams not originating in another community—in order to examine how environmental conditions of a particular neighborhood affected human values and quality of life rather than environmental conditions that might have originated upstream.

We affectionately referred to our investigation as the "Mastodon study," reflecting our view of being—from our distinct disciplinary perspectives—a little like the blind men seeking understanding of a large, extinct pachyderm by touching only a part of the creature—a leg, a trunk, a tusk, a tail. We hoped that by combining all of these disparate pieces of knowledge we could achieve sufficient understanding of the entire obscure beast. In addressing this complicated question of how human and natural systems shape each other, we collected an enormous amount of chemical, hydrological, biological, social, and economic data.

We set out to explore how the structure and function of natural systems affect human environmental values and socioeconomic conditions (as well as the reverse). We hypothesized that even in a modern industrial society people continue to be inextricably dependent on their ongoing experience of natural systems. We believed natural systems cause and, in turn, are the consequence of varying states of human performance and productivity. We viewed people as physically and mentally reliant on the quality of their interactions with the natural environment—even in south-central Connecticut, where few persons directly exploit local environments for their sustenance and security, and where many travel long distances to work at jobs associated with an increasingly global economy. As emphasized in chapter one, one illusion commonly held by contemporary society is that people are ever more independent of nature because we have a small fraction of the population producing huge food surpluses, because we can massively extract resources and create new consumer products and compounds, because we have achieved relatively good health and a longer life expectancy, and

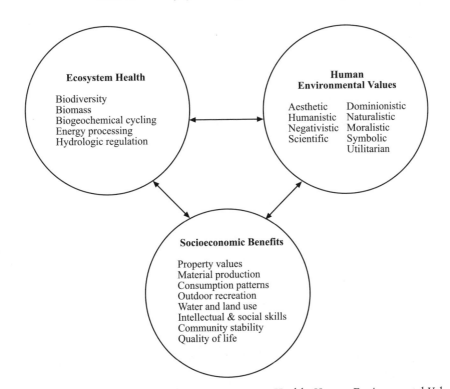

Figure 2. Hypothetical Relationship between Ecosystem Health, Human Environmental Values, and Socioeconomic Benefits

because most people live in highly transformed urban areas. Despite this seeming independence from nature, our study set out to demonstrate that human physical and mental well-being still heavily relies on the quality of people's continuing experience and contact with relatively local natural systems and processes.

We examined both positive and negative interactions of human and natural systems. As noted earlier, most people-nature research focuses on how humans degrade nature and, to some extent, on how damaged environments harm human well-being. We rejected the notion of people and nature as in inevitable conflict, treating people instead not as an inherently negative or positive environmental influence but, rather, as having the potential—like any biological organism—to exert both destructive and beneficial impacts on natural systems and processes. We also believed that this interaction between people and nature occurs everywhere, in urban and nonurban settings, and among modern as well as traditional peoples. How did we envision this relationship occurring between people and nature? Broadly speaking, we hypothesized that the health and integrity of natural systems exercise a crucial influence on people's values of nature (i.e., the basic ways they attach meaning and derive benefit from the natural world), which in turn influences their economic, social, and psychological well-being within a community context. This hypo-

Table 2.1

A Typology of Values in Nature

Aesthetic	Physical appeal of and attraction to nature
Dominionistic	Mastery and control of nature
Humanistic	Emotional attachment to nature
Moralistic	Moral and spiritual relation to nature
Naturalistic	Direct contact with and experience of nature
Negativistic	Fear of and aversion to nature
Scientific	Study and empirical observation of nature
Symbolic	Nature as a source of metaphorical and communicative thought
Utilitarian	Nature as a source of physical and material benefit

thetical relationship is depicted in Figure 2; however, as will be seen below, the results of this investigation substantially altered this presumed dynamic.

Before turning to the major findings of this research, the measurement of certain key variables, including environmental health, environmental values, and human physical and mental well-being and quality of life, is briefly revealed. The relative health of natural systems was determined by measuring various chemical, hydrological, and biological indicators that roughly indicate environmental functioning, quality, and productivity. These measures included species richness, species diversity, biomass (quantity of biological material), biogeochemical or nutrient flux (how efficiently chemical elements such as carbon, hydrogen, nitrogen, and others move through and are assimilated by natural systems), hydrological flow and regulation, aquatic chemistry (e.g., dissolved oxygen, nitrate, phosphate, fecal coliform, heavy metals, suspended solids, turbidity), the relative proportion of native versus nonnative species, and other measures of ecosystem functioning and productivity.[48]

People's environmental values were assessed based on a conceptual framework developed by this author of nine basic ways people attach meaning to and derive benefit from nature.[49] These values are defined briefly in Table 2.1 and are described in more detail later in this chapter. As will be explained more fully later, these nine values are regarded as "weak" biological, or inherent, tendencies that are greatly influenced by learning and experience within a cultural and community context.

The various indicators used to measure people's physical and mental well-being included neighborhood and household quality, land use, availability of schools, shopping, libraries, museums, roads, health, recreational activity, connection to place and community, environmental interest, and other factors. A composite quality-of-life measure was developed based on forty indicators, including such factors as community relationships, transportation networks, recreational opportunities, civic and cultural institutions, athletic opportunities, medical care facilities, availability of the arts, levels of crime and safety, presence of parks and open space, changes in neighborhood quality, and a semantic differential of contrasting community characteristics (e.g., clean versus dirty, safe versus dangerous, stable versus unstable, secure versus insecure, attractive versus ugly, interesting versus boring, prosperous versus poor, cared for versus rundown, and others). Information relevant to measuring values of nature, physical and mental well-being, and quality of life was obtained through a forty-five-minute survey administered to more than two thousand residents, through observational data, and through secondary sources.

A mountain of information on more than ninety major biophysical and socioeconomic variables was collected and examined, with many factors being combinations or aggregates of various indicators. Despite all of the data collected, the results must be viewed as tentative; the limited product of an "observational-correlational" rather than an "experimental-causal" study.[50] In other words, we examined the relationship of people and nature at just one point in time rather than observing how these variables shifted and changed as a consequence of altering conditions. To illustrate the distinction between this kind of correlational study and a more experimental one, consider the historic association prior to the age of air-conditioning between ice cream consumption and the murder rate on especially hot summer days. Even truly delicious ice cream rarely makes people murderous, but a high correlation was nonetheless observed between these factors because, of course, of the influence of other factors, such as summer heat. Similarly, it would be erroneous to draw strong causal conclusions from reported correlations in our investigation of environmental quality, environmental values, and human physical and mental well-being. To do so, we would have to examine changes in human-nature relationships over time and under highly controlled conditions—for example, by measuring social conditions and human environmental values and quality prior to, immediately following, and after natural factors had been greatly changed for the better or worse and then controlling for the possible confounding influence of other factors. Despite the limitations of our study, however, it still represents a highly unusual large-scale attempt to examine the relationship between environmental health, human values of nature, and people's physical and mental well-being in diverse urban, suburban, and rural communities.

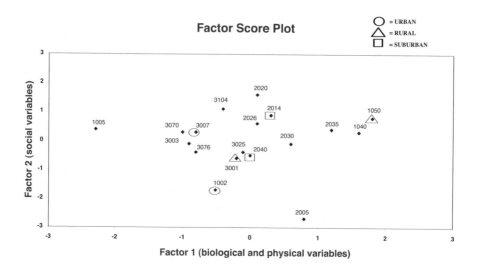

Figure 3. Distribution of Subwatersheds by Two Factors

So what did we learn? Initial results partially confirmed our hypothesis of negative and positive correlations of natural and human systems in a wide variety of urban and nonurban contexts. The results of two powerful multivariate statistics were particularly revealing. These findings together provide a compelling—albeit tentative—confirmation of the link among ecosystem functioning, people's environmental values, and human quality of life, although they also prompted us to revise our basic conceptual framework significantly. The two multivariate measures are known as factor analysis and redundancy analysis. These two statistical tools helped reduce the vast amount of diverse disciplinary data collected (more than ninety chemical, hydrological, plant, animal, social, and economic factors across eighteen communities), revealing relationships and identifying variables most closely related to one another that helped to explain the information collected.

The results of factor analysis first revealed that twenty-five variables were particularly related to one another and fell into three distinct clusters, or factors. One factor consisted of eleven biological and physical variables; a second factor, of eight social variables; and a third, of a mix of six biophysical and socioeconomic variables. The first two factors explained nearly two-thirds of the variability in the data collected (the third factor explained only another 5 percent and thus has been omitted from this discussion). The eighteen subwatersheds were compared on the two factors discussed here. Figure 3, which shows the comparison results, indicates that most subwatersheds were quite distinct from the others,

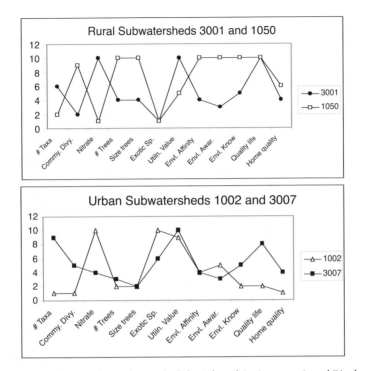

Figure 4. Two Rural and Two Urban Subwatersheds by Selected Socioeconomic and Biophysical Variables

although some were highly similar. The communities were, in effect, found to be distinguishable by the biophysical and socioeconomic variables identified by these two factors and thus could be meaningfully compared in relation to these variables.

Because space prohibits comparing all eighteen communities in relation to the nineteen variables identified by these two factors, for illustrative purposes here only four subwatersheds—two urban and two rural—are contrasted on six environmental and six social variables. Because the variables were scored differently, employing varying metrics, all results are standardized on a one-to-ten scale to facilitate comparisons. These comparisons (shown in Figure 4) provide partial support for the hypothesized relationship between environmental quality, certain human values of nature, and varying socioeconomic conditions. In general, factor analysis revealed that better environmental quality in the communities studied—as measured by such variables as species diversity, biomass, chemical pollution, native versus nonnative species, and other measures—was related to a greater appreciation and awareness of the natural environment, outdoor enjoyment, and superior household conditions and quality of life in these communities. Conversely, this statistic revealed that relatively disturbed environments in the neighborhoods examined were associated with less environmental interest and

Illustration 6. This neighborhood studied in Bethany, a small town in southern Connecticut, had relatively good environmental quality and a strong sense of place.

appreciation, lower quality of life, and poorer household conditions in the neighborhoods. Importantly, these correlations occurred in both rural and urban communities, although to a lesser degree in suburban neighborhoods, and (as will be seen in our later discussion of the redundancy analysis findings) somewhat independent of a community's income and education levels.

It may help to describe more fully the two urban and two rural subwatersheds to provide a deeper sense of how these communities might foster or impede positive connections among people, nature, and human quality of life. Subwatershed 1050 is located in the northeastern section of the small rural town of Bethany, Connecticut, at the headwaters of the smallest of the three rivers of the Greater New Haven Watershed. Much of this Bethany neighborhood has been environmentally protected to safeguard the surface drinking water for the region. The topography of the community is uneven and occasionally steep, with a major stream, several ponds, and natural as well as artificial lakes. Few public facilities occur in the subwatershed, although considerable open space, forests, hiking trails, and easy access to natural areas and a major state forest exist. Most of the neighborhood is secondary forest, with frequent stone walls and old farmsteads providing a generally pastoral character (Illustration 6).

Most households in this Bethany community are middle to upper middle income, and most of the homes are moderate to large in size and sparsely situated (some relatively newer subdivisions and smaller, older, and closely situated houses are also encountered). The distinctive architecture comfortably fits into the history, culture, and ecology of the region. A seeming congruence exists between the homes, surrounding fields, forests, and cultivated landscapes. Yards are generally well maintained, and a sense of neighborliness and pride seems to prevail. People appear largely content, although somewhat physically and socially isolated from one another and the surrounding region. Schools and commercial development are mostly absent, with most shopping and civic activity occurring elsewhere, although several commercial centers can be found a short distance away. Most residents rate the quality of life in the community as very good to excellent even though neighborhood interactions are sparse and the neighborhood possesses few cultural amenities.

The environmental quality in this small town is generally very good; it is characterized by a high degree of species diversity, abundant populations of preferred wildlife (e.g., deer and songbirds), low levels of pollutants, and good stream quality and water flows. Most residents possess considerable environmental knowledge, awareness, and concern, and they report active involvement in several kinds of outdoor activities. Many of the residents birdwatch, fish, or hunt, as well as support the practical use of the land for farming and forestry.

By contrast, subwatershed 3001 is located at the eastern border of the overall watershed along a tributary of its largest river in a relatively rural section of the small city of Meriden. Although classified as rural, this neighborhood has some urban features, including its thirty-one streets organized into a grid pattern with most homes situated on small lots. Extensive commercial development has occurred along some of the major roads, although rural features—including farmland, significant amounts of open space, several major lakes, and densely forested hills—predominate. Average income and household quality are modest. Most of the residents rate the overall neighborhood and quality of life as moderate to good.

The subwatershed's environmental quality has been compromised, a condition reflected in low levels of species diversity and biomass, diminished stream quality and flow, and relatively high rates of pollution, including elevated levels of fecal coliform, phosphate, and suspended solids. The nearby river has a long history of chemical contamination and industrial development (Illustration 7). Residents' environmental interests and concerns are limited, and they reported significantly less outdoor recreational activity than in most other communities studied.

Thus, striking differences in environmental quality, environmental interest, development patterns, and neighborhood characteristics distinguish the two rural subwatersheds. The Bethany neighborhood possesses a relatively healthy environment, easy access to natural amenities, and a comparatively high quality of life, whereas the Meriden community—although it has several positive environmental features and relatively good neighborhood quality—was far more polluted and environmentally compromised. Residents of this latter

Illustration 7. This community studied in rural Connecticut had a degraded
environment and widespread social ills.

neighborhood were substantially less interested and knowledgeable about the natural
environment and reported fewer outdoor activities.

Turning now to the two urban communities, subwatershed 1002 is located in a working-
class neighborhood in the moderately sized city of New Haven. The area is densely populated, consisting of mainly middle- to lower-middle-class and a smaller proportion of lower-
income residents. Homes are situated on small lots, and the community also contains several
row houses and apartment complexes (Illustration 8). The homes are among the oldest in the
study, with several streets neglected and unsafe, and a number of large roads having fast-
moving and congested traffic, which tends to fragment the community. Still, many side streets
seem comfortable, pleasant, attractive, and well maintained. This New Haven neighborhood
also includes a disproportionately larger mix of ethnic groups than the other communities
studied as well as a larger fraction of elderly residents.

The New Haven neighborhood does have a relatively intact forest nearby as well as many
large trees, although a major highway impedes access to the natural areas. The community relies
on city sewers rather than natural drainage or household septic systems to handle its wastewater.
Environmental quality is among the worst encountered in the study, with low levels of species
diversity, high levels of pollutants (such as fecal coliform and phosphate), and poor stream flows.

Illustration 8. This New Haven, Connecticut, neighborhood suffered from extensive pollution and social stress.

Most residents rated quality of life in the community as poor—in fact, as the lowest in the study. Environmental activity, concern, and knowledge were limited, with most respondents expressing comparatively little outdoor interest and a greater willingness to subordinate the needs of the natural environment to human socioeconomic activities and interests.

By contrast, subwatershed 3007 is located in the suburb of Cheshire, a town ten to fifteen miles inland from the Long Island Sound and the city of New Haven. This section of Cheshire is densely populated and is classified by the U.S. Census Bureau as urban, but it still retains many qualities of a small town (Illustration 9). Most residents are middle income, although considerable variation occurs, with most of the homes being generally well maintained. The neighborhood contains several public buildings, including a major high school and a large commercial district. It also has several parks, significant open spaces, ball fields, children's playgrounds, and picnic areas. Several heavily trafficked commercial areas cross the community, but the overall feeling is relatively tranquil, neighborly, and family oriented. Tall trees surround the mostly small, closely situated homes, with lawns and shrubs dominating the understory and vegetation.

Overall environmental quality is good, despite several impaired and degraded natural features. The neighborhood and household features of the area are also generally good, although some signs of socioeconomic deterioration and lower quality of life were observed. Most residents expressed limited interest, knowledge, and awareness of the natural environment,

Illustration 9. This densely populated section of suburban Cheshire, Connecticut, possessed positive environmental and social amenities.

although their interest was significantly greater than that found in the New Haven neighborhood (subwatershed 1002).

This qualitative comparison echoes many findings of the factor analysis regarding the relationship of environmental quality, people's environmental values, neighborhood characteristics, and quality of life. The findings of redundancy analysis further provide an informative quantitative understanding. Redundancy analysis is a powerful tool that identifies variables in one data set that are highly related to and predictive of variables in another data set and the reverse. We were interested here in determining whether or not a strong predictive relationship existed between the social and biophysical variables. In other words, could we identify social variables and human relationships to nature that confidently predicted the quality of the natural environment and, conversely, particular dimensions of the biophysical environment that were strongly related to and predictive of human social relationships and environmental perceptions?

This relationship was indeed found, with one particular biophysical factor powerfully related to human social variables and one human factor strongly predictive of the quality of the natural environment. Specifically, people's "environmental affinity" was found to be very strongly connected to and a powerful predictor of environmental conditions throughout the eighteen communities studied. Also, in the biophysical data, the diversity of native tree species was determined to be a very strong predictor of human socioeconomic conditions and environmental perceptions. Environmental affinity measured interest and involvement in the natural environment and was a scale based on twenty-five factors, including "nonconsumptive" outdoor recreational activity (e.g., levels of birdwatching, bird feeding, visiting the seashore, picnicking, photographing or observing nature, boating), visiting zoos and natural history museums, viewing nature-related television programs, reading about the natural world, cultivating wildflowers, belonging to environmental organizations, taking environmental classes, pursuing nature-related tourism, and other factors. Local diversity of native tree species measured both levels of biological diversity and environmental disturbance as reflected in the relative proportion of native versus nonnative species.

We discovered that the relationship between environmental affinity and diversity of native tree species occurred independent of (i.e., unrelated to) income and education across the eighteen neighborhoods studied. In other words, these powerful predictors of the interconnection of environmental quality, human-nature experience, and quality of life occurred among impoverished as well as affluent communities and among persons of limited education as well as the highly educated. This finding is reminiscent of the Chicago housing project findings (reported earlier in this chapter) of a connection between the quality of the natural environment and human well-being among those of lower socioeconomic status. Combined with the factor analysis results reported above, we thus found that the relationship between environmental quality and human quality of life occurred relatively independent of population density and affluence.

The redundancy analysis also found that few measures of environmental quality were directly related to human values and social conditions; instead, most were highly influenced by the intervening relationship between certain landscape features and land use practices (a finding pictured somewhat obscurely in Figure 5). Specifically, we found that indicators of ecosystem health, such as species diversity, chemical pollution, and nutrient cycling, were rarely directly related to human social factors, such as neighborhood quality, environmental affinity, environmental knowledge, or quality of life. Rather, these biophysical and socioeconomic variables were connected to intervening landscape features, such as road quality, the presence of large and attractive trees, the occurrence of open space, the appearance and quality of streams, and other land use variables. On reflection, the intervening influence of landscape features and land use practices makes a great deal of sense. Most people do not fully grasp what is a healthy ecosystem, such as biological diversity, hydrological flow, soil or aquatic chemistry, nutrient flow, and so on. Yet most people notice and appreciate prominent

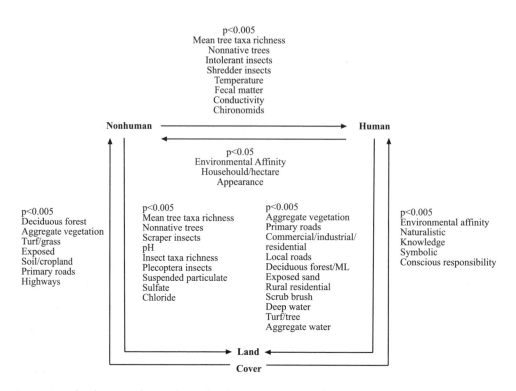

Figure 5. Redundancy Analysis Relationship between Human and Nonhuman Factors and Land Cover Characteristics

landscape features and land use practices that often are a consequence of these aspects of environmental quality—for example, the presence of large attractive trees, fast-flowing and clean streams, abundant parks, open space, and aesthetically pleasing roads.

To summarize, various findings from the Mastodon study revealed a strong relationship between environmental quality, people's environmental values, and human physical and mental well-being in various urban and nonurban communities. The major results of this investigation included the following:

- Communities with higher environmental quality had more positive environmental values and a higher quality of life, whereas those with lower environmental quality tended to reveal less environmental interest and a lower quality of life.
- The relationship between environmental quality, people's values and appreciation of nature, and socioeconomic conditions occurred among both urban and rural communities, although to a lesser extent in suburban neighborhoods.
- Certain environmental factors (e.g., diversity of native tree species) were strongly related to and strong predictors of human social conditions, while certain social factors (e.g.,

affinity for the natural environment) were powerfully related to the health and productivity of the natural environment.

• The relationship between environmental and social variables in the various communities studied occurred independent of income and education levels.

• The connection between natural and human factors was highly influenced by the association of each with prominent landscape features and land use practices.

The final result prompted us to revise our original conceptual framework regarding the relationship of environmental health, people's environmental values, and socioeconomic conditions. As the revised framework shown in Figure 6 suggests, we now view healthy natural
systems as fostering the occurrence of landscape features that people highly appreciate and
value; in turn, these land use features foster various social, psychological, and economic benefits that encourage people to positively identify with the places they live and that motivate them to sustain these communities socially and environmentally. This feedback relationship can, of course, also occur in a negative manner.

The results of the Mastodon study provide additional support for the hypothesized relationship between natural systems and human physical and mental well-being in people's
neighborhoods and communities. It appears that communities with relatively healthy ecosystems have a greater affinity for the natural environment and a higher quality of life, while
neighborhoods of relatively poorer environmental quality are generally less concerned about
the natural environment and possess a lower quality of life. This appears to occur in urban
and nonurban communities as well as among persons of all educational and income levels.

Explaining the Relationship

The various findings reported in this chapter covered a wide variety of human-nature relationships occurring in gardens, parks, and natural areas; in relation to companion animals;
and in health care facilities, in the workplace, and in neighborhoods and communities. These
studies generally support the contention that—even in our modern, increasingly urban age—
human physical and mental well-being continues to depend highly on the quality of people's experience of the natural environment. While most of the studies were limited in scope,
data covering many situations and circumstances collectively offer compelling evidence
to support the connection between the quality of people's contact with nature and their
health and productivity in contemporary society.

How do we explain this relationship? This complicated question requires a book in itself and
may be beyond our current knowledge and understanding. Still, three linked explanations can

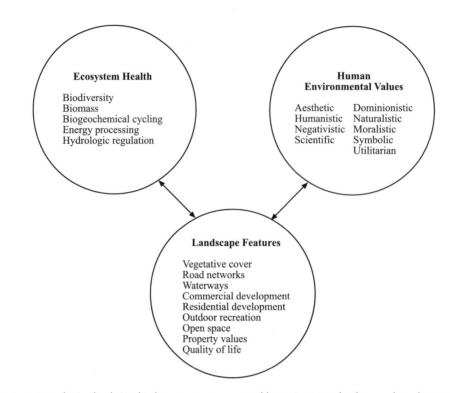

Figure 6. Hypothesized Relationship between Ecosystem Health, Environmental Values, and Landscape Features

be tentatively and briefly offered to elucidate the interdependence of nature and humanity. First, we explore the notion of ecosystem services and the various ways natural systems provide people with a host of services vital to their continuing welfare even in a technologically oriented society. Second, we examine the notion of biophilia and how the various ways people value the natural environment and express these connections confer important physical and mental benefits on them. Finally, we discuss the concept of spirit of place, or how people are more likely to derive critical ecosystem services and beneficial biophilic values when these occur in familiar communities that are cherished both culturally and ecologically. These factors occur in a linked, hierarchical fashion, with healthy ecosystems providing essential ecological services that foster the development of various biophilic values, which in turn encourage an attachment to and stewardship of these places where people work and reside. The reverse pattern is also just as likely to occur where vicious cycles of damaged human and environmental interactions prevail.

Ecosystem Services

The concept of ecosystem services is considered only briefly here, as it is discussed widely elsewhere.[51] Functioning natural systems provide people with an array of services critical to their well-being and survival. Moreover, these ecological services remain essential to people in an urban, industrial society that has become ever more reliant on manufactured goods and materials and that obtains much of its food and other products from distant rather than nearby sources, and where many travel relatively long distances to work. When examined carefully, however, we see that most people continue to depend on a wide range of basic ecosystem services that occur in their local neighborhoods and communities for their physical and material well-being. Some of these essential ecological services include the following:

- Waste decomposition
- Soil formation
- Remediation of chemical and biological pollution
- Control of injurious organisms
- Plant pollination and seed dispersal
- Hydrological (water) regulation and control
- Water supply and purification
- Nutrient retention and cycling
- Oxygen production
- Products from wild animals (e.g., honey, finfish, shellfish)
- Products from wild plants (e.g., wood, paper, lubricants)
- Pharmaceuticals and other medical materials
- Crop and livestock production

For example, decomposition, the breaking down of the wastes we produce, continues to rely even in modern society largely on the activities of countless other organisms (mainly microbes) found in the soil and water despite our increasing reliance on specialized, technologically sophisticated treatment facilities. In the United States, people generate an estimated 130 million tons of organic waste annually, while livestock generate another 12 billion tons of manure. Nearly 99 percent of this material is decomposed primarily by microbial life, leaving one to wonder where we would be if not for the assistance of our tiny "friends."[52] Moreover, much of the chemical and biological pollutants modern society produces is broken down by various terrestrial and aquatic organisms. The entomologist David Pimentel has estimated that three-quarters of the more than seventy thousand pollutants resulting from human activities are rendered largely harmless by the processes of the natural environment.

Soil fertility is also critical for producing food and lumber as well as for growing lawns, gardens, and other plants that benefit human life in many ways. Soil productivity largely depends on natural processes despite contemporary society's increasing reliance on artificial fertilizers. By disintegrating fibrous tissues, mixing organic materials, recycling nutrients, and increasing porosity and drainage, worms, ants, and other invertebrate organisms generate and maintain soil fertility, which is especially instrumental in agriculture and wood production.

Limiting or controlling injurious plants and animals, or "pests," is additionally essential to protecting human health, agriculture, and wood production. Pests can be controlled by applying artificial chemicals and mechanical procedures, but these applications are often expensive, have limited effect, and can cause environmental damage and human health problems. Most effective pest control continues to rely on largely natural organisms and processes. The feeding activities and populations of most harmful organisms are frequently limited by naturally occurring organisms (e.g., many bird, bat, and other species). Natural predators are estimated to control almost 90 percent of insect-borne diseases and agricultural pests. The scale of this pest control is illustrated by a single songbird, which can consume an estimated 100,000 to 250,000 insects annually.

Pollinating plants and dispersing seeds (and thus helping produce many desirable and valuable food products) are other essential ecological services performed mainly by wild organisms. For example, many species of bee pollinate an estimated 150 agricultural crops in the United States, including apples, berries, melons, and alfalfa.

Clean, naturally replenishing water is essential for human consumption, irrigating crops, and other activities critical to human well-being. This function continues to occur largely because of natural hydrological functions and regulatory controls.

Many, if not most, agricultural crops and domestic livestock remain reliant on genetic enhancements provided by wild relatives through crossbreeding and gene technology. People also harvest many wild species of trees, fish, and other wildlife for an assortment of food, clothing, fiber, and other products as well as for such highly valued recreational purposes as hunting, fishing, and wildlife watching.

Additionally, modern medicine continues to depend on exploiting the therapeutic properties of many plants, animals, and microorganisms. Indeed, an estimated one-third to one-half of all modern pharmaceuticals are thought to originate in exploiting or synthesizing chemicals associated with wild organisms. Finally, the most basic need of all—oxygen to breathe—continues to rely on the photosynthetic activities of countless plants.

These examples represent some of the many essential services people derive from healthy and diverse natural systems. Assessing the economic value of modern society's reliance on these ecosystem services is extremely difficult. Still, crude estimations have been generated and are worth noting to illustrate the continuing human dependence on the health and productivity of the natural environment. For example, David Pimentel and his colleagues estimated in 1999 that the natural world—from resources to tourism—directly contributed more than $300 billion to the American economy (at the time, 4.5 percent of the U.S. gross domestic product) and nearly $3 trillion (or about 15 percent) to the world's economic output.[53]

The smaller U.S. figure reflects the tendency of modern society to rely on synthetically produced goods and services through complex extraction and manufacturing processes and industrial controls. This characteristic prompted the ecologist Raymond Dasmann to label citizens of technologically advanced societies as "biospheric" people, who obtain most of their basic goods and services from distant sources and manufactured goods. He contrasted this situation with that of "ecosystem" people, who rely mostly on local natural systems for their subsistence and security.[54] Despite this distinction, as we have seen, contemporary urban societies continue to rely on the functioning and diversity of local natural systems. Nearly all of the ecosystem services reviewed earlier, with the possible exception of pharmaceutical production and the exploitation of most wild plant and animal products, continue to be an outgrowth of local, healthy, and productive natural systems. Although most people in modern urban society do not directly depend on exploiting local ecosystems for their sustenance and often travel long distances to jobs associated with an increasingly global economy, the quality of their lives continues to depend on the health and productivity of the local ecosystems where they work and reside. As discussed earlier, the services of these local ecosystems include decomposing wastes, breaking down pollutants, forming soils, controlling pests, dispersing seeds, pollinating plants, regulating water, and sustaining ecological functions essential to people's comfort and security, if not their very survival.

Biophilia

The inclination to value nature is known as *biophilia,* a presumably inherent biological affinity for the natural environment that is reflected in nine basic values (see Table 2.1).[55] The adaptive occurrence of these nine values is considered a vital basis for human physical and mental well-being. When people possess adequate and satisfying contact with the natural environment, they derive important physical and mental benefits from the functional occurrence of these biophilic values. Yet these values are "weak" genetic tendencies that depend highly on sufficient learning, experience, and cultural support to become functionally man-ifest.[56] Lacking adequate contact and experience of nature, the values remain atrophied or undeveloped, resulting in material, emotional, and intellectual deficits. When adaptively expressed, however, these biophilic values confer diverse physical and psychological advantages, including the greater likelihood of securing basic goods and services, of thinking critically and solving problems, of being creative and discovering, of expressing affection and developing social ties, and even of recognizing and affirming a just and mean-ingful existence. Each of the biophilic values developed over long periods of evolutionarily time and have persisted into the modern age because they contribute in subtle and complex ways to individual and social fitness in the ongoing struggle to adapt and survive.

Thus, the concept of biophilia can be simply defined as a complex of weak genetic ten-dencies to value nature that are instrumental in human physical, material, emotional, intellec-tual, and moral well-being. Because biophilia is rooted in human biology and evolution, it represents an argument for conserving nature based on long-term self-interest. The biophilic values are "biocultural" constructs, inherent tendencies whose outgrowth and functional devel-opment greatly depend on human choice and free will. Depending on the opportunities and choices individuals and groups make, the values will be either adaptively or dysfunctionally expressed. The biophilic values are, in effect, learning "rules" that reflect tendencies that a per-son can acquire quickly once the values are stimulated and triggered by experience and social support. Because each value is the product of both learning and genetics, extraordinary diver-sity does occur in their content and intensity among individuals and groups due to variations in culture and experience. The dictates of human biology, however, limit the adaptive expres-sion of this variability. Each value, thus, occurs hypothetically along a continuum that reflects functional variation within biological limits among individuals and groups, with dysfunction occurring at the outer extremes when either insufficient or atrophied development or exces-sive or inordinate expression occurs. This continuum is reflected in Figure 7.

Each of the nine biophilic values will be briefly described later.[57] These descriptions emphasize the physical, emotional, intellectual, and moral benefits conferred by each value. The order of presentation consists first of those values that generate largely physical and mate-rial benefits; next, of the values that offer a more intellectual and emotional advantage; and finally, of the values with a more moral and spiritual significance. Together, these nine val-ues reflect the richness of the human reliance on the natural world for fitness and security, a web of interdependence so pronounced that an ethic of concern for the natural environ-ment can emerge from an extended realization of self-interest.

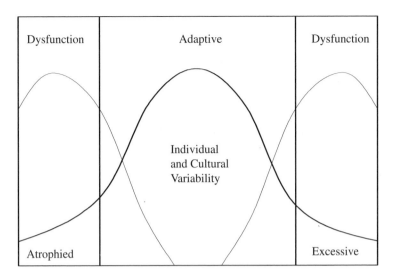

Figure 7. Hypothetical Expression of Biophilic Values

First, a *utilitarian* value reflects the inclination to affiliate with nature for various physical, material, and commodity advantages. The term *utilitarian* is something of a misnomer, however, because all of the biophilic values can advance human welfare and well-being. The term is used here in the conventional, narrow sense of physical and material benefits derived from the natural world. A utilitarian value reflects nature as a source of agricultural, medicinal, industrial, and other commodity advantages. In addition, demonstrating craft and skill through the utilitarian exploitation of the natural world can yield emotional and intellectual benefits even in the absence of immediate material reward.

Most people recognize the natural world as an important source of human sustenance and security. However, many people in contemporary society regard this reliance as more historic, as a characteristic of primitive cultures and less economically developed nations. For many modern people, the distinguishing feature of contemporary life is the seeming departure from this ancient dependence on nature. Yet, as we have argued earlier, this assumption is largely erroneous. Both traditional and modern peoples continue to rely on natural systems and processes for critical food, medicine, building material, and other services. Moreover, this material dependence is likely to greatly expand as advances in molecular genetics and bioengineering allow for increased material exploitation of the natural environment. Less than one-fifth of the planet's species have been identified, let alone assayed for their possible utilitarian benefits, with each species constituting a treasure of untapped physical and biochemical solutions to life's varied demands that have been developed through evolutionary trial and error. Also, as we have seen, the ecosystem services provided by healthy natural systems continue to sustain life in myriad irreplaceable ways, includ-ing producing water, decomposing wastes, propagating plants, and cycling nutrients.

People further express a utilitarian value of nature in the absence of need because it fosters various beneficial physical, emotional, and intellectual capacities. By cultivating proficiencies such as gardening or the harvesting of wild plants and animals, people also har-vest physical and mental skills. What they obtain through extracting a portion of their needs from the land and water, beyond the obvious material benefits, includes physical and mental fitness and a feeling of connection to timeless cycles and rhythms. People are bio-logically programmed to engage nature as a source of practical utility beyond the obvious mate-rial rewards because such actions can also produce self-sufficiency, self-confidence, and a feel-ing of independence gained by exercising their ability to survive with competence and craft.

A *dominionistic* value reflects the desire to master and control the natural world. People derive a host of benefits from expressing this tendency, including the ability to be safe and secure, exer-cise a sense of independence and autonomy, take risks and demonstrate resourcefulness, and cope with challenge and adversity. People have always honed physical and mental fitness through subduing and mastering nature. By competing, outwitting, and contesting other species and habitats, they emerge surer of themselves and their ability to confront the unknown and overcome hardship. Although modern people no longer rely on besting prey, eluding menac-ing predators, or surviving in the wild, the strengths and prowess obtained from confronting wild nature continue to produce physical and mental fitness. We derive self-esteem from the ability to persevere in the face of adversity. By besting a formidable opponent, whether a high peak, a rushing river, a wilderness setting, or another creature, we cultivate the ability to cope with challenge, risk, and the unknown with strength and resolve.

A *naturalistic* value reflects the perception of nature as a source of stimulation, detail, and diversity. People obtain various physical and mental rewards from immersing themselves in the natural environment's many functions and processes, above all its most conspicuous plants, animals, and landscapes. Through deep participatory involvement, each creature and habi-tat can become a magic well of imagination and discovery, where the more one explores the more one is likely to uncover boundless sources of stimulation and understanding. Adaptive benefits include heightened awareness and attentiveness, the willingness to examine and dis-cover, curiosity and inventiveness, and enhanced creativity and imagination.

Participatory involvement in the natural world can also engender feelings of calm, peace of mind, and a sense of timeless and boundless absorption. The greater the involvement, the more likely a person feels alive and attuned. Dull, colorless rocks become more varied; amorphous vegetation emerges loaded with meaning; the stillness of the landscape is transformed into many sensations; and even the air becomes substantive and palpable. This heightened awareness often leads to a greater sense of clarity, strength, and resolve. By contrast, people lacking a naturalistic appreciation typically confront a monotonous and dull world.

A *scientific* value reflects nature seen as a source of empirical knowledge and intellectual understanding. People possess a need to know and understand their world with authority. This tendency is facilitated through identifying, labeling, categorizing, and elucidating various aspects of the natural environment and, in the process, cultivating various cognitive abilities, including enhanced critical thinking, problem solving, and analytical skills.

Empirically observing and systematically studying nature are often considered a feature of contemporary life that depends on rigorous training and membership in an elite profession. The scientific inclination to study nature, however, occurs among all peoples in all cultures and throughout human history. Scientific tendencies have been observed, for example, among so-called primitive peoples, such as tribes in parts of New Guinea who can recognize and identify most of the scientifically classified bird species found there regardless of any immediate material significance they offer. Elaborate, science-like taxonomies have also been observed among indigenous peoples of North America and elsewhere.[58] All these and other people share the urge to empirically understand and categorize their world and, in the process, to hone their capacities for critical thinking, problem solving, and the development of other intellectual skills.

Carefully observing and comprehending even a fraction of the natural world provides countless stimulating ways to nurture learning and cognitive development. Developing intellectual competence can occur in other ways too—for example, through the use of computers and formal education in the modern world. Yet natural diversity remains an unrivaled source of intellectual stimulation, likely the most information-rich environment people will ever encounter, especially during childhood. The outdoors provides endless, challenging variety and wonder, a place where people free from the constraints of excessive formality can indulge their need to observe, understand, and learn. The knowledge gained from such empirical study can further occasionally and serendipitously yield tangible, practical advantage.

A *symbolic* value reflects the natural world as a source of imagination, communication, and thought. Throughout history, people have symbolized nature—using the sights, sounds, and sensations of nature in language, imagery, metaphor, and other symbolic ways—to aid the exchange of information and understanding.[59] This interaction and exchange occurs through speech, story, and fantasy, in sometimes obvious but at other times abstract and disguised ways. Adaptive benefits include language development through nurturing the ability to label and categorize, psychosocial maturation through the use of narrative and story, and enhanced communication through imagery and speech.

Symbolizing nature is critical in language development, arguably the most prized attribute of the human species. Learning to speak, write, and communicate depends on ever more refined distinctions, classifications, and taxonomies. This linguistic capacity is encouraged for the very young by distinguishing salient subjects—often, living creatures and life-like environmental objects. Nature offers a powerful, emotionally charged, and intellectually stimulating source of imagery for imposing classifications and categories. Even in our modern age, the very young rely strongly on images drawn from nature for developing their language ability, counting skills, and taxonomic capacities.

Symbolizing nature also occurs in children's stories and fables that confront critical maturational issues such as personal identity, conflict, and desire. This tendency, which occurs among all cultures and across history, reflects how symbolizing nature helps adolescents in particular to explore basic issues of maturation in emotionally powerful yet often disguised and acceptable ways. Anthropomorphism—the attribution of human feelings and motives to the natural world—is used frequently to help young persons confront complex, often threatening and painful subjects in a familiar yet tolerable fashion.

Finally, symbolizing nature can aid the language of everyday life. People incorporate nature's imagery into the language of the street, in the marketplace, and in oratory and debate. The origin of words and phrases in the natural world can be quite explicit at times and obscure at others, with their environmental sources becoming apparent only on close etymological examination. Images of nature in language and speech can be crude and trivial but also can produce eloquent and imaginative discourse. All these uses of nature's imagery in language share the ability to render communication more vivid, to bring to life, what is otherwise often abstract and bland discourse. Symbolizing nature aids human communication not unlike how natural diversity provides a template for physical and material discovery. Each biophilic value offers people clues for exploiting the raw material of the natural world to fashion solutions to life's varied challenges.

An *aesthetic* value reveals the natural world as a source of beauty and attraction. By cultivating this value, people enhance their capacities for curiosity, imagination, and creativity as well as the ability to recognize order, harmony, symmetry, balance, and even grace. Few experiences in life exert as consistent and powerful an impact on the human psyche as nature's aesthetic appeal. Even antisocial persons are typically unable to resist, even if fitfully manifest, an aesthetic attraction to natural features generally considered beautiful, such as a lovely sunset, a symmetrical rose, or a pyramidal, snow-capped mountain. The intensity of people's aesthetic attraction varies, but its occurrence seems certain. An aesthetic value is universal and, thus, is genetically encoded and, unless vestigial, is adaptively related to human fitness and security.

What are the functional advantages of an aesthetic value? At its most basic level, an aesthetic response to nature is being attracted and, as such, is an expression of interest and curiosity. With experience and cultivation, this attraction often leads to deeper and more complex levels of curiosity, exploration, and imagination. Over time and with persistence, this aesthetic attraction can even produce refined capacities for observation, discovery, and creation, all of which are highly adaptive in the ongoing struggle to persist and thrive.

An aesthetic attraction to nature has also been linked over the course of human evolution to the increased likelihood of obtaining safety, sustenance, and security.[60] People are aesthetically drawn to environmental features that have proven instrumental in human survival—for example, clean flowing water, promontories that foster sight and mobility, areas that offer refuge and shelter, and bright flowering colors that frequently signify the presence of food. Studies have found such consistent aesthetic preferences in a diversity of cultures. These aesthetic leanings in the contemporary world are also observed in the willingness to pay a premium for homes and offices that have distant vistas, are located near water, or are surrounded by colorful flowering plants and shrubs.

Discerning beauty in nature can further engender an awareness and appreciation of balance, symmetry, harmony, and grace. People are inspired and instructed by recognizing order and unity. These features in the natural world can serve as models or prototypes that inspire people to capture similar features in their own lives through mimicry and invention. The ideal in nature often functions as a design template helping people to discover clues to a more physical and psychologically rewarding existence. Perceiving beauty in nature advances an ideal of perfection that stands in contrast with the more normative reality of universal disorganization and chaos.

A *humanistic* value reflects the natural world as a source of emotional affection and attachment. This tendency fosters the capacities for giving and receiving affection, forming intimate and companionable bonds, and developing cooperation and trust. All of these attributes are adaptive for a largely social human species.

Emotionally bonding with nature often begins with highly familiar domesticated animals that are viewed as friends or even as family members. These individual animals become the subjects of intense loyalty, commitment, and identification and are highly valued as sources of caring, affection, and belonging. By contrast, isolation and aloneness are heavy burdens for most people who crave the companionship of others. By strongly identifying with individual animals, people achieve a sense of appreciation and significance. The affection of another creature rarely substitutes for the companionship of other people, but it often provides an important complement for expressing and experiencing closeness, intimacy, and a sense of kinship.

Bonding with nature also nurtures the capacities for cooperation and sociability. Caring and seemingly being cared for by another enhance self-confidence and self-esteem. These benefits accrue under normal circumstances but become especially pronounced during moments of crisis and disorder. The tender, intimate responses of another can be physically and emotionally restorative. When distressed, people often seek the therapeutic power of nature, whether through companion animals, gardens, seashores, or other "healing" creatures and landscapes.

A *negativistic* value reflects the inclination to avoid and fear nature. Aspects of the natural world likely to provoke anxiety and aversion include snakes, spiders, large predators, habitats like swamps and steep precipices, stormy seas, lightning, and more. These disturbing features in nature often produce aversive reactions with little provocation. This response may seem the antithesis of biophilia, which is translated literally as the "love of life." Yet biophilia reflects the inherent inclination to affiliate with nature, a tendency that includes apprehension and aversion as much as it does positive interest and affection.

Aversive reactions to nature can at times lead to destructive practices. Still, the inclination to fear and occasionally harm elements in nature is more typically expressed at moderate levels. Avoiding threatening aspects of the natural world is a functional tendency in any species that helps avoid harm, injury, and even death. When it is rationally manifest, people benefit from isolating and sometimes eliminating fearful natural elements. Human well-being depends on acquiring skills and abilities associated with some degree of distancing from potentially injurious environmental features. Lacking this awareness, people frequently behave naively, taking unnecessary risks and ignoring their inevitable vulnerability before powerful and unpredictable natural forces.

Fear of the natural world at times can also provoke positive feelings of awe and respect. By recognizing a power greater than ourselves—forces that can defeat and destroy us—we can cultivate feelings of deference and respect. Awe connotes reverence mingled with fear, the realization of a power and strength beyond oneself. Nature stripped of its power can become an object of condescension and superficial amusement. A lion, wolf, or bear confined to a small, barren cage rarely evokes much respect. Species and habitats that have been utterly subdued provoke little admiration, humility, and regard. An ethic toward the natural environment, thus, depends as much on some degree of fear and awe as on love and aesthetic appreciation.

Finally, a *moralistic* value reflects nature as a source of moral and spiritual inspiration. As environmental philosopher Holmes Rolston suggested: "Nature is a philosophical resource, as well as a scientific, recreational, aesthetic, or economic one. We are programmed to ask why and the natural dialectic is the cradle of our spirituality."[61] People obtain purpose and spiritual significance in their lives by developing feelings of connection with creation. Adaptive benefits include a heightened sense of meaning, increased self-confidence and self-esteem, and a willingness to treat nature with kindness and respect.

A moralistic value fosters recognition of unity in life and creation. Human existence is perceived to possess underlying meaning and purpose, a sentiment that supports spiritual and, at times, religious belief. This feeling of relationship to something universal occurs among all cultures and spiritual traditions throughout history. More recently, it has been rationalized through the understandings of modern science. Studies of the natural environment have revealed a remarkable degree of diversity reflected in 1.7 million classified species, an estimated 10 to 100 million existing species, and the extinction of 99 percent of all species that have ever existed. Despite all this variability, science has also revealed an astonishing commonality uniting much of life on earth. Most living creatures share common molecular, chemical, and genetic structures, similar circulatory and reproductive parts, and parallel bodily features. This extraordinary web of relationship can be seen to unite a beetle on the forest floor, a fish in the ocean, an ungulate on the savanna, a bird on high, and a human in a modern metropolis. This perception of relationship fosters a sense of an underlying unity governing life on earth, if not the entire universe. Faith and confidence are nurtured by discerning commonalities that transcend the aloneness of ourselves as single individuals isolated at a moment in time.

A moralistic perspective further encourages the willingness to conserve and protect nature. People temper their tendencies to harm or destroy the natural environment when they perceive a fundamental connection, or even kinship, binding them to other aspects of creation. An ethic emerges from a perceived link between human well-being and the natural world. The willingness to sustain nature derives as much from moral and spiritual inspiration as from any calculated materialism and regulatory mandate.

Each of the nine biophilic values has been associated with various physical and mental benefits derived from people's ongoing, satisfying experience of the natural world. Each value developed evolutionarily because each has been instrumental in advancing human welfare and well-being. The nine values collectively affirm the human reliance on natural process and diversity to achieve physical, material, emotional, intellectual, and moral benefits crucial to human existence.

Spirit of Place

A third concept that elucidates how people's ongoing experience of nature enhances their well-being is a secure, satisfying connection to the places where they work and reside.

When people live in familiar, accessible, and cherished social and geographical settings, they are more likely to reap the rewards of both the ecosystem services and the various biophilic values described earlier. A sense of satisfying and secure relation to one's physical and cultural environment has been called a "spirit of place," independently by the landscape architect Frederick Law Olmsted and by Nobel Prize–winning biologist René Dubos. Each described how when people feel tied to the places where they live, they convert these locations from mere inanimate landscapes to something like a living entity, which becomes a source of personal identity and endowed with a personality and spirit (Illustration 10). Dubos suggested: "People want to experience the sensory, emotional, and spiritual satisfactions that can be obtained only from an intimate interplay, an identification with the places in which they live. This interplay and identification generate the spirit of the place."[62]

Landscape historian John Brinckerhoff Jackson listed important characteristics of a sense or spirit of place. These included a heightened awareness of familiar environments, a strong sense of fellowship based on shared experience, and the occurrence and reoccurrence of reinforcing customs, habits, and rituals.[63] All of these features reflect human-centered, or cultural, dimensions of a spirit of place. They reveal how people living close to one another develop a special sense of bonding to their particular cultural milieu over time.

When examined closely, cherished places are not just social and cultural settings but also physical and ecological environments endowed with characteristics people associate with the place's distinctive identity. What makes a place special is the unique integration of culture with nature. Places of lasting significance reflect human society in continuous, iterative interaction with the natural environment that over time produces a unique, emergent outcome that cannot be explained as the consequence of either social or environmental forces alone. The spirit of a place is the singular outgrowth of the marriage of nature and human culture. As Dubos insightfully argued: "The environment acquires the [spirit] of a place through the fusion of the natural and human order."[64]

A spirit of place thus signifies the following:

- A comfortable, compatible connection between the cultural and natural heritage of an area
- The successful fusion of culture and nature within a biogeographical context resulting in the fundamental alteration of each
- Constructed buildings and landscapes that reflect the distinctive natural and social characteristics of a particular biocultural setting

Illustration 10. A spirit of place reflects the satisfying convergence of physical and cultural attributes, as this area of Connecticut suggests.

A spirit of place is reinforced by shared relationships among people within communities offering a diversity of economic, educational, recreational, civic, and environmental services and opportunities. A spirit of place engenders a sense of pride and identity with a neighborhood and region. As philosopher Mark Sagoff suggested, it "results in an idea of surroundings that arises from harmony, partnership, and intimacy."[65]

Still, it must be acknowledged that most people in modern society highly value opportunities for novelty, mobility, and the chance to explore the unfamiliar and unknown. Yet, even in contemporary society, most people appreciate when they return to the secure, reassuring place they call home. This sense of enduring relationship and connection to a particular place is sometimes referred to as possessing "roots," a concept reflecting both social and biological significance. The desire to have roots is a fundamental and often underappreciated aspect of human existence, as French philosopher Simone Weil suggests:

> To be rooted is perhaps the most important and least appreciated need of the human soul. It is one of the hardest to define. A person has roots by virtue of his real, active, and natural participation in the life of the community, which preserves in living shape certain particular expectations for the

future. . . . Every human being needs to have multiple roots. It is necessary for him to draw well-nigh the whole of his moral, intellectual, and spiritual life by way of the environment of which he forms a part.[66]

Various forces of contemporary society seem to have eroded this sense of rooted relation and identification with the spirit of the places where people reside. We have witnessed this regrettable phenomenon in a growing unfamiliarity and disconnection with the places we inhabit. This anonymous relation has been called "placelessness," described by geographer Edward Relph as the "weakening of distinct and diverse experiences and identities of places" (Illustration 11).[67] Aspects of modern life that contribute to a sense of placelessness include transience, excessive mobility, the loosening of neighborhood and community ties, economic globalization, the decline of extended family networks, urban sprawl, loss of open space, environmental and biological degradation and pollution, and an anonymous and alienating architecture.

When placelessness prevails, people are rarely committed to maintaining the cultural or ecological features of the places where they reside. They lack feelings of responsibility and stewardship for sustaining the spirit of their place. Writer Wendell Berry describes the consequences of placelessness in this way: "Without a complex knowledge of one's place, and without the faithfulness to one's place on which such knowledge depends, it is inevitable that the place will be used carelessly, and eventually destroyed."[68] Mark Sagoff further suggests that placelessness makes us feel like "strangers in our own land" and is often a core characteristic of the contemporary environmental crisis. He writes: "Much of what we deplore about the human subversion of nature—and fear about the destruction of [both the natural and human built] environments—has to do with loss of security one has when one relies upon the characteristic aspects of places and communities one knows well. What may worry us most is the prospect of becoming strangers in our own land."[69]

Despite the seeming decline in secure, satisfying connections to the places where people work and reside, contemporary society also offers many opportunities for meaningful relation to nature. Even in our highly mobile and somewhat rootless culture, the following positive trends in people's experience of nature can be cited:

- More Americans visit zoos and aquariums each year than attend all professional baseball, basketball, and football games combined.
- A majority of Americans annually watch at least one nature-related television program.
- Visits to national parks have soared, with more than 400 million visits occurring annually.

Illustration 11. In contrast to spirit of place, "placelessness" reflects an unfamiliarity with and disconnection from one's physical and social environments, which can occur in neighborhoods like the one shown here.

- Ecotourism has become one of the fastest-growing segments of the international travel industry.
- Three million people participate in whalewatching trips each year, an activity virtually unknown just fifty years ago, when these creatures were being slaughtered to near extinction.[70]

These statistics reflect the many opportunities for contact with nature in modern society that occur beyond the boundaries of local communities or that require a pronounced connection to the spirit of particular places. Yet these activities are typically peripheral to most people's lives and of fleeting, if not superficial, significance. By contrast, achieving the ecological benefits that come from experiencing a healthy environment or nurturing our various biophilic values requires regular, repeated contact with nature in secure, satisfying, and reinforcing local settings. For most people, this means having access to place-based environmental and cultural contexts marked by familiarity, access, and security. When strongly connected to the places where they work and reside, people are far more likely to derive the services of a healthy environment and to reap the benefits of their developed biophilic values.

Places of meaning and significance are more than lifeless aggregates of physical material. When healthy, familiar, and relevant, these places become a part of our very identities, and we imbue them with an animate quality or spirit. Recognizing the tendency of healthy ecosystems and meaningful places to become life-like, the great ecologist Aldo Leopold

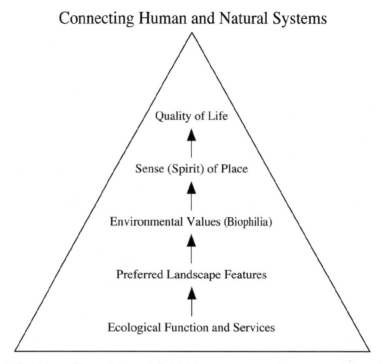

Figure 8. "Thinking like a Mountain": Linking Ecosystem Structure and Function with Environmental Experience and Quality of Life

referred to "thinking like a mountain."[71] The spirit of a place, like a healthy ecosystem, gives rise to and sustains life. The phrase "thinking like a mountain" links the various factors emphasized in this chapter—ecosystem services, biophilic values, and spirit of place—to the enduring connection between nature and human well-being (see Figure 8).

Conclusion

We have reviewed various findings and offered several explanations for why the positive experience of nature continues even in modern society to be essential for human physical and mental well-being.

This chapter has explored the interdependencies of nature and humanity that originate in human biology but are greatly influenced and conditioned by our species' unique capacities for learning, culture, and free will. Although people are capable of lifelong learning, the most critical period for forming any genetically encoded tendency is likely to be childhood. Chapter three explores the particular importance of ongoing contact with nature for healthy, functional maturation and development during childhood.

Nature and Childhood Development

I dreamed I was in an elephant.

I dreamed I was stepped on by a giant chicken.

I dreamed I was dreaming.

I dreamed I had no brain.

I dreamed that my ears were bigger than me.

I dreamed that I had static hair forever.

I dreamed that I ate too much food.

I dreamed that when I sneezed it was a tornado.

I dreamed when I spit it was a great flood.

I dreamed that I flew to a different galaxy.

I dreamed that I was a brownie and I ate myself.

I dreamed I turned into a hockey puck and got a lot of concussions.

I dreamed I had to be cross-eyed forever.

I dreamed I finished my poem.

—Peter Weinberg, age 7

T he previous chapter offered both evidence and theory to support the contention that human physical and mental well-being inextricably depends on the quality (if not the quantity) of people's experience of the natural environment and that this dependence remains critical in our modern, increasingly urban world. To explain this reliance, we considered the notions of ecosystem services, biophilia, and the spirit of place, all concepts rooted in

Much of the material in this chapter is also partially covered in S. Kellert, "Experiencing nature: Affective, cognitive, and evaluative development in children," in P. Kahn and S. Kellert, eds., *Children and Nature: Psychological, Sociocultural, and Evolutionary Investigations* (Cambridge, MA: MIT Press, 2002).

human biology but highly shaped by people's experience, learning, and culture. Assuming that the human affinity for nature is partially genetically encoded—a product of our having evolved in a natural rather than an artificial world—the importance of childhood must be recognized as the period when this contact with nature first occurs. Even for the human animal, which appears uniquely capable of constructing its world and learning throughout its lifetime, the fundamental development of any biologically rooted tendency is likely to occur during childhood.

This chapter explores this importance of childhood contact with nature, particularly for children's emotional, intellectual, and evaluative development. We consider how children's physical and mental well-being depends on the quality of their experience of the natural world. Several important questions guide our exploration:

- How much and what kind of contact with nature is necessary for healthy childhood development?
- Does a child's experience of nature vary in importance at different ages or stages during childhood?
- What are the effects during childhood of varying forms of direct, indirect, and symbolic contact with nature? Do these impacts differ at varying ages?
- Do children today encounter fewer direct and spontaneous opportunities for experiencing nature? If so, does this reduced contact affect their maturation?
- What are the developmental consequences of an increase in indirect and, especially, vicarious forms of contact with nature? Can this shift compensate for a decline in direct experience of the natural world?
- What happens when children become separated and estranged from the natural environment because it has become significantly degraded or difficult to access?

Although critical for attempting to understand the developmental importance of childhood contact with nature, these questions have received surprisingly little scholarly attention. For example, a review of widely cited publications with such provocative titles as *The Ecology of Human Development* and *Ecological Psychology* found the words *ecology* and *environment* used to describe the effect of the human-built and social environment rather than the natural environment on children.[1] Fortunately, this situation is changing, although most social science research still devotes little attention to the subject, while the field of environmental education largely emphasizes cultivating children's knowledge and appreciation of the natural environment rather than the environment's role in their physical and mental development. Commenting on the inattention to nature's role in childhood development, psychiatrist Harold Searles remarked that

> most writings concerning human personality development limit themselves for all practical purposes to considerations of interpersonal processes. The nonhuman environment is, by implication, considered as irrelevant to human personality development, as though the human race were alone in the universe, pursuing individual and collective destinies in a homogenous matrix of nothingness, a background devoid of form, color, and substance.[2]

Given the relative lack of available research, this chapter's conclusions will be preliminary and tentative. We will draw on a spate of recent research and writing on the topic, including essays in a book this author recently coedited with psychologist Peter Kahn, *Children and Nature: Psychological, Sociocultural, and Evolutionary Investigations,* to explore how varying types of contact with nature affect children's emotional and intellectual development.[3]

Children's experience of nature involves three kinds of contact: direct, indirect, and vicarious (or symbolic) experience. Direct contact refers to interaction with largely self-sustaining features and processes of the natural environment. These forms of direct contact include plants, animals, and habitats that function mostly independent of human input and control, although they may sometimes be affected by human activity. Direct experience of nature is often spontaneous and unplanned, occurring in relatively unmanaged areas, such as a meadow, a creek, a forest, or sometimes even a park or a child's backyard. Ecologist Robert Pyle describes these settings as places where "kids . . . [are] free to climb trees, muck about, catch things, and get wet." These areas include "watercourses, such as creeks, canals, ravines, and ponds, a big tree, a clump of brush, bosky dell, or hollow; parks, especially undeveloped ones; and old fields, pastures, and meadows."[4]

By contrast, children's indirect experience of nature, although involving actual contact, occurs in created and highly controlled environments that depend on ongoing human management and intervention. Indirect experience of nature tends to be highly structured, organized, and planned; it may occur in settings such as zoos, botanical gardens, nature centers, museums, and parks. These indirect encounters sometimes involve domesticated animals (pets), household plants, or other elements of the nonhuman world that have been incorporated into the human household. Domesticated creatures usually mean cats and dogs but can also include horses, birds, and even fish or a potted plant that retains qualities of "wildness." Children's indirect experience of nature can also occur through flower and vegetable gardening, raising livestock, and interacting with creatures and habitats that require human input and control.

The vicarious, or symbolic, experience of nature does not involve contact with actual living organisms or environments but, rather, with the image, representation, or metaphorical expression of nature. Vicarious experience can be clearly evident or, at times, highly stylized and obscure. Children today encounter a wide range of vicarious images and symbols of the natural world—a teddy bear, the three pigs, the big bad wolf, Mickey Mouse, Lassie, Winnie the Pooh, depictions in such films as *Free Willy* and *Never Cry Wolf*, and in National Geographic specials and other television programs such as *Animal Planet*. Such vicarious representations of nature are surprisingly prolific despite modern society's diminishing direct contact with nature, a consequence both of revolutionary new electronic media (film, television, computers) and of the widespread occurrence of more traditional forms of written communication (books, magazines, comics).

Counter to the notion that vicarious natural contact may be a particularly contemporary phenomenon, the symbolic experience of nature has an ancient lineage, perhaps as old as human society itself, which is encountered in the oldest rock art and more figuratively in innumerable myths, fables, tales, and totems over the long course of human evolution. Still, the unprecedented development of mass communications technology appears to have produced an extraordinary proliferation of natural images. Some people worry that such vicarious experience is rapidly replacing the more direct and spontaneous forms of childhood contact with the natural world, an issue that will be discussed later in this chapter. First, we will explore the relative role of each form of contact with nature in children's development. In this regard, we will link these forms of contact with nature to three kinds of childhood development: (1) cognitive or intellectual, (2) affective or emotional, and (3) evaluative or moral development (Figure 9).

Nature and Cognitive Development

A taxonomy of cognitive development developed by psychologist Benjamin Bloom and his colleagues identified six stages in children's normal intellectual development, moving from relatively simple to more complex levels of understanding, problem solving, and thinking.[5] The shift from one cognitive stage to another is typically sequential and hierarchical, with one intellectual stage usually following the preceding one. A summary of the six stages includes the following:

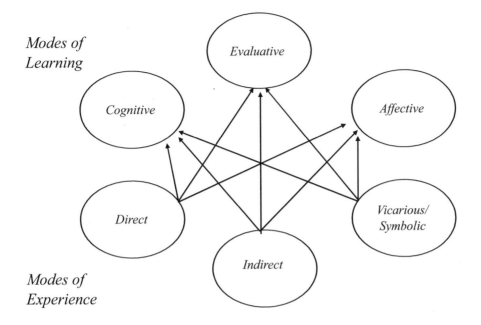

Figure 9. Modes of Experiencing Nature and Modes of Learning in Maturation and Development

- *Stage one: Knowledge.* The first stage emphasizes the child's emerging capacities to understand basic facts and terms and then apply this knowledge to presenting ideas, rendering broad classifications, and expressing a rudimentary understanding of causal relationships.
- *Stage two: Comprehension.* The second stage involves the child's developing capacity to interpret and paraphrase information and ideas and then extrapolate these understandings to other situations.
- *Stage three: Application.* The third stage stresses the child's maturing capacity to apply knowledge in generating ideas, concepts, and even principles applied to a wide range of situations.
- *Stage four: Analysis.* The fourth stage involves the child's evolving ability to examine and then break down knowledge into constituent parts and then use this understanding to elucidate underlying relationships.
- *Stage five: Synthesis.* The converse of analysis (stage four), the fifth stage emphasizes the child's ability to integrate and collate knowledge from discrete parts, organize it into structured wholes, and then use this knowledge to identify and understand relationships.

• *Stage six: Evaluation.* The final stage in cognitive development involves the child's ability to form judgments about the functional significance of parts of patterned and structured wholes based on carefully examining evidence, impacts, and outcomes.

As noted, the major task of the first stage of cognitive development is forming basic understandings of facts and terms, creating rudimentary classifications, and crudely discerning causal relationships. The natural world greatly aids this emerging capacity because it affords numerous highly stimulating and engaging opportunities to identify and order basic information and ideas. At a relatively early age, children encounter in nature a vast array of objects for labeling and discriminating features and properties. The young child continually confronts opportunities to assign names and categories to basic and nearly ubiquitous features of his or her life, including trees, bushes, plants, flowers, birds, mammals, habitats, and landscapes.

Moreover, this process occurs in direct ways as well as through more representational, metaphorical means. Part of nature's attraction for the young is its wide range of subjects encountered in so many forms. For example, in North America almost all children encounter to some degree oaks, maples, pines, poison ivy, dandelions, roses, tulips, dogwoods, robins, cardinals, turtles, snakes, fish, ants, mosquitoes, clams, crabs, rivers, lakes, streams, valleys, rocks, cliffs, boulders, wind, rain, clouds, and more. They also confront this wealth of subject matter, and a nearly equal richness of more remote or fantastic creatures, such as tigers, bears, hippos, giraffes, dinosaurs, and monsters, in realistic as well as stylized ways. The abundance of actual and symbolic opportunities nature offers for naming, sorting, and classifying is unrivaled by any other aspect of the child's world. Moreover, a major appeal is that these objects are fundamentally similar to the child either because they are alive or because they relate closely to his or her everyday world. Nature offers all children an especially salient and dramatic focus for developing the capacities to know, label, and classify, which are basic to the first stage of cognitive maturation.[6]

This opportunity occurs not only through direct contact or observation of nature but also through more metaphorical means. Children's preschool books, for example, offer many images drawn from nature to help develop the ability to name, categorize, and count. The stories include such characters as "one bear," "two giraffes," "three lions," "four hippos," or "five mountains," but rarely contain contrived artifacts of an entirely human constructed world. Nature's depiction is often anthropomorphic in these tales, but this represents a stimulating approach that almost always engages children.

Anthropologist and veterinarian Elizabeth Lawrence uses the provocative term *cognitive biophilia* to suggest that images and symbols of nature are often used to aid human communication and maturation.[7] Even in our modern society, which is characterized by extraordinarily inventive fabrication, images drawn from the natural world continue to provide an unrivaled, irreplaceable context for challenging children's cognitive development. For children, nature is the richest, most detailed, and most readily available informational context they are ever likely to encounter.[8]

Contact with nature in children's cognitive maturation can also be identified in the second stage of intellectual development, comprehension. Comprehension emphasizes the translation, interpretation, and extrapolation of facts and ideas involved in collating and validating information through observation and experience. Both real and imagined encounters with the natural world offer children a wide range of accessible and emotionally salient opportunities to develop this ability to analyze, assimilate, and comprehend facts and ideas.

A major challenge of childhood is developing the ability to translate and interpret experience by systematically assessing objective, empirical evidence. Examining the world through the eyes of a child, we see again that nature provides numerous opportunities to develop this capacity through objects that are frequently encountered in a child's ordinary life. For example, the North American child learns to comprehend that snow falls at certain temperatures and rain at others; that trees grow in soil and not in water or through asphalt; that ducks and geese inhabit wet rather than dry or upland places; that butterflies fly during the day and moths at night; that many, rather than one or a few trees, constitute a forest; that cattle and sheep group together in herds while large predators generally stand alone and apart; that crabs and clams muck about in marshy rather than dry habitats; and more.

Indeed, no other aspect of a child's life offers this degree of consistent but varied chances for critical thinking and problem solving—a steady diet for the mind as well as the body. The child engages in an ongoing dynamic of intellectual development by distinguishing creatures, natural features, and environmental processes; by lumping and classifying life and non-life into categories of relation and distinction; by observing and interpreting the processes of feeding, reproducing, surviving, and dying. The child observes many normal and abnormal events in nature, helping him or her progress from simple acts of identification and classification to more complex conceptualizations and predictions. This spiral through the various stages of cognitive maturation aided by a matrix of direct, indirect, and symbolic experiences of nature helps condition and strengthen the muscle we call the mind.

To expedite our discussion, we will bypass similar descriptions of the four remaining stages of cognitive development to consider how contact with nature can influence children's affective development.

Nature and Affective Development

The natural world strongly affects children's emotional maturation. Again, we can draw from the work of developmental psychologists in examining this relationship. David Krathwohl and his colleagues identified five stages in emotional maturation:

- *Stage one: Receiving.* The first stage focuses on the child's developing awareness of and sensitivity to facts, information, and ideas, and the willingness to receive and consider this information.
- *Stage two: Responding.* The second stage emphasizes the child's capacity to react to and gain satisfaction from receiving and responding to information, situations, and ideas.
- *Stage three: Valuing.* The third stage involves the child's ability to attribute worth or importance to information, ideas, and situations, reflecting a clear and consistent set of preferences and commitments.
- *Stage four: Organization.* The fourth stage emphasizes the child's ability to internalize and organize preferences and assumptions of worth into a consistent, stable, and predictable pattern of values and beliefs.
- *Stage five: Characterization by a value or value complex.* The final stage reflects the child's ability to integrate values and beliefs into a coherent worldview or philosophy of life.[9]

Only the first two stages of this taxonomy are considered here in examining children's experience of nature in affective development. Stages three through five are treated as a separate growth process that is neither entirely affective nor cognitive but, rather, is a combination of the two. In other words, values are viewed as a combination of intellect and feeling.[10]

In the first two stages of affective development, children develop the capacities to receive and respond to information, ideas, and situations. These emotional states encourage intellectual maturity as children form emotional interests that motivate them to seek and understand information and ideas. Children's feelings can be considered building blocks for acquiring knowledge, as suggested by psychologist Leonard Iozzi: "[There is] significant evidence that the affective domain is the key entry point to learning and teaching."[11]

What aspects of a child's world provide an emotional basis for receiving and respond-ing to new information and ideas? Certainly, significant people (parents, siblings, friends, teachers, neighbors) represent an irreplaceable core that encourages emotional receptivity and attachment. However, children are also highly attracted to the natural world, most particu-larly to its living forms. A child's experience of nature, especially of other animals, provides an emotionally powerful, if secondary, basis for affective development.

How does this occur? A child responds to stimuli with such basic emotional states as like, dislike, attraction, aversion, doubt, joy, sorrow, fear, wonder, and more. For most children, the natural world consistently elicits these and other basic emotional states. For example, young people encounter in nature various creatures that look, move, and feel like themselves. These resemblances prompt children to respond emotionally, most importantly by extending to these creatures the presumed capacities to feel and to think, which produces an emotional bond and assumption of reciprocity. As psychologists Gene Myers and Carol Saunders explain: "Animals are so fascinating [for children because] they are highly responsive and offer many dynamic opportunities for interaction."[12] These researchers identified four prop-erties of familiar animals that generally prompt children to identify emotionally with them: (1) "agency," the seeming ability of certain animals to initiate and sustain patterns of behav-ior; (2) "affectivity," the apparent capacity of certain creatures to express and reveal feelings; (3) "coherence," the tendency of particular animals to react and respond to children; and (4) "continuity," the willingness of some animals (particularly companion animals) to repeat behaviors in response to a child. All four factors typically result in certain animals becom-ing subjects of children's emotional attachment, which aids the children's evolving capaci-ties for receiving and responding to information, situations, and ideas.

These affective encounters with animals, and with nature in general, tend to be so signifi-cant that most adults looking back on their childhood cite the natural world as an emotion-ally critical aspect of their youth. Psychologist Rachel Sebba reports that an extraordinary 96.5 percent of all adults she studied, who represented a wide range of age, gender, and other demo-graphic groups and were raised in both urban and nonurban settings, identified the outdoors as being of critical emotional significance during their childhood. Moreover, the natural set-tings recalled were typically quite simple and ordinary, such as a backyard or nearby park.[13]

For many adults, these early childhood experiences of nature constitute a treasured emotional legacy that they draw on for personal creativity. Pioneering psychologist Edith Cobb reports in her study *The Ecology of Imagination in Childhood* that many highly gifted persons cite the mem-ory of particular childhood environments as an emotional basis for their creative production. These childhood experiences enabled them "to renew the power and impulse to create at its very source." Childhood contact with nature formed for these persons an affective crucible on which they forged a sense of wonder, exploration, and discovery. The encounters were frequently joyful, adventurous, and surprising as well as a source of curiosity, mystery, and inventiveness. As Cobb suggests:

> The child's sense of . . . nature is . . . basically aesthetic and infused with joy in the power to know and to be. These equal, for the child, a sense of the power to make. . . . The child's sense of wonder, displayed as surprise and joy, is aroused as a response to the mystery of [the] stimulus [of nature] that promises "more to come" or, better still, "more to do"—the power of perceptual participation in the known and unknown.[14]

Cobb also invokes the poetry of Walt Whitman to explain the emotive power of nature for children and its ability to infuse them with wonder and joy:

> There was a child went forth every day,
> And the first object he looked upon, that object he became,
> And that object became part of him for the day or a certain part
>   of the day,
> Or for many years or stretching cycles of years.
> The early lilacs became part of the child,
> And grass and white and red morning glories, and white and red
>   clover, and the song of the phoebe-bird,
> And the Third-month lambs and the sow's pink-faint litter, and
>   the mare's foal and the cow's calf.[15]

The environmental scientist Rachel Carson similarly observed how often a child's capacity for wonder, exploration, and discovery begins with and is encouraged by an emotional experience in and identification with nature. She suggested that feelings of interest, enthusiasm, and joy typically originate in the natural world and become motivating forces in childhood learning and cognitive development. She also noted how often these feelings precede and motivate intellectual maturation. Carson wrote:

> For the child . . . it is not half so important to *know* as to *feel*. If facts are the seeds that later produce knowledge and wisdom, then the emotions and the impressions of the senses are the

fertile soil in which the seeds must grow. The years of early childhood are the time to prepare the soil. Once the emotions have been aroused—a sense of the beautiful, the excitement of the new and the unknown, a feeling of sympathy, pity, admiration or love—then we wish for knowledge about the object of our emotional response. Once found, it has lasting meaning. It is more important to pave the way for the child to want to know than to put him on a diet of facts he [or she] is not ready to assimilate.[16]

Experiencing nature during childhood engenders both curiosity and the passion to learn that reflects a willingness to give and receive information, facts, and ideas. By interacting with the natural world, children encounter a matrix of diverse and stimulating opportunities to engage such affective capacities as wonder, imagination, and joy. Children's experience of nature provides a source of deep and enduring emotional significance throughout people's lives. As Rachel Carson suggests:

A child's world is fresh and new and beautiful, full of wonder and excitement. . . . What is the value of preserving and strengthening this sense of awe and wonder, this recognition of something beyond the boundaries of human existence? Is the exploration of the natural world just a pleasant way to pass the golden hours of childhood or is there something deeper? I am sure there is something much deeper, something lasting and significant. . . . Those who contemplate the beauty of the earth find reserves of strength that will endure as long as life lasts. There is symbolic as well as actual beauty in the migration of the birds, the ebb and flow of the tides, the folded bud ready for the spring. There is something infinitely healing in the repeated refrains of nature.[17]

In addition to wonder, fascination, and emotional attachment, a child's experience of nature can elicit far less pleasant feelings, such as uncertainty, anxiety, pain, and fear. The emotional power of nature to inspire and instruct depends on sentiments ranging from pleasure and satisfaction to vulnerability, foreboding, and a feeling of danger. If not overwhelming, all of these positive as well as negative emotions contribute to maturation and development.

Why does the natural world emotionally arouse children so strongly and consistently? Part of the answer lies, as psychologist Rachel Sebba suggests, in its being "an unfailing source of stimulation."[18] Nature provides an endless bounty of circumstances that prompt an emotional as well as an intellectual response. Imagine for a moment the wide variety of emotional states associated with the following scenario: A young girl and her friends make a long, fatiguing climb up a wooded mountain at the edge of town. They enter a dark, foreboding forest and eventually emerge into the light at the mountain's peak, where they look far into the distance. They return along the edge of a steep, dark canyon, where they spy a soaring hawk above and also occasionally look down at curious crawling insects as they challenge and explore the unknown. Fearing they are lost, they eventually stumble on a road that leads back home. In the course of their short journey, they experience pleasure, wonder, fascination, apprehension, anxiety, and more, all raw material in the process of emotional and intellectual maturation.

Nature provides young people with diverse and challenging opportunities for affective and cognitive growth. These experiences present many ways for children to cope and adapt, often in contrast to the ambiguity and complexity of their dealings with adults. As psychiatrist Harold Searles observes: "The non-human environment is relatively simple and stable, rather than overwhelmingly complex and ever shifting . . . and generally available rather than walled off by parental injunctions."[19]

The emotional importance of nature for children is also found in stories and fantasy. Nature's mystery and wonder are frequently revealed through children's stories, fables, fantasies, and even dreams.[20] This world of make-believe includes high mountains soaring into the mist; frightening creatures plotting people's demise; and young boys and girls aided by animal friends who manage to save the day for their families and friends. These fantasies provide ways for children to engage their sense of mystery, wonder, uncertainty, adventure, and fear of failure. Fantasizing about nature offers children highly emotional encounters in important and often disguised ways.

A potentially disturbing aspect of contemporary life is the rapid growth of fictional and fantastic depictions of the natural world accompanied by a pronounced decline in direct and real encounters.[21] Children too often today confront a contrived, artificial nature in place of an actual, ordinary experience. Confronting nature as fantasy creatures in story and film or as herds of exotic wildlife on television may be entertaining and sometimes instructive, but it can never adequately substitute for direct and real contact. The contrived experience of nature rarely provokes in children strong and lasting emotional responses, such as wonder, joy, surprise, challenge, and discovery. This sense of excitement, adventure, and imagination that a familiar experience of nature can provide is illustrated by poet Dylan Thomas's recollection of a local park from his youth:

> Though it was a little park, it held within its borders of old tall trees, notched with our names and shabby from our climbing, as many secret places, caverns and forests, prairies and deserts, as a country somewhere at the end of the sea. . . . And though we could explore it one day, armed and des-

perate, from end to end, from the robbers' den to the pirates cabin, the highwayman's inn to the cattle ranch, or the hidden room in the undergrowth, where we held beetle races, and lit the wood fires and roasted potatoes and talked about Africa, and the makes of motor cars, yet still the next day, it remained as unexplored as the Poles. . . . And that park grew up with me; that small world widened as I learned its secrets and boundaries, as I discovered new refuges and ambushes in its woods and jungles; hidden homes and lairs for the multitudes of imagination.[22]

Again, this question of the relative importance of direct versus indirect symbolic experience of nature in children's maturation in modern society will be considered in more detail later in this chapter. Next, we examine the role of contact with nature in evaluative development.

Nature and Evaluative Development

Evaluative maturation refers to a child's evolving capacity to form values, a fundamental aspect of moral development. Understood as the attribution of worth or importance to—as well as the realization of benefits from—information and situations, values reflect a clear, consistent set of judgments and preferences. Values are the synthesis of emotion and intellect, an organizational property that cannot be explained by or reduced to either affect or cognition alone. Healthy maturation involves the formation of children's values of nature. The nine biophilic values described in chapter two form the basis of this development; when they become functionally evident, they enable children to adapt more readily as they mature into adults.[23] Because these biophilic values are weak biological affinities, their operative development in children depends on adequate experience, learning, and social support. Although they were described fully in chapter two, let us briefly review the prominent benefits of each value here.

Developing an *aesthetic* value stimulates a child's curiosity, imagination, and ability to create and discover; to discern order and organization; to form ideas about symmetry, harmony, and balance; and to recognize the potential for achieving safety, sustenance, and security. Developing a *dominionistic* value fosters a child's resourcefulness and the ability to cope with adversity, to take risks and confront the unknown, to explore and discover, to achieve a sense of independence and autonomy, and to gain self-confidence and self-worth. Forming a *humanistic* value enhances a child's capacity for bonding, companionship, and giving and receiving affection; caring for others and expressing intimacy and trust; and being sociable and cooperative. Developing a *moralistic* value increases a child's ability to form judgments about good and bad, to treat the world with kindness and respect, to develop a sense of faith and trust, and to experience spiritual meaning and purpose.

Developing a *naturalistic* value enhances a child's curiosity, exploration, and discovery; demonstrating competence and craft; and achieving self-confidence and self-esteem. Forming a *negativistic* value helps a child avoid harm and injury; minimize risk and uncertainty; and experience feelings of awe, humility, and respect for forces greater than the self. Developing a *scientific* value fosters a child's capacity for observation, analysis, and empirical examination; critical thinking and problem solving; and appreciation and respect for the diversity and complexity of creation. Forming a *symbolic* value enhances a child's classificatory and taxonomic skills, communication and cognitive capacities, and ability to cope with complicated aspects of psychosocial development through imagery and story. Finally, developing a *utilitarian* value enhances the child's ability to achieve physical comfort and security, to demonstrate craft and skill, and to eventually reap material and physical rewards.

Three major stages occur in the maturation of children's values of nature. The first stage generally occurs before age six or during early childhood and focuses on developing utilitarian, dominionistic, and negativistic values of nature. These values reinforce a child's sense of physical and material security and the avoidance of threat and danger. Although not absent during this period, affection for nature is subordinated to the more fundamental concerns for safety, sustenance, and security. The very young are anxious about direct and uncontrolled contact with nature, with the exception of restricted contact with highly familiar creatures and settings (e.g., companion animals encountered close to family members and trusted others). Exploratory encounters typically occur in the protective, guiding environment of the home. During early childhood, children are fascinated by drawings and photographs of nature, particularly of big and familiar animals—such as fat hippos; long, preposterous giraffes; and frightening yet thrilling wolves—that help develop their abilities to identify and acquire language and numeric skills.[24]

The second stage in the development of children's values of nature occurs during middle childhood (roughly ages six to twelve). During this period, the child forms basic ideas about nature and gains a rudimentary empirical understanding of the natural world. Middle childhood marks a time of rapidly developing humanistic, symbolic, and aesthetic values of nature. Children at this age learn to recognize other creatures and habitats, although still primarily those near their own homes and neighborhoods rather than in wild settings. Children in middle childhood also begin to appreciate other creatures as independent and autonomous, existing apart from their own immediate interests and needs, and they start to comprehend the "differentness" and "otherness" of life. They also develop the capacity to form strong bonds with animals, especially with companion animals and well-known species. As their grasp of the separateness of the natural world grows, they further begin to develop a sense of responsibility and caring for nature based on conscience rather than simply on punishment for doing something wrong.

During middle childhood, children also begin to venture away from the immediate home into the relatively unfamiliar terrain of the backyard and neighborhood, as they start to engage and immerse themselves in more natural and less domesticated settings. Here, they can expand their interests, curiosities, and feelings of competence independent of adult supervision. Children of this age rapidly develop a cognitive interest in the natural world, including basic information and ideas about nature that assist in problem solving and creative ventures (often in neighborhood open spaces). These local natural settings provide many chances for children during middle childhood to explore, discover, imagine, and create.[25] As psychologist David Sobel explains:

> Middle childhood is a critical period in the development of the self and in the individual's relationship to the natural world. The *sense of wonder* of early childhood gets transmuted in middle childhood to a *sense of exploration.* Children leave the security of home behind and set out . . . to discover the new world. . . . Middle childhood appears to be the time when the natural world is experienced in highly evocative ways. It appears to be the time when children strike out, alone or with peers, to explore an ever-expanding repertoire of reachable places, in search of new experiences and adventure.[26]

During middle childhood, children also use natural settings to develop an identity apart from their parents and immediate household. Eminent psychologist Erik Erikson describes middle childhood as a time when the young person becomes engaged in making things, demonstrating industry and competence, and establishing a self apart from adult control.[27] Nearby nature in particular affords children of this age a varied and stimulating source for creating a place away from but near the home—for example, forts, dens, hideouts, and playhouses. Commonly secreted in the foliage of ordinary nature, these constructions provide the chance for independent creation, producing a sense of autonomy and confidence in children of this age as they manipulate objects in the effort to create their own world of safety and security. As Sobel further describes:

> During . . . middle childhood, the self is fragile and under construction and needs to be protected. . . . The secretive nature of the hiding place is significant. . . . To go farther in their explorations, many children at this age create an outpost, a place to be "at home" in the outdoors.

Forts and playhouses serve as places to look at the world from a place of one's own, as places for experimenting with how to put things together. The satisfaction of being able to transform the environment successfully and comfort in being able to make a place for oneself.[28]

These constructive, creative encounters with nature during middle childhood often produce great satisfactions—as well as memories commonly retained into adulthood. As writer Wallace Stegner observes: "There is a time somewhere between five and twelve . . . when an impression lasting only a few seconds may be imprinted . . . for life. . . . Expose a child to a particular [natural] environment at this susceptible time and he will perceive in the shapes of the environment until he [or she] dies."[29]

Psychologist Louise Chawla reported that adults almost universally cite the outdoors of middle childhood as one of the most significant settings of their childhood. She suggests that adults use these recollections of nature for what the poet Wordsworth called "tranquil restoration," a time to reflect and draw strength from the presumed simplicity and beauty of youth. Citing research by Hoffman, Chawla asserts that adults reminiscing about childhood emphasize "moments [in nature] in which [they] seemed to experience a . . . sense of rapture or great harmony." These instances of intimate immersion in nature often become seared in memory and are recalled throughout a person's life, particularly at moments of crisis or injury.[30]

Symbolizing nature is also important for children's development during middle childhood.[31] Unlike the very young, whose images of nature focus mainly on naming and counting, the fantasies of middle childhood dwell on more complicated matters of psychosocial development. Children at this age use nature symbolically to confront issues of identity, selfhood, good, evil, trust, betrayal, innocence, guilt, order, and chaos. They accomplish this through stories, tales, and myths involving characters such as Cinderella, Snow White, Winnie the Pooh, the Lord of the Rings, and others. Children confront in these often anthropomorphic stories disturbing and risky situations of conflict, need, desire, power, and authority, though almost always in beguiling and enchanting ways. Psychologist Bruno Bettelheim, in his classic essay "The Uses of Enchantment," emphasizes the symbolic utility of the nonhuman world, described here by human ecologist Paul Shepard:

The [children's stories] dramatize the intrinsic childhood worries which the youthful listener unconsciously interprets as his [or her] own story and his [or her] own inner self . . . [Bettelheim] believes the problems to be universal, having to do with protection from malicious relatives, the uncertain intentions of strangers, [the child's] verbal or physical limitations, . . . the bodily changes and functions associated with growth, . . . rivalry, jealousy and envy. . . . Every story is a magical prophecy of personal transcendence. . . . Their message is that special skills, often the powers represented by different animal species, will come to the rescue, solve the problems, save the day.[32]

The third stage in children's development of their values of nature occurs during adolescence (ages thirteen to seventeen). Children at this age significantly develop their ecological, moralistic, and naturalistic perspectives of the natural world. Rapid, pronounced development of abstract and conceptual reasoning about nature occurs, helping adolescent children form ethical and moral judgments about their relationship to the natural world.

They understand and appreciate larger spatial and temporal scales, which are reflected in their evolving grasp of such concepts as ecosystems and evolution. They also become more concerned about moral obligations to care for and to protect nature, particularly treatment of other animals and issues of inflicting pain, suffering, or causing pollution and despoiling the natural environment. This does not suggest that younger children are incapable of forming moral judgments about the natural world; rather, this evaluative tendency becomes far more pronounced and manifest during the late teenage years.

Adolescents also become far more ambitious and adventurous in challenging unfamiliar terrain. These outdoor experiences offer important opportunities to develop physically and psychologically, to exercise independence and autonomy, and to build self-confidence and self-esteem. Research on outdoor programs (reported in chapter two) reveals the considerable effects on maturation these experiences often produce during late adolescence, including enhanced capacities for coping and problem solving, critical thinking, and interpersonal skills. The following comments attest to the perceived benefits these outdoors encounters provide for late adolescents in particular:

[My outdoor program occurred at] a pivotal point in my life. It gave me the opportunity to take a risk. It strengthened my sense of self. It gave me a feeling of purposefulness, self-respect, and strength that I had never had before. When you have confidence in yourself it affects every aspect of your life.

[My outdoor experience] was the most amazing, awe-inspiring, thought provoking, and challenging experience of my life. It helped me to believe that if there is anything I really want to do in life, I have the ability to do it. All I have to do is look deep inside myself and I can find it. [It] helped me realize who I was and how I fit into the world around me. This realization affects every decision I make in my life.

[Being in nature] gave me an unbelievable confidence in myself. I found a beauty, strength, and an inner peace that I never knew was present. I learned the most I ever learned about life, myself, and skills that I still use everyday. It made me more confident, focused, and self-reliant. I have become more compassionate towards not only nature, but towards other people. I learned about respect, setting goals, working to my maximum and past it. These are skills I consider to be important in everything I do, and I feel they will help me continue to be successful throughout life.[33]

On the other hand, some research has reported diminishing interest and involvement in nature among teenagers. Psychologists Rachel and Stephen Kaplan report that adolescence is a "time-out" period when concern about peer relationships and social competence replace attraction to the outdoors.[34] Further exploration, however, suggests that these interpersonal concerns do not substitute for or replace adolescent interest in nature so much as they indicate the need for these children to share these outdoor experiences with others of their own age. This may suggest why group-oriented outdoor programs, such as those offered by the National Outdoor Leadership School and Outward Bound, are so popular among late adolescents.

The three-stage development of children's values of nature shares several characteristics in common with the processes of affective and cognitive maturation described earlier in this chapter.[35] First, values formation appears to progress from more concrete and direct relationships with nature to more abstract understandings and interactions. Second, the initial focus on individual needs and immediate interests in relation to nature widens with age to become a broader concern for social interactions and relationships. Third, the focus on the natural world shifts at an early age from local and parochial settings to a more regional and even global emphasis during adolescence. Finally, early childhood emphasis on emotional and affective development in relation to nature broadens during middle childhood to more cognitive concerns, and during adolescence to a greater stress on abstract ecological and moral reasoning about nature.

The Importance of Direct Experience

We have considered how various kinds of direct, indirect, and vicarious contact with nature exerts a shaping influence on children's emotional, intellectual, and moral development.

Echoing the assertion of psychiatrist Harold Searles, we have found: "The non-human environment, far from being of little or no account to human personality development, constitutes one of the most basically important ingredients of human psychological existence."[36]

Considerable data underscored the particular influence that direct experience of familiar natural settings has on children's maturation, especially during middle childhood.[37] Direct, often spontaneous contact with nature appears to constitute an irreplaceable core for healthy childhood growth and development. Commenting on the importance of direct experience, conservation biologist and writer Robert Pyle argues: "It is through close and intimate contact with a particular patch of ground that [children] learn to respond to the earth. . . . We need to recognize the humble places where this alchemy occurs. . . . Everybody has a ditch, or ought to. For only the ditches—and the fields, the woods, the ravines—can teach us to care enough."[38]

Ecologist and anthropologist Gary Nabhan has similarly observed the importance of familiar and ordinary—rather than unusual or spectacular nature—in his own children's maturation. He reflects: "I've come to realize that a few intimate places mean more to . . . children . . . than all the glorious panoramas."[39] Both theory and evidence support the view that direct, ongoing experience of nature in relatively familiar settings remains a vital source for children's physical, emotional, and intellectual development.

Why does direct contact with nature affect childhood maturation so strongly? The work of psychologist Rachel Sebba can help address this question, particularly several critical characteristics of the direct experience of nature that exercise a powerful effect on children.[40] First, Sebba emphasizes that the natural world is extraordinarily diverse and variable, thus, exerting an especially stimulating impact on a child's senses of sight, sound, smell, touch, and taste. Moreover, these responses are unavoidable and occur in nearly all settings, from rural to urban. Children are rarely far from the sight of plants, the feel of wind, the smell of soil, the sounds of songbirds, even the disturbing presence of spiders. A child's sensory experience of nature is so ubiquitous that it often remains intuitive and unnoticed, a constant aspect of life. Second, Sebba points out that the child's normal experience of nature occurs in a continuous, dynamic way: "The natural environment is characterized by a continual change of stimuli (over time or across area)." Nature's sensory effect is constantly shifting and modulating across geographic areas and throughout the day and season, forcing on the child its recognition, awareness, and response.

Third, Sebba emphasizes that the natural world is revealed in random, unpredictable ways. As she suggests: "The external environment is characterized by instability." A dynamic, altering natural environment demands the child's "alertness and attention" and, as a consequence, requires that the child adapt his or her perception and behavior to respond to new, emerging, and often challenging situations.

Finally, Sebba points out that nature is replete with animate life and life-like features. She observes: "The natural environment is . . . one from which life springs and one which exerts forces that cause inanimate objects to move." This aliveness is revealed in forms familiar to children, which they can easily identify with as an integral part of their lives. This quality of animation fundamentally distinguishes for children the natural from the built environment. No degree of finely executed fabricated or artificial product can fully replicate the vital, ambient qualities of living nature. The natural world constitutes that singular place where life is born, grows, feeds, seemingly feels and thinks, and then dies. Even nonliving elements in nature, including the air, water, and landscapes, often seem life-like for most children, even if not precisely alive. The child intuits that these features support and sustain life, and though not an ecologist, he or she can readily observe that all creatures need water, that some animals eat plants and others eat other animals, and that the air is the irreplaceable foundation for life and behaves at times like a great ambient beast.

A basic dilemma of the modern age is whether children still experience enough direct contact with the natural world. Some argue that a disturbing aspect of contemporary life is a profound decline in both the quantity and quality of children's direct experiences of nature. Children are increasingly separated from the natural environment, direct contact with nature being gradually replaced by indirect and vicarious experience.[41]

Many factors have contributed to this decline in modern children's direct experience of nature, including extensive pollution and degradation, decline of open spaces, habitat fragmentation, loss of biological diversity, the growth of artificial and impervious surfaces, the replacement of native fauna and flora by exotic and introduced species, the disappearance of familiar species and environments, crowding and congestion, and an increased reliance on motorized transportation. Changing social and cultural patterns have also added to the decline. Traditionally, adults have served as the critical role model for a child's developing interests in the natural world mainly by introducing and familiarizing the child with various outdoor activities and communicating this knowledge from one generation to another. Yet adults—especially parents—now appear to be less and less involved in shaping children's outdoor interests. This situation is likely a consequence of increasing geographic and social mobility, declining extended-family networks, less stable communities, urbanization, and destruction of local habitats. Increased concern about children's safety also seems to have made adults less willing to allow children to play spontaneously outdoors without supervision.[42]

Play in nature, particularly during the critical period of middle childhood, appears to be an especially important time for developing the capacities for creativity, problem solving, and emotional and intellectual development. This has apparently been the norm throughout human history, as designer Randy White describes based on an extensive review of relevant literature:

> Throughout most of history, when children were free to play, their first choice was often to flee to the nearest wild place. . . . Two hundred years ago, most children spent their days surrounded by fields, farms, or in the wild nature at its edges. By the late twentieth century, many children's environments had become urbanized. . . . But . . . as recently as 1970, children [still] had access to nature and the world at large. They spent the bulk of their recreation time outdoors, using the . . . playground, parks, . . . vacant lots and other spaces "left over" during the urbanization process.[43]

Unfortunately, during at least the past twenty-five years, the chances for children to directly experience nature during playtime has drastically declined. For many reasons, most children today have fewer opportunities to spontaneously engage and immerse themselves in the nearby outdoors. This change reflects a declining availability of appealing, accessible habitats as well a reduction in children's time and inclination to play outdoors. As White again observes:

> Not only have children's play environments dramatically changed in the last few decades, but also the time children have to play has decreased. Between 1981 and 1997, the amount of time children ages 6 to 8 in the U.S. played decreased 25%, by almost four hours per week, from 15 hours a week to 11 hours and 10 minutes. . . . A recent study surveyed mothers and found that 70% of mothers in the U.S. played outdoors everyday when they were children, compared with only 31% of their children, and that when the mothers played outdoors, 56% remained outside for three or more hours compared to only 22% of their children.[44]

Modern especially urban society appears to rely more and more on indirect and vicarious forms of contact with nature instead of direct, spontaneous experience. More than ever, contemporary children encounter nature through organized, supervised, and formal visits to places like zoos, nature centers, and museums, or through the lens of television, film, and the computer. Children today are more likely to encounter exotic wildlife from Africa or Asia (whether in the zoo or on television) than to have contact with common creatures in nearby settings. As political scientist David Orr observes: "The reigning political economy has shifted the lives and prospects of children from direct contact with nature to an increasingly abstract and symbolic nature; routine and daily contact with animals to contact with things; . . . direct exposure to reality to abstraction and virtual reality."[45]

Robert Pyle invoked the evocative phrase "the extinction of experience" to describe these tendencies toward diminished and compromised direct contact with ordinary nature.[46] Pyle, a conservation biologist and author of the World Conservation Union's book on endangered invertebrates, certainly understands the biological meaning of the term *extinction* as it is reflected in some twenty-seven thousand annual projected species extinctions today.[47] Yet he also recognizes from a more anthropocentric view that the significant decline in the human (and especially childhood) experience of nature constitutes a profound loss of psychological and social bearings as much as it does the elimination of unique gene pools. He writes:

> Simply stated, the loss of neighborhood species endangers our experience of nature. . . . Direct, personal contact with living things affects us in vital ways that vicarious experience can never replace. I believe that one of the greatest causes of the ecological crisis is the state of personal alienation from nature in which many [children] live. We lack a widespread sense of intimacy with the living world. . . . The extinction of experience . . . implies a cycle of disaffection that can have disastrous consequences. As cities and metastasizing suburbs forsake their natural diversity, and their citizens grow more removed from personal contact with nature, awareness and appreciation retreat. . . . So it goes . . . the extinction of experience sucking the life from the land, the intimacy from our connections.[48]

Yet we know little about the long-term developmental impacts of children having far fewer opportunities to directly experience the natural world. Our knowledge is also scant regarding the possible compensatory effects of an apparent increase in indirect and vicarious experiences of nature fostered by the rapid growth of electronic media, organized programs, and formal institutions. Nonetheless, children's affective, cognitive, and evaluative development appears to have suffered greatly from reduced direct contact with the natural environment due to increasing habitat degradation, biodiversity loss, declining open space, urban sprawl, pollution, and shifts in familial and community patterns.

Would it be exaggerating to label this decline in direct contact with nature an extinction of experience? Although major losses of biological diversity measured in thousands of species extinctions undeniably represents a biological catastrophe, this appalling event primarily afflicts obscure invertebrates in remote places (e.g., tropical rain forests), far removed from the ordinary lives of most contemporary children. Still, children encounter the decline of the natural world every day through widespread extirpations of familiar species and habitats. Most children today experience an impoverished, highly simplified natural world as a result of pollution, urban sprawl, and the widespread conversion of natural habitats to artificial ones. Children regularly confront nature's declining and precarious condition; the abundance of pollutants in the air, water, and soil; and the decline of legendary creatures such as the tiger, grizzly bear, gorilla, elephant, rhinoceros, panda, whale, and more. How does this daily exposure to pervasive environmental abuse (in the place of natural health, beauty, and diversity) affect a child's sense of hope and optimism over the long term? What is lost when children no longer experience direct, ongoing access to local species in nearby settings?

Can a rapid, significant increase in opportunities for indirect and vicarious contact with nature replace or at least compensate for substantial reductions in direct ordinary experience of the natural world? Children today participate more than ever in many organized, planned activities in nature through school programs; visits to zoos, natural history museums, and nature centers; and outdoor programs, wildlife watching, and nature tourism. Contemporary children also have unprecedented access to the natural world through television, film, computers, and the Internet. These media represent revolutionary technological developments never before encountered in human history that give children unparalleled access to species and habitats from across the globe in the comfort and security of their homes and schools.

But do these encounters exert the same quality of developmental impact on children as do more direct, unstructured contacts, especially in local settings? Recalling the four features of the direct experience of nature cited by Louise Chawla—intensity, variability, instability, ambience—indirect or vicarious contact rarely offers the same degree of opportunity for experiencing challenge, adaptation, immersion, creativity, discovery, problem solving, or critical thinking as that afforded by direct encounters in the natural world. Confronting nature through television or computer, or at the zoo or nature center, does not provide children with intimacy, adventure, or surprise, all of which (and much more) form the basis for substantive learning and development. As Robert Pyle describes:

> Electronic mediation . . . may effectively convey facts and impressions and generally reinforce interest in animals and geography. But when the world comes edited for maximum impact and bundled into quick bites and bytes, it fails to convey the everyday wonder of the much maligned

ordinary. Just as real life does not consist primarily of car chases and exploding buildings, quo-
tidian nature is much more about grasshoppers in the pigweed than it is rhinos mating on a pix-
ilated screen.[49]

The direct experience of nature also extends to the child the possibilities of uncertainty, risk,
and failure. These realities necessitate adaptation and problem solving as well as the need
to construct solutions and to think critically, all of which are essential to lasting learning and
maturation. These conditions rarely arise when children passively watch television, visit a
zoo, manipulate a computer screen, or even in most classrooms. As Pyle suggests: "Everyone
has . . . a chance of realizing a pleasurable and collegial wholeness with nature. But to get
there, intimate association is necessary. A face-to-face encounter with a banana slug means
much more than a Komodo dragon seen on television. . . . Direct, personal contact with other
living things affects us in vital ways that vicarious experience can never replace."[50]

What about the compensatory effects of high-quality zoos, museums, nature centers, or
outdoor programs? These activities can and do influence knowledge and appreciation of the
natural world.[51] But do these activities sufficiently substitute for direct contact in ordinary
natural settings? Let us examine some relevant findings from studies of zoos. First, zoological parks are not a modern invention; menageries originated as long as four thousand years
ago, the modern zoo emerged in Europe during the sixteenth and seventeenth centuries, and
some four hundred accredited zoos exist today. Zoological parks are also extremely popular, with annual visits in the United States alone totaling more than 130 million people, and
with 98 percent of Americans having visited a zoo at some point in their lives. Research on
modern zoos that have naturalistic exhibits and ambitious educational programs has found
that these places can positively affect children's knowledge and appreciation of wildlife. Yet
research also suggests that this understanding is transitory and rarely contributes significantly
to children's maturation and development. Moreover, visits to less progressive zoos often
result in marginal to no improvement in learning and even at times to negatively affect children's appreciation and concern for the natural environment.[52]

Zoos and other indirect forms of natural contact have limited developmental effects
because they provide few opportunities for spontaneous immersion and challenge and
because they occur infrequently, existing only on the periphery of children's lives. Indirect
organized contact with nature also tends to be passive, requires little feedback, and commonly emphasizes entertainment more than sustained learning and maturation. Visits to zoos,
aquariums, and museums often focus on exotic, unusual species and habitats unrelated to chil-

dren's daily lives. These indirect, highly regulated, and often contrived forms of contact with nature are commonly more of a simulation and a "show" (no matter how sophisticated the fabrication), and most children recognize them as such. The zoo or museum lacks the reality and relevancy of direct experience in ordinary settings.

What about outdoor programs in relatively undisturbed natural settings, such as those described earlier in this chapter, which have been proven to exert significant developmental impacts on adolescent children in particular? Clearly, these programs are important learning experiences, but several factors limit their capacity to substitute for direct ordinary contact. First, these programs typically are available to only a small fraction of today's youth because of their high costs and their location in pristine settings. The programs also constitute highly unusual forms of contact with nature that take place in settings only marginally related to the everyday reality of most children. As one participant suggested: "[Participation] shifted my perspective a little bit. . . . I went and gathered some strength. But, the experience now seems so distant. Everything we learned is relevant, but it is so abstract. We learned how to organize and be careful with what we do with our bodies. But with the everyday hustle [and] bustle of daily life it is hard to incorporate this into my life."[53]

Structured, organized, planned encounters in the natural world generally do not offer the spontaneity, challenge, and relevancy afforded by direct experience in ordinary familiar settings. Positive developmental effects certainly occur from indirect and vicarious contact with nature, but these benefits should be viewed as complementary to rather than substitutes for direct experience of local environments. As Robert Pyle describes:

> Nature reserves . . . are not enough to ensure connection. Such places, important as they are, invite a measured, restricted kind of contact. . . . Children . . . need free places for puttering, netting, catching, and watching. . . . Spots near home where [they] can wander off a trail, lift a stone, poke about, and merely wander: places where no interpretive signs intrude their message to rob [their] spontaneous response.[54]

Experiencing nature in ongoing, unregulated, direct ways offers children irreplaceable opportunities for exploring and discovering, for creating and developing their personalities and identities, for probing and testing the margins of their world. Direct access to modest and even compromised natural settings can strongly influence childhood development. Even vacant lots, what one researcher called "unofficial countryside," can allow children opportunities to construct, create, and develop a sense of independence and identity.[55]

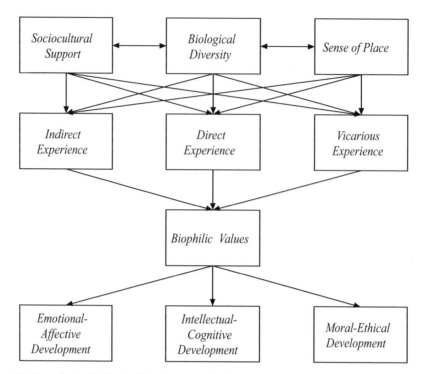

Figure 10. Hypothetical Relationship of Sociocultural Support, Biological Diversity, and Sense of Place to Experience of Nature and Development of Biophilic Values and Emotional, Cognitive, and Evaluative Development

Conclusion

This chapter, thus, concludes somewhat ambivalently. We have explored how children's emotional, intellectual, and evaluative development depends on varied, ongoing experiences of natural process and diversity. The need for such experiences can be satisfied through a broad matrix of direct, indirect, and vicarious encounters with nature in settings and circumstances from early childhood through adolescence. This contact produces the greatest maturational benefits when it occurs in stable, accessible, and culturally relevant social and physical environments. This array of factors, along with their hypothetical impacts on children's development, appears in Figure 10.

Yet a review of the various contemporary forces that have greatly diminished children's ongoing direct experience of nature prompts a more sobering conclusion. We have offered considerable evidence here and in chapter two suggesting that the ultimate raw material for much of human intellect, emotion, personality, industry, and spirit is rooted in a healthy, accessible, and abundant natural environment. Can children achieve meaningful, satisfying lives despite the degradation of their direct experience of nature? Like adults, children can endure and survive polluted air and water as well as the extirpation of many life forms. But will they prosper physically, psychologically, or morally under such conditions? Given the perspective and material presented in this chapter, it seems unlikely.

The decline in children's experience of nature will not change until a fundamental shift occurs in the attitudes and practices of developers, designers, educators, political leaders, and ordinary citizens. The enormous challenge facing us is how to minimize and mitigate the adverse environmental impacts of the modern built environment and how to provide more positive opportunities for contact with nature among children and adults as an integral part of everyday life. How can we reconcile—if not harmonize—the natural and human built environments through changes in how we design and develop our increasingly urban world? This is the subject of chapter four.

4

Harmonizing the Natural
and Human Built Environments

The relationship of manmade structures to the natural world offers . . . the richest and
most valuable physical and intellectual experience that architecture can show, and it
is the one that has been most neglected by . . . architectural critics and historians.
There are many reasons for this. Foremost among them, perhaps, is the blindness of
the contemporary world to everything that is not itself, to nature most of all.

— Vincent Scully, *Architecture: The Natural and the Manmade*[1]

Education's greatest crime is to have removed men from nature. . . . All great ideas
and impulses were born in the open air, close to nature.

— Louis Sullivan, architect, paraphrased in D. Hoffman, *Frank Lloyd Wright:
Architecture and Nature*[2]

Many contemporary influences have diminished positive contact between people and
the natural environment, including forces of destruction and alienation. Symptoms
of environmental destruction include widespread habitat destruction, large-scale loss of biological diversity, soil and water pollution, resource depletion, atmospheric degradation, and
global climate change. These and other factors of an increasingly urban culture, at least as
conventionally designed and developed, have increased human separation—and even
alienation—from the natural world.

One major cause of alienation from nature has been how we design and develop our built
environment. We have constructed our modern buildings, communities, and cities by excessively

consuming natural resources, significantly transforming natural landscapes, producing enormous quantities of waste and pollutants, and disconnecting people from positive contact with nature.[3] The human built environment today consumes 40 percent of the world's energy resources, 25 percent of its freshwater resources, and 30 percent of its natural resources. Buildings further generate an estimated 20 percent of freshwater effluents, 25 percent of solid wastes, 40 percent of air emissions, 60 percent of ozone-depleting emissions, and 30 percent of greenhouse gas emissions. Increases in developed land and roadways in the United States alone now approach 3 percent annually, an area roughly half the size of Pennsylvania. The scale of this construction and development is reflected in environmental lawyer William Shutkin's suggestion that: "Land use and development in the twentieth century have been so extensive it is believed that 80% of everything built in the United States was constructed within the last fifty years."[4]

These impacts have been exacerbated by the spread of the urban environment, at least as it has been conventionally developed until now. Some 70 percent of people in the industrially developed world today reside in a city or suburb.[5] It is also sobering to realize that it took an estimated 1 million years for the human species to number 1 billion people, a mark reached in the mid-1800s. Yet today we total more than 6 billion and add roughly another billion every fifteen years. The most optimistic population projections suggest that we could stabilize at 8 to 9 billion people twenty-five to fifty years from now, with the majority living in cities.

Human population growth, urbanization, and massive development do not necessarily mean widespread environmental destruction and alienation from nature. However, the prevailing paradigm for designing and developing the human and especially the urban built environment has until now produced such outcomes. Today, construction and development move more resources and materials than do the traditional forces of weather and geology combined. They are, thus, the primary consumer of the estimated 40 percent of the planet's net primary productivity currently appropriated by the human species.[6] A partial listing of the environmental effects of this population growth, consumption, and construction of the built environment includes the following:

- Widespread atmospheric and environmental damage associated with the consumption of fossil fuels, particularly the generation of heat-trapping gasses and acidification of the atmosphere
- Toxic and chemical contamination dispersed into the air and waters
- Pollution resulting from an excess discharge of nutrients and fertilizers

- Depletion of stratospheric ozone caused by the release of atmospheric contaminants
- Photochemical smog generated by massive construction, energy use, and transportation
- Loss of biological diversity and natural habitats resulting from diverse land use and development practices
- Depletion of renewable and nonrenewable resources from the excessive manufacture of building products and materials
- Generation of liquid and solid wastes beyond the capacity of natural systems to assimilate and absorb
- Release of noxious chemicals and microbes into the indoor environment

Modern construction and development have also separated people from beneficial contact with the natural environment, leaving the majority of urban residents to spend most of their waking hours in buildings lacking daylight, fresh air, and exposure to nature. As psychologist Judith Heerwagen observes: "Modern workplaces are often seas of bland cubicles that isolate rather than integrate people with anything natural—not unlike the cages in the old style zoo."[7]

Heerwagen's reference to the traditional zoo reminds us that although it is no longer acceptable to restrict such species as tigers, bears, and elephants to barren cages because of it being presumably "inhumane," it has become acceptable to treat ourselves in this way. Perhaps this reality attests to how removed we have become from nature, inclined to view our species as somehow no longer subject to the dictates of our biology or evolutionary origins. Yet a mounting body of evidence discussed earlier in this book reveals how contact with natural systems remains a fundamental basis for human physical and mental well-being, maturation, and productivity.

The great design and development fallacy of our time is the presumption that the human built environment can exist independent of the natural environment (Illustration 12). The result of this presumption has been buildings and landscapes that routinely abuse and degrade people's experience of nature, fostering alienation and destructive environmental practices. Political scientist David Orr captures the reality of this paradigm when he points out that most buildings today

reflect no understanding of ecology or ecological processes. . . . Most buildings tell its users that . . . knowing where they are is unimportant. . . . Most buildings tell its users that energy is cheap and abundant and can be squandered. . . . Most buildings are provisioned with . . . materials and water and dispose of their wastes in ways that tell its occupants that we are not part of the larger web of life. . . . Most buildings resonate with no part of our biology, evolutionary experience, or aesthetic sensibilities.[8]

This conventional design and development paradigm is neither necessary nor desirable and is certainly not sustainable. Our challenge is to move beyond diagnosing this lamentable condition of diminishing ties to the natural environment to prescribing how we can restore these tattered connections. Creating less damaging, more positive relationships between nature and humanity, however, will require dramatic changes in how we construct our buildings and landscapes. Whether constructing commercial, manufacturing, civic, retail, educational, residential, or recreational structures, we will need to learn how to both minimize and mitigate the damaging effects of modern design as well as how to foster more positive connections between people and nature in the built environment. We refer to this new paradigm as *restorative environmental design*. It will be the focus of this and the following chapter.

Restorative Environmental Design

The fundamental goal of restorative environmental design is to achieve a more harmonious relationship between people and nature in the built environment. Two basic objectives drive restorative environmental design: (1) to reduce the adverse effects of modern design and development on natural systems and human health, and (2) to promote more positive contact between people and nature in the built environment. These complementary goals address the two ways contemporary development has contributed to the modern environmental crisis: impairing the integrity and functioning of natural systems, and compromising people's capacity to derive many benefits from their ongoing contact with nature.

The first objective—avoiding, minimizing, and mitigating the adverse effects of building and landscape development on natural systems and human health—is called *low environmental impact design* and is the primary focus of this chapter. Low environmental impact design involves many important challenges, which include promoting energy efficiency, creating renewable energy, reducing resource use, eliminating pollution, minimizing waste, maintaining healthy indoor environments, and avoiding habitat destruction and loss of biological diversity.

Restorative environmental design, however, goes beyond minimizing environmental harm. It also seeks to restore positive contact between people and nature in the built environment. Without this more affirmative dimension of design and development, long-term sustainabil-

Illustration 12. (*above and opposite*) A common result of contemporary design is an indifference to the natural environment that leads to environmental abuse and alienation. The two design styles shown here illustrate the difference between an antagonistic and a compatible relation to the natural environment.

ity can rarely, if ever, be achieved, no matter how much improvement occurs in reducing resource consumption, enhancing energy efficiency, minimizing waste, or abating pollution. Without the positive experience of nature, people will not be inclined to commit the necessary energy, emotions, and resources to sustaining buildings and constructed landscapes over time, regardless of how technologically sophisticated these efforts may be. As architect James Wines suggests: "People will . . . never want to keep an aesthetically inferior building around no matter how well stocked . . . with cutting edge thermal glass, photovoltaic cells, recycled materials, and zero emissions carpeting. The mission [of sustainable design] . . . is [also] to recover those fragile threads of connectedness with nature."[9]

William McDonough and Michael Braungart advance a similarly broad vision of sustainable design when they distinguish "eco-efficiency" from "eco-effectiveness." They describe eco-efficiency as minimizing and avoiding environmental harm caused by the built environment, a necessary and challenging objective but one, they suggest, that is too narrow and fails to provide a more compelling vision of a satisfying future. As McDonough and Braungart rhetorically ask: "If I look at eco-efficiency as a design assignment, what would it be? I'd have to say, 'I spend

my day trying to feel better by being less bad and my goal is zero.' . . . Humans are trying hard to be efficient because the buildings we make are typically so dangerous." They argue for a broader, more affirmative goal of sustainable development, one that combines avoiding environmental harm with generating ecological health. They suggest that we "design a building that's a net exporter, producing more energy than it needs to operate and becoming fecund, giving back. . . . [Why not, they ask, design] a building like a tree?—one that produces food and energy, creates no adverse wastes, and fosters beauty and diversity."[10]

Though admirable, McDonough and Braungart's concept of ecological health needs to be extended to include a greater emphasis on human experience, incorporating the recognition of how much people's physical and mental well-being depends on their contact with nature. Unfortunately, prevailing approaches to conventional, and even sustainable, design rarely address the human need for nature as an integral dimension of people's well-being. Yet an ultimately successful approach to sustainable design and development must also produce a beneficial experience rooted in people's innate biophilic affinity for the natural environment.

Other architects and ecologists—including John Lyle, John and Nancy Todd, Sim Van der Ryn and Stuart Cowan, and those of the Rocky Mountain Institute—have identified important dimensions of this expanded approach.[11] Their basic principles are listed in Table 4.1.

These principles help define major elements of restorative environmental design but lack an overall integration and conceptual focus. Missing from these formulations is a detailed delineation of what we call here *positive environmental impact (or biophilic) design*. Positive environmental impact or biophilic design involves building and landscape designs that enhance human well-being by fostering positive connections between people and the natural environment. Biophilic design encompasses two basic dimensions: organic (or naturalistic) design and vernacular (or place-based) design. Famed architect Frank Lloyd Wright coined the term *organic design,* defined here as features in the built environment that foster the direct, indirect, or symbolic experience of nature.[12] Many building and landscape qualities can elicit this organic response, including natural lighting, ventilation, and materials; shapes and forms that mimic natural features and processes; certain manipulations of light and space; views and prospects of nature; and more. The other major dimension of biophilic design is *vernacular design,* defined here as building and landscape features that foster the distinctive culture and ecology of what (as discussed in chapter two) landscape architect Fredrick Law Olmsted and biologist René Dubos called the "spirit of place."[13] People who lack a strong connection to the spirit of place rarely make good stewards or commit the necessary resources or energies needed to sustain their natural or built environments over the long term.

Table 4.1
Principles of Sustainable Design

Lyle	Todd and Todd	Van der Ryn and Cowen	Rocky Mountain Institute
• Letting nature do the work	• Design should follow, not oppose, the laws of life	• Solutions grow from place	• Recognize context
• Considering nature as both model and context	• Biological equity must determine design	• Ecological accounting informs design	• Treat landscape as interdependent and interconnected rather than fragmented
• Aggregating, not isolating	• Design must reflect bioregionality	• Design with nature	• Integrate native landscape with development
• Seeking optimal levels for multiple functions, not the maximum or minimum level for any one	• Projects should be based on renewable energy sources	• Everyone is a designer	• Promote biodiversity
• Matching technology to need	• Design should be sustainable through the integration of living systems	• Make nature visible	• Reuse already disturbed areas
• Using information to replace power	• Design should be coevolutionary with the natural world		• Make a habit of restoration
• Providing multiple pathways	• Building and design should help to heal the planet		• Expand design considerations to recognize distant effects
• Seeking common solutions to disparate problems	• Design should follow a sacred ecology		• Eliminate concept of waste
• Managing storage as a key to sustainability			• Rely on natural energy flows
• Shaping form to guide flow			• Educate building industry, clients, and consumers about sustainable design
• Shaping manifest form to manifest process			
• Prioritizing for sustainability			

Two basic assumptions guide restorative environmental design and point the way toward reconciling the natural and human built environments. First, the contemporary environmental crisis of damaged and impoverished natural systems and alienation from nature is fundamentally a design failure rather than an intrinsic feature of modern life, and it can be resolved through more efficient and benign building and landscape development. Second, we cannot construct deeply meaningful buildings and landscapes if they lack fundamental connections to the human affinity for the natural environment. The two principles of restorative environmental design—low environmental impact design and positive environmental impact (or biophilic) design—hold the promise of achieving a more harmonious relationship between nature and humanity in the built environment. Either approach alone cannot achieve long-term sustainability or resolve the contemporary environmental crisis. By combining both approaches, however, restorative environmental design can help heal modern society's generally adversarial stance toward nature. This perspective, thus, places the human relation to nature at the core of building and landscape design.

The Bren School

Before beginning a detailed description of various aspects of low environmental impact design in this chapter and of biophilic design in chapter five, the difference between the two can be illustrated by using the example of the Donald Bren School of Environmental Science and Management at the University of California at Santa Barbara, an 85,000-square-foot building constructed in 2001 and designed by the architectural firm Zimmer Gunsul Frasca Partnership. This project is among the nation's best examples of low environmental impact architecture, having succeeded in reducing various adverse effects on the natural environment.

The Bren School consists of classrooms, offices, laboratory space, and a large auditorium occupying a magnificent three-acre site alongside the Pacific Ocean (Illustration 13). The building cost roughly $30 million, with an additional $800,000 needed for its sustainable design features. The structure encouraged the University of California at Santa Barbara to have its new construction meet the standards recently established for green architecture known as Leadership in Energy and Environmental Design, or LEED (described more fully later in this chapter). The building received the LEED highest (platinum) rating, signifying its significant accomplishments in sustainable design.

The project accomplished much in the areas of energy efficiency, reduced resource use, improved indoor environmental quality, and building controls. The structure includes highly

Illustration 13. The Donald Bren School of Environmental Science and Management at the University of California, Santa Barbara—a 85,000-square-foot facility designed by Zimmer Gunsul Frasca Partnership—received LEED's highest (platinum) rating.

efficient lighting and HVAC systems, is extensively day lit, contains photovoltaic rooftop panels, and relies on purchased renewable energy. Innovative laboratory designs have resulted in substantial energy reductions through the use of efficient air-volume controls, exhaust fans, low-maintenance devices, and other high-performance innovations. Operable windows and natural ventilation have further reduced energy consumption as well as improved occupant comfort.

The project impressively conserves resources and materials, including recycled and reused plastic, glass, and carpeting used in floors, fixtures, furniture, and insulation. A substantial proportion of the building's concrete is derived from recycled fly ash (a waste associated with coal power production). Wood paneling was obtained from forests certified as sustainably managed. Reclaimed water is used for landscape irrigation and toilet flushing, while waterless urinals and automatic flush valves reduce water use. About 93 percent of construction waste and all of the demolition waste was reused and thereby diverted from landfills. Carefully selected roofing material has reduced the climate-warming effects of conventional roofs, and the building's site exploits the ventilating effects of sea breezes. Landscape design retained existing trees and used native xeric vegetation to reduce water consumption and avoid erosion. Using products without volatile chemical compounds and formaldehydes and installing an air-quality monitoring system fulfilled indoor environmental quality objectives.

Despite these achievements, the Bren building illustrates the limitations of an almost exclusive focus on low environmental impact design. The building is deficient in biophilic design features, lacking qualities that are likely to foster people's well-being through enhanced contact with nature. Although the structure abuts the Pacific Ocean, its window-less auditorium faces that direction, with only administrative and some faculty offices taking advantage of this remarkable site feature. Most classrooms, student areas, and offices are by contrast isolated from the oceanfront. The building's internal courtyard is hard surfaced and unappealing. Much of the building lacks a positive connection to the natural environment and remains aesthetically impoverished. The occupants are not likely to be motivated to restore and renew this construction once the building's low environmental impact design technologies are no longer especially innovative. The building's LEED platinum rating illustrates the inadequate emphasis of current sustainable design on low environmental impact approaches to the near exclusion of positive environmental impact considerations.

Low Environmental Impact Design

Still, low environmental impact design remains a fundamental and arguably first priority and, thus, is the initial focus of our description of restorative environmental design. Many conventional building design and development practices contribute to nonsustainable levels of resource use, waste, consumption, pollution, and illness. Collectively, these practices exert enormous pressures on local, regional, and even global systems, threatening the abundance and diversity of life on earth, including long-term human welfare. The consumption and pollution-related effects of modern design and development have resulted in widespread habitat fragmentation, disrupted food chains, compromised nutrient and energy flows, and impaired reproductive and feeding strategies of many species. Much of this consumption, waste, and pollution has impaired human health and welfare by depleting critical resources and contributing to human disease. The objective of low environmental impact design is to avoid or reduce these harmful effects.

Often, however, the disruptive environmental effects of modern design and development go unnoticed by the average person. An interesting current example is the impact of glass office towers on many bird species. Highly glazed buildings represent a miracle of modern architecture, only recently made possible by advances in structural engineering and glass man-

Illustration 14. Tall glass office towers can result in significant bird mortalities because of their highly transparent or reflective glass and excessive night illumination.

ufacture (Illustration 14). Highly transparent, strong, and energy-efficient tall glass towers can now be constructed with often extraordinary views in heavily populated urban areas.

Unfortunately, the adverse environmental impacts of glass buildings have been recently identified.[14] New data suggest that highly glazed office buildings constitute a significant hazard to bird life.[15] While the data remain sparse, in North America alone some 225 of 971 bird species have been found to experience mortality due to striking glass buildings. The total number of birds killed annually is estimated at a minimum of 4 million and a maximum of 976 million. If the latter figure is correct, this single building practice could represent a serious threat to bird life today.

Tall glass buildings pose several hazards to birds, especially to migratory species during fall and spring migration and particularly in certain habitats, such as flyways and estuaries, and when overcast and stormy weather prevail. Many birds are vulnerable to highly transparent glass during the day because the barrier is invisible and impenetrable. Highly reflective glass can also confuse birds and precipitate collisions, particularly when vegetation is reflected. Finally, during the evening hours, birds are often attracted and confused by brightly lit buildings, especially when the glass towers are above five-hundred feet, when conditions are overcast, and after midnight, when many species descend to lower elevations.

The seeming ubiquity of bird life may suggest a relatively minor problem that should not interfere with the construction of useful and often beautiful buildings. However, the possibility of millions—even close to a billion—birds being lost each year in our continent alone because of a single building practice not only is lamentable but aptly illustrates how a seemingly innocent modern technology can adversely effect the natural environment and remain practically unknown to the public.

One laudable attempt to reduce this impact is the recent construction of an eight-hundred-foot-high glass office tower in Jersey City, New Jersey, for the financial services company Goldman Sachs (Illustration 15). Designed by architect Cesar Pelli and associates, the tower's glass facade features significant modifications as well as lighting design that should substantially reduce bird mortality. These design changes include the use of inserted ceramic frits in the external glazing to make the facade more visible to birds, less-reflective glass, reduced night illumination, and intermittent instead of continuous rooftop beams.

The construction of glass buildings, although a seemingly innocent building practice, illustrates how large-scale modern technology and development often have profound yet unrecognized impacts on the natural environment. Like much of contemporary life, its harmful consequences are not so much the result of deliberately malicious intent but, rather, the unintended consequences of enormous environmental transformations combined with an inadequate understanding of their long-term impacts. The adverse impacts of modern building design must be adequately assessed at multiple spatial and temporal scales—from the building itself to the larger site and to even more distant ecosystems and landscapes—to avoid these unfortunate effects.

We will now consider the adverse environmental and health-related effects of the built environment by focusing on five broad categories of impact:

- Energy use and efficiency
- Use of products, materials, and resources
- Waste and its management
- Indoor environmental quality
- Ecological and wildlife impacts

Avoiding and reducing these impacts on natural systems and human health constitutes an immense technological, socioeconomic, and political challenge. Volumes have been written about the complexities of such low-impact approaches as energy and resource efficiency,

Illustration 15. Significant changes in glass and lighting design of the Goldman Sachs building in Jersey City, New Jersey, will likely greatly reduce harm to migratory birds.

products and materials use, pollution avoidance, waste minimization, and indoor environmental quality. This section can only briefly review some aspects of these low environmental impact strategies.

In time, our society will need to move beyond merely controlling and mitigating these
adverse environmental effects to more ambitiously seeking to convert dangerous practices
into future sources of technical and ecological productivity. For example, we will need to
eliminate the very concept of waste, creating a "closed loop" system instead in which discarded building products and materials are reused or safely returned and assimilated into the
environment. As Charles Kibert, director of the University of Florida's Center for
Construction and Environment, suggests, this long-term approach will require a sense of
"stewardship that emphasizes . . . life cycle environmental impacts . . . and the development
of clean technologies . . . in sync with natural systems."[16] For now, we will consider the more
modest yet immensely difficult challenge of how to mitigate five areas of environmental
impact through more sustainable design and development practices.

Energy Use and Efficiency

Energy is used in lighting, heating, cooling, and other basic building functions. The vast
amount of energy used in contemporary construction and building operations, as well as the
wastes and pollutants generated, makes energy efficiency a priority objective of low environmental impact design.[17] Hydrocarbon resources, such as coal, oil, and gas, have been our
primary sources of energy in modern design and development, often generated by large-scale
centralized power plants and distributed by power grids and lines over long distances.
Relying on nonrenewable and often polluting energy sources has produced major ecological and human health impacts at various stages of energy extraction, production, distribution, and consumption.

Obtaining power from renewable and less polluting energy sources is a major goal of sustainable design and development. This objective has until recently focused on hydroelectric and
nuclear power, but these alternatives have now been proven to exert major ecological impacts
and cause contamination-related effects. Recent advances in energy efficiency and alternative
renewable energy production have begun to reduce nonrenewable energy use and to diminish
human health effects. Shifting from nonrenewable and highly polluting fossil fuels to cleaner
energy sources and production techniques has represented major progress. Using more efficient
lighting—as well as heating, ventilation, and air conditioning systems—and generating electric power from waste heat have also reduced energy consumption and waste.

Rapid strides in low-emission renewable energy production—particularly systems that exploit sunlight, wind, water, the relatively constant temperature of the earth, and potentially highly abundant chemicals like hydrogen—represent promising alternatives to the use of conventional fossil fuels. Advances in energy efficiency and renewable energy production could result in revolutionary shifts in energy use during the next quarter century, including combined heating and power generation and the use of nonpolluting energy sources. However, these developments remain technically and economically difficult to achieve, and several will prove impractical over time.

Conventional energy use can be substantially reduced through more efficient building design, construction, and operations, particularly in lighting, heating, ventilation, cooling, and machine and appliance use. An estimated one-quarter or more of building energy use can be attributed to lighting and appliances. Energy consumed in this single area can be significantly reduced by substituting more efficient lighting fixtures, using machines and appliances that consume substantially less energy, and employing more effective heating, ventilation, and air conditioning systems.

Sophisticated energy modeling in the design and construction of buildings can also improve the energy performance of buildings. Useful models have been developed by the U.S. Department of Energy, the American Society of Heating, Refrigerating, and Air-conditioning Engineers (ASHRAE), and others. These standards seek "minimum requirements for the energy-efficient design of . . . buildings so that they may be constructed, operated, and maintained in a manner that minimizes the use of energy, while not constraining either the building's functions or the comfort and productivity of its occupants."[18] "Intelligent" building controls can further reduce building energy consumption through better matching of energy use with various human activities and shifting climatic conditions. These controls include lighting and occupancy sensors, energy-monitoring systems, the creation of heating and cooling zones, and the cooling of buildings during the late, nonuse hours. Lighting controls also include photoelectric dimmers and task lighting that reduces electric demand.

The use of more effective lighting fixtures, lamps, ballasts, fans, filters, and motors can further reduce energy use. High-efficiency appliances and product leasing can also encourage product development and substitution that reduces energy use. Energy savings can be additionally achieved by minimizing water consumption through the use of low-flush toilets, automatic water shutoffs, flow-restricting nozzles, temperature controls, wide-diameter piping, and innovative systems such as composting toilets. One promising water use practice is the collection and reuse of stormwater. Captured rainwater can be used for cooling, washing, flushing, insulation, irrigation, or simply creating aquatic environments that enhance human physical and mental satisfaction. This energy-saving approach illustrates how a traditionally perceived waste can instead become a valuable resource.

An effective way to achieve energy efficiency is through more intelligent design of buildings that use and depend on less energy intensive mechanical systems. Labeled "passive" energy design, this approach in fact requires highly dynamic, complex, and sophisticated building designs. Passive design aims to achieve efficient energy use by exploiting such variables as a building's shape, orientation, airflow, and materials to control and manipulate water temperature, light, heat, wind, air, climate, and soil. Both modeling and the tools of computational fluid dynamics can be used to adjust these variables so that they minimize a building's need for mechanically produced energy. These design strategies reduce energy consumption and foster more renewable and non-polluting energy sources by optimizing a building's orientation to the sun, storing and releasing hot and cool air through the use of certain materials and forms, exploiting natural light and ventilation, and using the relatively constant temperature of belowground earth and water. Energy can also be saved by using heavy materials (e.g., brick and stone) in the building structure that, when combined with such design innovations as ventilating chimney stacks and atriums, can more efficiently distribute hot and cool air and control temperature changes.

An impressive illustration of passive design that has greatly reduced energy use is the Queen's Building in the industrial city of Leicester, England (Illustration 16). This 107,000-square-foot engineering laboratory located at De Montfort Engineering School was designed by the firm Short and Ford in the late 1990s. The building design achieves significant reductions in energy use by extensively relying on natural ventilation and daylighting. Energy savings also result from the building's unusual shape, the heavy materials used, and extensive building controls. The structure's long, narrow, open shape is unusual for a laboratory building, which more typically is rectangular and wide. The shape of the Queen's Building, however, permits a greater reliance on natural lighting and cross ventilation. Natural ventilation is also aided by the building's large number of ceiling and roof ventilators, chimney stacks, 1,600 operable windows, and extensive air vents and panels. These structural innovations have resulted in the near elimination of mechanical cooling. The natural ventilation system also includes more than one thousand monitoring stations located throughout the structure, which help control its airflow and temperature.

The extensive use of brick—characteristic of historic Leicester—as well as concrete further assist in absorbing, storing, and releasing warm and cool air. These building materials combined with a highly efficient gas-fired system reduce energy use and diminish temperature fluctuations. The building's design and operation, thus, dynamically manipulate

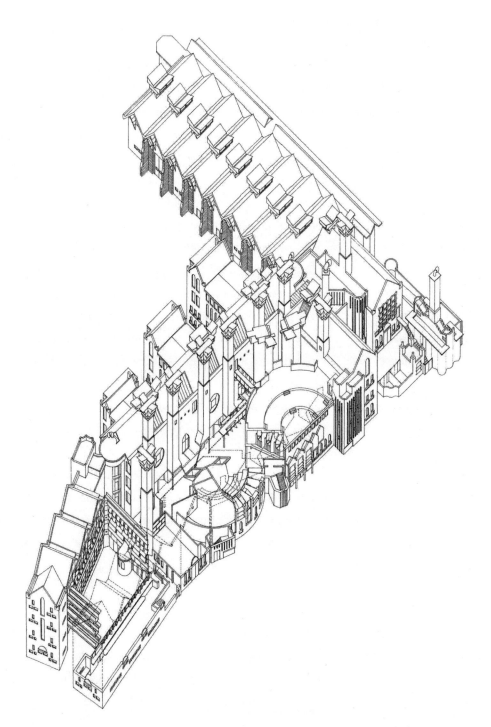

Illustration 16. Queens Building—a 107,000-square-foot engineering laboratory at De Montfort University in Leicester, England, designed by Short and Ford—has achieved exemplary energy efficiencies through reliance on natural ventilation, daylighting, extensive building controls, and a sophisticated design.

variables of light, air, temperature, and climate to achieve energy reductions greater than those in buildings of similar size and function. Major airflow and control modifications have been needed, however, to achieve consistent user comfort, especially in the auditorium areas.

The building's remarkable energy accomplishments were aided by an innovative decision-making process, including multidisciplinary collaboration and extensive planning that involved architects working closely with engineers, contractors, and clients. Sophisticated simulation and modeling analyses of airflows, natural ventilation, solar penetration and gain, and seasonal climatic fluctuations greatly contributed to the building's design. Extensive monitoring and controls were also a critical aspect of the building's performance.

In addition, the Queen's Building is aesthetically striking. Its large number and variety of windows, skylights, chimney stacks, light shelves, louvers, and vents give the brick facade an arresting shape and quality. This complexity of the design and materials was largely the outgrowth of efforts to exploit, manipulate, and control air, light, and temperature to minimize reliance on mechanical heating and cooling. This design strategy, which in many ways mimics the variability often encountered in many natural systems, prompted architectural critic Charles Jencks to label the building "post-modern Gothic." As Jencks describes:

> The large, rambling De Montfort [building is] Post-Modern Gothic . . . with [its] gables, pinnacles, pointed arches and polychromatic brickwork. . . . Gable-forms are transformed around the site—pointed, triangular, splayed, staggered—and ten different window-forms are used. Self-similarity and fractals appear again, laying against a stable background of ruddy brick, and made more stable because the mortar is coloured to match the brick. . . . This is a robust architecture that resists easy interpretation, showing that hallmark of . . . organizational depth. Today's "ecologically correct" building has an affinity with the Organic and Expressionist traditions of architecture, which were marginalized by Modernism.[19]

More conventional energy-efficiency strategies employed in many modern buildings include minimizing heating and cooling loss through the use of extensive insulation, window seals, double- and triple-pane glazing, and other energy-saving products and materials. Major improvements in glazing technology—such as high-performance, "low-emissivity" glass that fosters light transmittance yet deflects the radiant heat of the sun—can dramatically reduce energy loss while maintaining good visual access to the outside environment. When combined with optimizing a building's orientation to the sun and prevailing winds, innovative glazing technologies can produce considerable energy savings. Window shading, light shelves, and louvers that exploit natural lighting and ventilation while avoiding overheating and glare can also improve energy efficiency. Building designs that include high ceiling-to-floor ratios, attempt to cool the structure during the late evening hours, and have operable windows can further reduce energy use.

Energy-efficient design depends on careful consideration of an area's climatic conditions over the course of a day and season and in response to varying building uses. Buildings can be imaginatively and creatively designed to retain and release heat, foster natural ventilation and cooling, and reduce the need for mechanical systems and artificial lighting. Designs that manipulate varying natural resources and climatic conditions reflect a dynamic, multivariate approach that treats a building like a fine-tuned instrument or sailing craft. Rather than being perceived and operated as an inanimate object immutably frozen in space and time, the building is treated instead as a complex entity that is made to respond to changing environmental and human social conditions. This design strategy can reduce energy consumption, diminish waste, and lessen environmental harm and pollution.

Using waste heat for building heat and power, an approach often referred to as a "cogeneration" system, can also achieve considerable energy efficiencies. Most conventional single-use energy systems exploit approximately one-third of the energy produced. By contrast, cogeneration systems can potentially increase energy efficiency to an estimated 80 percent of the power generated. These systems can be further developed into an "eco-industrial" system in which the waste heat of one set of buildings becomes the heating and energy source for other, typically nearby structures.

Renewable energy production represents a long-term strategy for reducing the adverse environmental impacts of conventional nonrenewable energy fuels. Promising low-emission renewable energy sources exploit sunlight, wind, groundwater, earth temperatures, organic wastes (biofuels), and highly abundant substances, such as hydrogen used in fuel cells. Photovoltaic (PV) energy, which converts sunlight into electricity, represents an increasingly reliable, low-emission renewable energy technology. The cost and efficiency of PV systems still remains largely prohibitive, with the exception of remote locations that lack access to central power systems. Dramatic improvements in the cost and technical efficiency of PV have occurred in recent years, including the development of building-integrated PV systems that produce energy as well as provide material for the building facade.

Other promising renewable energy systems exploit wind, biomass, water, soil, and hydrogen. Although some of this energy can be produced on-site, it often involves purchasing from more remote locations and distribution through existing power grids. The feasibility of on-site energy generation depends on many factors, including technology, climate, geography, economic incentives, government assistance, and the tolerance and values of building users and nearby residents. A proven renewable energy alternative is exploiting the relatively constant temperature of the earth as well as groundwater by using pumps and tubes.

The use of wind energy has greatly increased in recent years following improvements in turbine technology, enhanced distribution systems, economic incentives, and government regulation. Wind energy costs have dropped an estimated 85 percent during the past twenty years, although on-site generation is often limited because of local meteorologic conditions, high costs, objections to noise, aesthetic damage, and fear of ecological impacts. A major expansion of remotely generated wind power could involve large wind farms in locations with especially suitable conditions, such as Wyoming, North Dakota, and South Dakota.

Another potentially important low-emission power source is the combustion of organic materials, or biofuel, from such waste products as vegetable oils, animal fats, wood chips, or methane from landfills. The United States contains an estimated seven hundred landfills that potentially could produce significant amounts of energy. Often technical and pollution-related obstacles need to be resolved.

Another promising alternative energy source is the hydrogen fuel cell. Hydrogen is the most abundant element in the universe. Rarely available in free form, it is generally found in combination with other elements, such as oxygen in water. Energy obtained from hydrogen results from the chemical conversion of hydrogen and oxygen in fuel cells. Significant technological and economic obstacles remain before the promise of hydrogen fuel cells can be realized. Still, the development of this new technology in buildings and vehicles could exert a revolutionary impact that would shift energy reliance from non-renewable, polluting fossil fuels to a nearly unlimited energy from a relatively pollution free source.

Materials, Products, and Resources

The design and construction of modern buildings consume enormous quantities of resources and materials, often resulting in significant adverse impacts on both natural systems and human health. The term *green materials* has been invoked to describe more environmentally benign and safer products, although the impacts of these as well as conventional materials are often difficult to ascertain.[20] Product labeling and certification programs can distribute relevant information based on a careful assessment of the environmental and health-related effects. Both governmental and nongovernmental organizations have been involved in these efforts, although the ratings and certification procedures sometimes involve contentious criteria.

The most widely used and accepted certification programs exist for natural resources (e.g., wood and fish) as well as for electrical appliances and machines.[21] The Forest Stewardship Council and the Sustainable Forestry Initiative have been two efforts to certify sustainably managed and harvested forest and wood products. The U.S. Environmental Protection Agency and ASHRAE have developed labeling systems to judge the energy efficiency of appliances and mechanical systems. The International Organization for Standardization (ISO) has created the ISO 14000 series to evaluate energy products, disseminate life cycle assessment procedures, and evaluate other aspects of product environmental performance.

Model contracts have also been developed to encourage vendors to specify and identify the environmental and health-related impacts of products and materials. Frequently specified performance criteria include energy efficiency, polluting and hazardous substances, recycled or recyclable content, and resources used. Low environmental impact products and materials should include the following:

- Few or no harmful emissions
- Few or no climate-altering or ozone-depleting chemicals
- High percentages of recycled, reused, or recyclable materials
- Biodegradable materials
- Durable materials requiring minimal maintenance
- Sustainably harvested resources
- Local rather than distantly manufactured and transported resources

The book *Green Building Materials: A Guide to Product Selection and Specification* specifies criteria for green product and material selection, including that they be durable, energy efficient, and recyclable; include recycled content; be obtained from local and regional sources; and contain few hazardous and synthetic chemicals as well as little embodied energy.[22] Various publications, directories, Web sites, and government and nongovernmental sources publish useful information regarding green product and material selection.

An impressive example of a building project that greatly reduced the amount of harmful environmental and health-related products and materials is Audubon House, the retrofit of a nineteenth-century Manhattan office building designed by Randy Croxton and associates working closely with their client the National Audubon Society (Illustration 17).[23] Most sustainable design focuses on new construction, which is often better able to take advantage of low environmental impact technologies. However, when sustainable design involves only new construction, it intrinsically fails to achieve the goal of reducing resource use and minimizing adverse environmental impacts. Audubon House is commendable as being one of the first sustainably designed renovations of an existing building—in this case, remarkable for occurring in the early 1990s, prior to many new products and materials becoming widely available.

Among the building's notable low environmental impact design accomplishments are the use of low-chemical-emitting products and materials, greatly improved energy efficiency, the reuse and recycling of resources and materials, and substantial waste reduction. Significant gains in indoor environmental quality resulted from careful—and, at the time, unprecedented— evaluation of chemicals found in carpeting, floors, paints, furniture, adhesives, and other products and materials. Energy was conserved by the installation of an advanced heating, ventilation, and cooling system, extensive reliance on natural lighting, widespread building lighting and ventilation controls, and extensive insulation and high-quality glazing. Audubon House also reduced waste by placing conveniently available recycling chutes on every floor.

The building's design goals were achieved even though construction costs were not allowed to exceed normal expenditures by more than 10 percent; much of this up-front expense was offset by savings over time, a healthier work environment, and enhanced employee health and productivity. These objectives were aided by a highly cooperative decision-making process that involved the collaborative efforts of architects, engineers, scientists, and clients well in advance of construction.

Audubon House unusually blends ideals, technology, and thoughtful design. Still, it achieves few biophilic design features. Although the design includes significant improvements in natural lighting and ventilation, as well as the partial installation of a rooftop garden, the building lacks organic and vernacular design features. Its low environmental impact gains largely occur beyond the experience of the average employee, who remains mostly isolated from contact with the natural environment. Audubon House, thus, neglects to offer its users a fundamentally different work environment based on an enhanced experience of nature (an issue we will discuss in detail in the next chapter).

The notion of embodied energy is another important consideration in green product and material selection. The energy and resources required to produce and consume commodities involves not just their immediate use but also all of the processes that are a part of their extraction, distribution, disposal, and possible reuse over the entire "life" of the product from "cradle to grave." This total amount of energy expended throughout a product's or material's "life cycle" is its *embodied energy*. Estimating only the "greenness" of a finished or consumed material can, thus, lead to misleading conclusions regarding its overall impact. For example, the embodied energy involved in

Illustration 17. New York City's Audubon House, a retrofit of a nineteenth-century office building designed by Randy Croxton and Associates, features many notable innovations in sustainable design.

the creation, use, and disposal of "virgin" aluminum usually far exceeds that of most wood products, steel, and, of course, recycled aluminum. Additionally, the embodied energy required for products obtained from distant or remotely manufactured and transported sources tends to be much higher than that involved in locally or regionally derived products and materials.

Technical, economic, and regulatory factors all affect the efficiency, reliability, cost, and availability of green products and materials. The values and ethics of producers and consumers are also as important as technical and regulatory factors in determining the manufacture and use of green materials. The public ultimately determines whether or not products are available that contain few pollutants, conserve energy, have a high degree of recycled content, minimize resource use or waste, and are durable and recyclable. People will need to be far more knowledgeable, caring, and ethically responsible if our society is to significantly alter the environmental impacts of various products and materials.

Waste and Its Management

The design, construction, and operation of buildings typically produces an enormous generation of waste, by-products, and discarded materials, often resulting from excess consumption and the tendency to construct new buildings rather than renovate them.[24] Each American on average produces some fifty thousand pounds of solid waste and twenty thousand gallons of liquid sewage each year. Much of this waste is disposed in landfills; incinerated; passed into the soil, water, and atmosphere; or treated through complex, expensive, energy-intensive technologies. Reducing waste and its environmental impacts requires vastly accelerating recycling, reducing consumption, and using more efficient and less harmful materials and technologies. The basic goals of efficient waste management include recycling and reusing solid wastes, processing and reusing liquid wastes, and minimizing unwanted by-products and materials.

An immediate, practical challenge is how to dispose of building construction and operational wastes to minimize pollution and environmental damage. Primary, secondary, and tertiary waste treatment technologies are available to meet this challenge. One useful practice is to divide building and construction wastes into different "waste streams"—for example, paper, glass, metal, plastic, wood, and food. Much of this material can be recycled and reused. A significant contemporary success has been policies that mandate the creation and recycling of several waste streams. In addition, establishing distinct, conveniently located, and easily utilized waste separation and collection facilities can better manage and process wastes more efficiently. Effective recycling depends on developing transportation, storage, and manufacturing systems that move and transform recycled materials into new products. Additionally, improving the durability and maintenance of products and materials can significantly reduce waste.

Demolishing existing buildings and constructing new ones produces considerable waste, which can often be reused and recycled. Building construction in the United States alone yields an estimated two pounds of waste per square foot of building annually, with much of this material discarded, accounting for one-quarter to one-half of all landfill debris. Construction and demolition waste often consists of asphalt, concrete, wallboard, roofing material, wood, and metals. In the United States, buildings consume one-quarter of all virgin wood, two-fifths of stone and gravel, and a large proportion of other natural resources. The potential economic and environmental benefits of recycling and reusing all of this material are enormous. These wastes can at times be salvaged and reused on site, and discarded wastes can often be reused to produce other construction material. For example, fly ash, a by-product of fossil fuel combustion, can be recycled to produce cement. The U.S. Environmental Protection Agency estimates this single recycled industrial waste could provide a high percentage of the cement used in the United States for paving, steel framing, and concrete construction, as well be incorporated into ceiling, floor, and wall material.

Wastewater can also be potentially reduced and recycled on-site from sinks, showers, stormwater, and even sewage. Stormwater can be exploited by installing rooftop cisterns, underground storage tanks, and constructed wetlands that capture and harvest precipitation, which is then used in internal and external building-related operations. Innovative on-site techniques have also used biodegradable processes to assimilate organic wastes, which are sometimes transformed into potentially useful materials.

One innovative example of wastewater reuse is the "living machine" system developed by John and Nancy Todd, which processes wastewater by moving it through several metabolic stages (Illustration 18). This system involves microorganisms and plants that "digest" and "cure" wastewater, which can then be used for other building uses, including flushing, irrigation, aesthetic and recreational enjoyment, and even fish production. The system typically includes aquatic tanks that provide a growth medium for bacteria, algae, plants, and sometimes crustaceans and fish. Sewage is decomposed by anaerobic and aerobic bacteria that generate nutrients for other organisms, which, in turn, progressively break down and remove wastes and pathogens. This waste management approach can convert waste into a resource as well as blur the distinction between the built and natural environments. As John Todd has suggested: "By studying waste recycling in a beautiful, ecologically diverse and dynamic Living Machine, [people can] begin to comprehend the meaning of natural systems in their lives."[25]

As this example illustrates, a long-term but critical waste management strategy is to shift from the very concept of waste to treating discarded products and materials as future

Illustration 18. Known as a "living machine," this wastewater treatment technology relies on microorganisms and plants to "digest" and "cure" wastewater so that it can be used for other building needs, such as flushing and irrigation.

stocks for producing other products and materials. As Charles Kibert suggests: "Much of [the] difficulty with waste is embedded in the word itself. Waste is defined as material considered worthless and thrown away after use. . . . This definition depends on the assumption that energy and materials, having once served our immediate purposes, can simply cease to exist in any functional sense."[26] Viewing waste as a resource shifts our perspective from managing an undesirable, feared substance to what William McDonough calls "food" that can be used to generate new and valuable products. McDonough advocates a waste management strategy that mimics natural systems whereby plants draw energy from the sun, produce needed products, and recycle their wastes into other forms of organic productivity yet leave few if any toxic materials behind. Such a strategy among people suggests two "waste to food" streams: one that safely recycles biodegradable materials back into ecological systems, and one that reuses nonbiodegradable materials as stocks for producing new products and materials.[27]

The shift to viewing unwanted and discarded wastes as sources for future products and materials requires a fundamental change in our values. It means discarding the prevailing attitude of wastefulness in an increasingly "throwaway" society, which is easily addicted to new products and technologies. We cannot minimize and eliminate wastes until we adopt an ethic of reusing and regenerating products that once served us well and can do so again.

Indoor Environmental Quality

We will consider indoor environmental quality (IEQ) only briefly, because this topic focuses primarily on a human health issue of building interiors rather than our emphasis here on human interactions with the natural environment. IEQ concerns historically emerged in response to the appearance of health-related problems associated with modern office buildings, including skin lesions, irritations, respiratory difficulties, and other neurological and respiratory problems. These buildings frequently had poor ventilation, extensive synthetic and chemically treated materials, and problematic heating and cooling systems. Ironically, IEQ problems occurred mostly in energy-efficient buildings that relied on airtight construction, extensive sealing and insulation, nonoperable windows, and technologies that limited the flow of air and fostered moisture buildup, contributing to the growth of molds and fungi. These health problems led to the identification of "building-related illness" and the designation of "sick building syndrome."

IEQ problems related to air and ventilation deficiencies can be exacerbated by products and materials containing chemically noxious substances, such as volatile organic compounds, formaldehydes, and known or suspected carcinogens.[28] Controlling the effects of these substances requires reducing, isolating, and eliminating certain chemicals. However, identifying the building or material source of these chemicals can be difficult, given the extraordinary range of products that include potentially harmful chemicals in flooring, carpeting, paints, drywall, furniture, fabrics, tiles, insulation, glazing, paneling, wood, glues, adhesives, sealants, caulks, preservatives, refrigerants, and fire retardants. Still, these harmful substances can be substantially reduced and sometimes eliminated. Moisture accumulation can also be reduced and prevented in heating, ventilation, and cooling systems and in airtight buildings by installing adequate numbers of air-handling ducts, filters, vents, and fans, and by implementing frequent fresh air exchanges.

Guidelines have been developed for avoiding certain paints, finishes, preservatives, drying agents, solvents, carpets, and furniture that potentially lead to health problems. Some of the most important criteria include minimizing the use of toxics and pollutants; including a high percentage of natural and biodegradable substances; avoiding formaldehydes, arsenics, and other known or suspected carcinogens; minimizing off-gassing and other chemical emissions; and assessing and certifying the safety of the indoor environment prior to building occupancy.

Ecological and Wildlife Impacts

The last low environmental impact objective considered here is minimizing the adverse effects of building construction on ecological systems and biological diversity. Species and ecosystem impacts should be considered at varying spatial and temporal scales, including direct and cumulative impacts at both on-site and off-site locations.[29] Reducing the amount of land and resources used in building construction and operations can substantially reduce ecological impacts. More deliberate planning can also minimize damage to sensitive species and critical habitats, such as riparian areas and migratory corridors. Design and development can also sometimes enhance and restore natural systems as well as create open space that benefits people as well as wildlife.

Building sites can be selected that lessen damage to particularly important ecosystems, such as wetlands and critical feeding and breeding areas. Development of undisturbed natural areas almost inevitably results in environmental degradation. Thus, whenever feasible, growth should focus on already developed sites. Restoring contaminated "brownfield" sites is generally preferred to "greenfield" development and can result in transportation and energy savings and the revitalization of frequently blighted urban areas (Illustration 19). An estimated 425,000 brownfield sites have been identified in the United States alone. Restoring and reusing this land could lessen the development of undisturbed areas, ameliorate past environmental wrongs, and assist in rebuilding economically and ecologically impoverished cities.

Minimizing soil erosion and the destruction of native organisms represents another important ecological objective. Soil that is removed from construction sites can almost always be safely stored and reused and, if contaminated, cleaned or recycled. Design modifications can reduce the direct wildlife mortality often resulting from building and landscape construction. In the earlier example of bird mortality, modifications include less-reflective, less-transparent glass; changed lighting design; and reduced night illumination. Excessive light pollution in urban areas has also been found to degrade the nocturnal environment for humans as well. For much of human history, the evening sky was an integral part of our culture and experience; its impoverishment in modern times may thus result in a subtly damaging effect on people's physical and mental well-being. The potentially insidious effects of modern light pollution could be mitigated by reducing building illumination as well as by using more shades and blinds and less exterior flood lighting.

Widespread reliance on pesticides and artificial fertilizers in landscape design and maintenance often leads to highly degraded water and soil quality. The quantity of water used in most landscaping can also be greatly reduced through more efficient watering techniques.

Illustration 19. Constructed on a contaminated industrial site, the Jubilee campus of the University of Nottingham, England, designed by Hopkins Architects, has been a significant catalyst for neighborhood revitalization.

An estimated one-fifth of water used in the United States is devoted to irrigating homes and buildings. Instituting more efficient operations, using recycled and collected stormwater, and avoiding discharges of damaging fertilizers and pesticides could all yield significantly improved water quality and quantity.

More intelligent and careful road design can also mitigate the ecologically damaging effects of modern road construction. Overreliance on impervious surfaces and the use of chemically harmful substances in asphalt and bituminous road products frequently lead to environmental damage. Reducing the amount of asphalt in roads and rooftops can also greatly diminish the "heat island" and "greenhouse" effects of modern cities that significantly contribute to local and global climate change. Using more porous paving materials can further reduce stormwater runoff and the harmful effects of toxic chemicals. Creating vegetative buffers beside roads can also lessen the environmental damage caused by impervious asphalt surfaces. Roads and highways can be more intelligently designed to minimize environmental damage and the ecological fragmentation of natural areas.

Contemporary transportation systems too often rely on highways to facilitate vehicular movement. The modern highway system has often resulted in significant adverse ecological, energy, and resource-related impacts. Unnecessary highway construction should be discouraged—as well as greater reliance on mass transit and increased, easier pedestrian movement. So-called smart growth and new urbanism strategies often complement restorative environmental design strategies. (Additional landscape development suggestions are included in the discussion of vernacular design in chapter five.)

Encouraging Low Environmental Impact Design

Before turning to the topic of positive environmental impact, or biophilic, design in chapter five, several important efforts should be noted that have greatly fostered low environmental impact design in recent years. These include the establishment of benchmarks and performance standards for designing, constructing, and operating the built environment. Important examples are the British Research Establishment Environmental Assessment Method (BREEAM); a development primer produced by the Rocky Mountain Institute (RMI); a guidebook to sustainable design developed by the architectural firm HOK; a sustainable design guide produced by the state of Minnesota and other states; and—most significant—the U.S. Green Building Council's Leadership in Energy and Environmental Design (LEED) system.[30] The RMI primer specifies design and construction criteria in such areas as site selection and development, transportation, building placement, land design, building configuration and shell, energy use, water, ecology, operations, and construction specifications. The *Minnesota Sustainable Design Guide* focuses on the six broad environmental impact categories of site, water, energy, indoor environmental quality, materials, and waste.

LEED has, however, become the most widely adopted and influential system. Created in the late 1990s, LEED is now employed extensively throughout the United States and more and more internationally. Major LEED categories include sustainable sites, water, energy and atmosphere, materials and resources, indoor environmental quality, and innovation and design process. LEED's appeal stems from its performance-based criteria resulting in numeric credits that at certain levels trigger LEED certification. Each LEED category includes design and construction objectives whose accomplishment beyond established standards generates LEED points. For example, in the sustainable sites category, a maximum of fourteen points is possible related to such impact areas as site selection, urban redevelopment, brownfield redevelopment, alternative transportation, site disturbance, stormwater management, landscape design, heat island effects, and light pollution. Similar point awards are related to the other categories. Across all the criteria, a total of twenty-six points results in LEED certification; thirty-three to thirty-eight points, a silver designation; thirty-nine to fifty-one points, a gold rating; and fifty-two to sixty-nine points, the highest, or platinum, award.

An example of how LEED can be an incentive for sustainable design that might not have otherwise occurred is the previously cited Goldman Sachs project in Jersey City, New Jersey. Initial interest in sustainable design was prompted by a concern of top executives about the potential large-scale bird mortality associated with tall glass office towers. However, driven by the goal of becoming LEED certified, the project collaborators expanded this wildlife concern to include a broader range of sustainable design objectives. In addition to mitigating bird impacts, the project's sustainable design objectives included energy efficiency, minimizing site disturbance, using recycled materials, reducing waste, improving indoor environmental quality, promoting mass transit, and redeveloping the brownfield site. These objectives were also emphasized within existing budget guidelines rather than being treated as an additional cost.

Brownfield redevelopment illustrates the project's low environmental design efforts. The Jersey City, New Jersey, site beside the Hudson River had been an industrial area for more than two centuries that was used to produce soap, cosmetics, chemicals, and machine parts. Cleaning its contaminated soil required the removal and cleansing of enormous quantities of mostly low level hazardous material. This soil was removed from a huge area—500 feet long, 325 feet wide, 45 feet deep—with much of it below the existing riverbed. The quantity of material removed occupied northern New Jersey recycling facilities for six months and required some three hundred thousand square yards of soil to be treated, recycled, stabilized, or capped. Some of this material was recycled as asphalt for a nearby airport runway, composted for a golf course's fairways, or used to construct a wastewater pond.

The client and designers are justifiably proud of their sustainable design accomplishments. Moreover, the client's prominence could influence other large firms to make similar efforts. Still, the project's nearly exclusive emphasis on low environmental impact technology reflects the biases and deficiencies of much sustainable design today. The Goldman Sachs project illustrates the LEED system's inordinate focus on low environmental impact design technologies and objectives. The Goldman Sachs project lacked such biophilic design considerations as improved natural lighting, natural ventilation, use of natural materials, landscape and riparian restoration, increased contact with nature, or an ecological and cultural connection with the site. This last omission was particularly regrettable in the Goldman Sachs project given its extraordinary location beside the Hudson River. The work setting or experience of the average Goldman employee will, thus, not differ substantially from that experienced in a conventionally designed office tower. The project's restorative environmental design deficiencies reflect the near-exclusive emphasis of LEED on low environmental impact goals and methodologies.

LEED and related sustainable design systems have unquestionably helped minimize the adverse environment impacts of much contemporary construction and development. These systems fail, however, to consider how by enhancing and restoring positive contact between people and nature we can foster human well-being and productivity. This additional challenge of restorative environmental design—positive environmental impact, or biophilic, design—is the focus of chapter five.

Biophilic Design

5

We will never achieve an ethical architecture that is beautiful and sustainable until nature is integral and at the core and at the substance and being of the architecture, not added on. If it ain't beautiful, it can't be sustainable. Buildings must shelter and inspire.

—Steve Kieran, architect, paraphrase of lecture, "Toward an Ethical Architecture." Yale University School of Forestry and Environmental Studies, New Haven, CT, February 3, 2005

As noted, restorative environmental design emphasizes two complementary goals: (1) avoiding, minimizing, and mitigating the adverse effects of building construction and development on natural systems and human health, and (2) promoting positive interactions between people and nature in the built environment. Unfortunately, the second objective is often neglected in modern design and development. Yet, humans evolved in a biological—not artificial or manufactured—environment and continue to depend on ongoing contact with nature for their physical and mental well-being. Sadly, however, the quality and character of the contemporary built environment has increasingly isolated people from the beneficial experience of natural systems and processes.

Reducing the adverse effects of modern development is arguably the first and more basic priority of restorative environmental design, but we must go beyond this limited objective to also identify how buildings and landscapes can foster human lives of meaning and satisfaction by celebrating our dependence on nature as an irreplaceable core of intellectual creativity and emotional capacity. The label "positive environmental impact" or, preferably, "biophilic"

design describes this second dimension of a comprehensive approach to restorative environmental design. The fundamental objective of biophilic design is to elicit a positive, valued experience of nature in the human built environment.

Incorporating biophilic design into modern development is critical. Over the long run,
few low environmental impact designs will prove to be sustainable or contribute significantly
to a more benign society if the developments lack significant biophilic design features and
characteristics. When people are not emotionally and intellectually attached to the buildings,
landscapes, and places around them, they will rarely be motivated to commit the resources
and energies needed to sustain ("keep in existence") these features. Low environmental impact
design innovations will inevitably become conventional, if not obsolete, in our rapidly changing world. When this happens, will a building's occupants be sufficiently motivated to maintain and restore the structure or will they neglect and eventually abandon it? Buildings and
landscapes that people do not associate with a positive experience of nature will almost
always be discarded overtime, because they are not perceived as aesthetically appealing or
connected to people's emotional and intellectual well-being. Low environmental impact
design that relies only on motivating people to avoid harm and damage to natural systems
and human health fails to offer a positive vision of how we can achieve lives of meaning and
satisfaction through our experience of the natural world. Therefore, the rhetorical question
must be: What is more sustainable—a technologically complex, low environmental impact
building isolated from the natural world and abandoned once its high technology systems
are no longer novel, or constructions that people revere and recycle generation after generation because they affirm an enduring and inherent affinity for the natural environment?
As psychologist Judith Heerwagen has argued:

> [Human] performance and well being . . . depend not only on the *absence* of significant [envi-
> ronmental] problems, but also on the *presence* of particular kinds of features and attributes in
> buildings. . . . The challenge of green design is . . . to integrate into buildings the positive bio-
> philic features of our evolved relationship with nature and to avoid biophobic conditions.[1]

Architect Rafael Pelli similarly remarked that sustainable design must achieve "more than a
series of solutions to technical problems. It must also seek to create something that transcends
the solving of specific problems, resulting in a valued reality in a special and beautiful place."[2]
The basic goal of restorative environmental design is to rekindle and renew our compromised
connections with the natural world.

The additional emphasis here on biophilic design should not be interpreted as advocating a subjective aesthetic over the more rational, objective standard of technical efficiency that characterizes low environmental impact design. Indeed, the opposite is the case. Satisfactions and benefits associated with biophilic design foster adaptive behavior that is instrumental to human welfare, including better health, reduced stress, improved emotional well-being, enhanced productivity, and increased problem solving and creativity. Design and development that satisfy only people's physical and material needs will not succeed if they deny other biophilic affinities for nature that are crucial to people's long-term physical, mental, and spiritual well-being.

The Bastille Viaduct

One project that restored contact with nature in an urban context is Bastille Viaduct, or Promenade Plantée, located in the eastern section of Paris, France (Illustration 20). The viaduct includes an elevated greenway (or "linear park") with commercial areas—glass street-level enterprises—located below its supporting arches. The promenade is situated on a former rail line originally constructed in the nineteenth century and is nearly three miles long, thirty feet high, and thirty- to one-hundred-feet wide. It consists largely of brick and was converted to a park-like promenade in 1998, designed by landscape architects Philippe Mathieu and Jacques Vergely.

The viaduct's conversion has revitalized the area socially and economically. The promenade on top of the viaduct contains a mosaic of gardens and pathways that include flowerbeds, trees, pergolas, bamboo forests, water gardens, and savanna-like areas. The walkway runs the length of the viaduct, periodically connecting to the ground, to the shops below, and to adjacent buildings via paths and stairs. The elevated viaduct allows the user to gaze out at the buildings and streets below while feeling removed from the noise and bustle of the city. The promenade's extensive vegetation and garden-like qualities add to this feeling of serenity. The greenway offers a remarkable pedestrian experience in an urban setting, in effect, an arrow of vegetation running through the heart of the city's clamor and congestion.

The promenade's popularity is enhanced by the successful conversion of the street-level vaults into commercial space. The resulting combination of shops, gardens, and pedestrian pathways has spurred a revival of the once-depressed East Paris area. Attracted by the promenade's open space, park-like qualities, and pedestrian access, new residents and businesses have renovated residential, commercial, and office space in the wider area. The environmental

Illustration 20. The Bastille Viaduct, an elevated greenway with commercial establishments located below, was designed by Philippe Mathieu and Jacques Vergely and constructed on a former railway line. The viaduct has stimulated revival of its East Paris neighborhood.

restoration of the viaduct has been a major catalyst and unifying element for the neighborhood's overall revitalization.

The aesthetic and recreational appeal of the promenade has been central to its success, providing a valued connection between people and nature in a highly urban setting. The three miles of linear open space offer an extraordinary amenity for both residents and workers. The integration of the promenade and the old brick viaduct fosters a strong vernacular connection to the city's past. Both environmental restoration and historic tradition informed the promenade's reconstruction in contrast to its possible destruction.

However, the promenade's design largely fails to incorporate many features of low environmental impact or ecological landscape design, which detracts from the project's overall relevance as a model of restorative environmental design. The walkway, which consists mostly of formal gardens and exotic plantings, makes little attempt to include native vegetation or to construct an ecologically self-sustaining environment. The nonindigenous plants require intensive management, including a regimen of watering, fertilizing, and treating with chemicals that reflects its imposed and contrived aesthetic. Nor does the promenade offer much in the way of food, shelter, or migratory corridors for native wildlife; thus, it does little to heal the prevailing breach between Parisian culture and its local ecology. The commercial spaces also lack low environmental impact design features, with scant attention paid to energy and resource use, waste generation and disposal, and material and product impacts. Still, the promenade represents an innovative and important accomplishment that has enhanced the economic and social well-being of its neighborhood by connecting people to nature in an urban setting.

Attributes of Biophilic Design

Biophilic design can be encountered in a building's facade, interior environment, decorative features, and exterior landscape. It can be directly, indirectly, or symbolically revealed and can sometimes occur unconsciously, without deliberate creation or even sometimes explicit recognition. This subjective element of biophilic design underscores its ancient qualities, which often tap into inherent human affinities for nature that people frequently fail to recognize. Consequently, many of the world's most admired buildings and landscapes possess prominent biophilic features that are often barely appreciated yet exert powerful effects on us (Illustration 21). Architectural historian Grant Hildebrand alludes to this more subjective, inherent quality of biophilic design when he suggests:

> We are biologically predisposed to liking buildings and landscapes with prominent natural elements. When we cannot actually place ourselves in a natural setting, we make some effort to provide ourselves with substitutes. There is evidence that we like to have around us natural archetypes or simulations of them. The point is not that a building or landscape resembles nature but that some architectural scenes accord (e.g., in form and space, in light and darkness) with an archetypal image of the natural world.[3]

The challenge is to more specifically identify those biophilic design features that reflect a human affinity for the natural world and, thus, to create a satisfying and beneficial architecture. What are some of these biophilic features? They include natural lighting, natural materials, natural ventilation, shapes and forms that mimic natural features and processes, views and prospects of nature, and more. Psychologist Judith Heerwagen has developed a list of biophilic design features, which are presented in Table 5.1.

To deepen our understanding of biophilic design beyond this broad listing, this chapter will describe two basic dimensions of biophilic design: organic design and vernacular design.

Illustration 21. The Sydney Opera House, designed by Jorn Utzon, possesses prominent organic qualities, particularly its bird and sail-like features viewed against the Sydney Harbor.

Organic Design

Organic design can be defined as building shapes and forms that directly, indirectly, or symbolically elicit a human affinity for natural features and processes. Direct experience is contact with largely self-sustaining features of the natural world, such as a wooded landscape, a natural stream, or unfiltered air and light. Indirect experience is contact with natural elements that require continual human input and control—for example, a potted plant, a manicured lawn, or an aquarium tank. Symbolic experience involves contact not with living, or real, nature but, rather, with its ornamental, metaphorical, or vicarious representation. This can include decorations simulating natural shapes and forms, interior furnishing of refashioned wood and stone, or pictures and symbols of landscapes and organisms. The direct experience of nature does occur in buildings and especially in landscapes, but more typically the built environment emphasizes the indirect and particularly the symbolic experience of the natural world.

The term *organic design* originated with the famed architect Frank Lloyd Wright, although he described it in often obscure and varied ways.[4] Still, his interest in the subject relates to

Table 5.1
Elements of Biophilic Design

Prospect (ability to see into distance)	• Brightness in the field of view (windows, bright walls) • Ability to get to a distant point for a better view • Horizon/sky imagery (sun, mountains, clouds) • Strategic viewing conditions • View corridors
Refuge (sense of enclosure or shelter)	• Canopy effect (lowered ceilings, screening, branchlike forms overhead)
Water (indoors or inside views)	• Glimmer or reflective surface (suggests clean water) • Moving water (also suggests clean, aerated water) • Symbolic forms of water
Biodiversity	• Varied vegetation indoors and out (large trees, plants, flowers) • Windows designed and placed to incorporate nature views • Outdoor natural areas with rich vegetation and animals
Sensory variability	• Changes and variability in environmental color, temperature, air movement, textures, and light over time and spaces • Natural rhythms and processes (natural ventilation and lighting)
Biomimicry	• Designs derived from nature • Use of natural patterns, forms, and textures • Fractal characteristics (self-similarity at different levels of scale with random variation in key features rather than exact repetition)
Sense of playfulness	• Incorporation of decor, natural materials, artifacts, objects, and spaces whose primary purpose is to delight, surprise, and amuse
Enticement	• Discovered complexity • Information richness that encourages exploration • Curvilinear surfaces that gradually open information to view

Source: Adapted from J. Heerwagen and B. Hase, "Building biophilia: Connecting people to nature," *Environmental Design + Construction* (March 2001): 33.

this discussion in two important respects. First, he asserted that the appeal of buildings and landscapes is frequently a function of their connection and relation to features of the natural environment. Second, he suggested that most successful architecture possesses a harmony and integrity originating in nature or, as he suggested, a characteristic of "being true to [their] nature." Wright often captured these organic qualities in his architectural creations, including Fallingwater (located in Bear Run, Pennsylvania), Taliesen East (Spring Green, Wisconsin), Taliesen West (Scottsdale, Arizona), the Johnson Wax office building (Racine, Wisconsin), his "Prairie" style of design, and other creations. These constructions frequently emulate or evoke features found in nature. To Wright, the most enduring designs possessed organic qualities of harmony and symmetry that are often encountered in the natural world and iteratively developed over time. He explained his approach to organic design as follows: "Nature is a good teacher. I am a child of hers, and apart from her precepts, I cannot flourish. I cannot work as well as she, perhaps, but at least I can shape my work to sympathize with what seems beautiful to hers. . . . Any building . . . should be an elemental, sympathetic feature of the ground, complementary to its nature-environment, belonging by kinship to the terrain."[5]

Wright's work emphasized incorporating natural shapes and forms, especially in his residential designs—in particular, Fallingwater, his personal residences Taliesin East and Taliesin West, and his Prairie-style homes. These creations reveal important elements of organic design and some dimensions of vernacular design. However, his work reflects almost no aspect of low environmental impact design, a limitation of Wright's greatness that certainly was not unusual for his time.

Nonetheless, several important organic design features emerge from examining Wright's residential structures. These concepts include an emphasis on natural materials (especially wood and stone), natural lighting, and qualities of the environment incorporated into building interiors and experienced through exterior views. Wright stressed fitting structures into the landscape, seen especially in the parallel relation of his Prairie-style homes to the relative flatness of their savanna landscapes, which make them appear to emerge out of, rather than dominate, the ground. Wright also insisted on what he called the organic principles of simplicity and directness of design, with the house or artifact needing to be molded and connected to its environmental context. He suggested: "Nothing is more difficult to achieve than the integral simplicity of organic nature amid the tangled confusion of the innumerable relics of forms that encumber life for us. To achieve it in any degree means a serious devotion to the 'underneath' in an attempt to grasp the nature of building a beautiful building beautifully, as organically true in itself, to itself and to its purpose as any tree or flower."[6]

Wright also emphasized simulating the dynamic character, or "plasticity," often encountered in nature—forms altering or adapting themselves to changing conditions over time and space. His designs can, thus, appear to transform or mature in response to changing lighting and seasonal features, an effect frequently enhanced by his extensive use of natural materials, natural lighting, and dramatic exterior views in complementary relation to warm interiors. Wright's structures reflect an intuitive understanding of nature's appeal. Features that enhance this affinity for nature in Wright's residential designs include the following, which are drawn from the work of Grant Hildebrand:

- High ceilings and a sense of spaciousness in main living areas
- Extensive natural lighting and vistas of the exterior landscape
- Living spaces high above the terrain that provide extended views
- The play of natural light seen through clear and decorative glass
- Fireplaces within low-ceiling interiors creating a feeling of refuge
- Large overhanging eaves and cantilevers engendering a sense of connection to the exterior landscape
- Conspicuous terraces offering distant views and a feeling of peril and excitement
- Winding paths and concealed entryways fostering feelings of safety and security
- Buildings integrated into the landscape through the use of long horizontal planes
- Visual connections between interior rooms, many with outside views, and few closed interior spaces (or what Wright called "destroying the box")[7]

Fallingwater—arguably Wright's most accomplished creation—particularly illustrates many of these organic design features. The house fits extraordinarily well into its surrounding hillside, particularly the adjacent ledges and forest (Illustration 22). Most dramatically, it sits astride a stream nearly on top of a waterfall. Precariously poised above the cataract, the house remarkably blends ledge, water, rock, moss, and forest. Cantilevered terraces thrust into space accentuate the home's dramatic proximity to the falls. Living room spaces feature abundant windows and natural lighting, the use of natural materials, and frequent fireplaces, achieving an overall satisfying confluence of limitless possibilities within the protective nest of a sheltered environment.

These organic design features attract thousands of visitors each year despite Fallingwater's remote Pennsylvania location. Most visitors want to see the home's dramatic connection to the natural environment, especially the waterfall and its near incorporation into the household. Yet,

Illustration 22. Frank Lloyd Wright's famous residential design Fallingwater fits extraordinarily well into its surrounding hillside and nearby stream and rests nearly atop a waterfall.

Wright's celebrated creation lacks many important aspects of restorative environmental design, particularly low environmental impact and vernacular design features. The structure uses some regionally derived materials, but achieves little sense of connection to indigenous culture or ecology. Indeed, most of Wright's constructions possess few low environmental impact or vernacular design features. Rather, they proclaim an attitude of wastefulness, a lack of concern for energy and other resource uses, and a philosophy of art over nature. Indeed, Fallingwater's most dramatic design feature—its location beside the watercourse and nearly on top of a waterfall—would not even be allowed today, given its destructive effects on the riparian environment.

Still, as Wright's creations demonstrate, people are attracted to and become attached to buildings and landscapes that successfully incorporate organic qualities into their design.[8] This can be seen in much traditional architecture, in which some of the most admired and enduring constructions possess prominent organic features. By contrast, the alienation associated with much contemporary architecture reflects an excessive reliance on fabricated materials, artificial lighting, controlled climatic conditions, straight-line geometries, homogeneity of design, scales rarely if ever encountered in nature, substitution of the synthetic for the natural, and an indifference to local ecology and culture.

Writer David Pearson describes organic architecture as "rooted in a passion for life, nature, and natural forms . . . full of the vitality of the natural world with its biological forms and processes." He identifies several broad features of organic design, including their tendency to be

- Inspired by nature
- Unfolding, like an organism, from the seed within
- Existing in the "continuous present"
- Following (natural) flows, flexible, and adaptable
- Satisfying social, physical, and spiritual needs
- Growing out of the site
- Celebrating a spirit of play and surprise[9]

He suggests that these attributes depend on such features as natural light, natural materials, wind, air, soil, geology, water, and other characteristics of the natural environment. Although useful, these attributions remain vague and elusive. The following discussion thus will use the simpler categories of direct, indirect, and symbolic experience of nature to describe various attributes and characteristics of organic design. But first, let us consider a recent example of organic design in modern architecture.

The International Netherlands Group (or ING) Bank complex, an office, commercial, and residential development outside Amsterdam, The Netherlands, was initially conceived during the late 1970s but not completed until 1987 (Illustration 23). Designed by architect Anton Alberts, who was inspired by the work of the philosopher and designer Rudolf Steiner, the project includes half a million square feet in ten connected buildings. The developers envisioned creating a community as much as a bank headquarters, uniting architecture, work, commerce, and residence in an overall complex. This goal was partially achieved, although most of the complex's residents seem to differ economically, culturally, and occupationally from the typical bank employee.

The ING complex incorporates organic design elements as well as, to a lesser extent, those of low environmental impact design. A striking organic feature is the lack of straight-line geometries that characterize so much of office construction today in favor of the curvilinear forms more often found in the natural world. Also, lighting fixtures, furniture, wall coverings, columns, and art objects consciously strive to simulate the shapes of nature. Water is frequently designed into the exterior landscaping and even occasionally is encountered in interior features, such as a handrail and staircase that incorporate the sight and sound of water. Building heights are modest to foster a more human scale, and gardens are often located near the buildings. Natural lighting, ventilation, and materials are used extensively throughout the complex, with the natural lighting having helped to substantially reduce energy consumption. Other low environmental impact features include the use of waste heat as an energy source, the use of locally and sustainably produced products and materials, and water conservation practices.

As noted, the ING complex was inspired by the ideas of German designer and philosopher Rudolf Steiner. Architectural critic Günther Feuerstein described Steiner's design approach as follows:

> Rudolf Steiner speaks of an "organic building style" and supplies this with a number of metaphors pointing to biological phenomena [of] plants, human beings, and animals. . . . Buildings can be described as close to Expressionism and to organic architecture. . . . Steiner repeatedly compared human physicality, though spiritualized, with his architecture. The buildings are interpreted as bodies.[10]

The ING project introduced many changes in the decision-making process to encourage its design goals. These included long-term planning and a close, consensual relationship among

Illustration 23. The International Netherlands Group Bank's complex of office, commercial, and residential buildings in Amsterdam, The Netherlands, designed by Anton Alberts, is an early and still relevant example of restorative environmental design.

architects, engineers, executive management, and employees. Organic and low environmental impact objectives were emphasized at the outset and infused into all phases of design, development, and construction. This interdisciplinary planning process—viewed as essential to the project's success—is described in the Rocky Mountain Institute's book *Green Development*: "This process . . . included, first, a vision for what was to be created . . . [and] second . . . integrated planning and design, in which the performance goals were identified up-front . . . involving four overlapping components: whole-systems thinking, front-loaded design, end-use/least-cost considerations, and multidisciplinary teamwork."[11]

The ING project is an inspiring though only partially effective attempt at restorative environmental design. Although its achievements have purportedly resulted in improved employee satisfaction, productivity, and morale, many organic design features remain incomplete and only partly successful. The project's low environmental impact design features are also limited in scope and effectiveness. Vernacular design elements are not extensive or well integrated, despite the use of local materials and the attempt to create a community. The ING complex feels imposed on its social setting and landscape, uncomfortable with either its cultural or ecological context. Still, the project is highly innovative and its organic design accomplishments impressive and relevant.

Direct Experience of Nature

Direct attributes of organic design result in the relatively immediate experience of nature in buildings and constructed landscapes. Natural lighting and natural ventilation are common expressions of direct organic design (Illustration 24). These features can be the result of deliberate design decisions, such as large operable windows, or the by-product of technical innovations, such as chimney stacks, light shelves, and buildings orientated to the sun and prevailing winds. Natural lighting and ventilation are basic properties of the natural environment, although the quality of their experience varies considerably depending on such factors as amount and kind of vegetation, relationships between building interiors and exteriors, and exhaust and road placements. The decision to enhance natural lighting and ventilation can profoundly affect occupant well-being, including health, motivation, morale, and other aspects of physical and mental well-being and satisfaction.

Other natural features that can be designed into buildings and constructed landscapes include plants, soil, water, geological forms, and even fire or animal life. These environmental elements—which can occur in building interiors but more often appear in exterior settings—often exert considerable physical and psychological effects. Their impact varies depending

Illustration 24. Natural Lighting and Ventilation: The atrium of the new Parliament building in London, designed by Hopkins Architects, provides extensive natural lighting in a striking organic design.

on the quality of the design. An isolated encounter with a single element of exotic vegetation is typically a sterile, contrived form of contact with nature that holds little consequence. For example, designs featuring only trivial contact with a "prisoner" plant confined within a planter tend to offer little more than a decorative, superficial experience (Illustration 25). By contrast, designing a coherent and functionally organized natural system that includes diverse vegetation, soil, water, and even animal life can stimulate people's senses, emotions, intellect, and spirit, resulting in considerable aesthetic, naturalistic, and other biophilic satisfactions. The quality of any direct contact with nature in the built environment is often constrained by the practicalities of cost, opportunity, and technology. Still, with commitment and imagination the direct experience of nature in buildings and landscapes can be achieved, resulting in many benefits to people.

Direct design of nature can also incorporate views of the exterior environment. One attraction and advance of modern glass buildings—despite their potentially adverse ecological

Illustration 25. Prisoner Plants: The palm disappearing into the hard surface floor and the isolated lobby planter reflect the widespread practice of treating plants as mere decoration.

impacts—is the extraordinary visual access they afford of the outside. This exposure to the natural environment has been invaluable in many urban locations that contain major natural landmarks, such as large rivers, estuaries, and mountains. However, the pleasure of seeing these vistas can sometimes be diminished by building heights that are greatly out of scale with the human experience, precipitating anxiety and threat as much as satisfaction. Still, visual access to the exterior environment is often a highly gratifying feature of organic design.

Exposure to water near or even within buildings can also foster the direct experience of nature in the built environment. The sight, sound, and even smell of water often exert positive psychological effects, especially when the water is conspicuous, moving, and inhabited by vegetative or animal life (Illustration 26). After reviewing many studies of the human attraction to water across diverse cultures, geographer and environmental psychologist Roger Ulrich concluded: "Water features consistently elicit especially high levels of liking or preference."[12] Similarly, critic and designer John Ruskin long ago observed: "As far as I can recollect, without a single exception, every Homeric landscape, intended to be beautiful, is composed of a fountain, a meadow, and a shady grove."[13]

Illustration 26. (*top and bottom*) Sight, Sound, and Smell of Water: The view of buildings across an urban lake and the presence of a more formal water fountain reflect the powerful effect of water in the built environment.

Creating the experience of water in the built environment can be technically challenging, and water that is poorly designed into buildings and landscapes can be disturbing. As Grant Hildebrand remarks: "Water is not a universal feature of pleasurable settings, and . . . can suggest danger in certain instances."[14] However, when well connected to other natural features (e.g., soils, geological forms, plants, and animal life), water incorporated into building interiors and landscapes can be profoundly satisfying. Most successful water designs mimic natural forms and processes. In some restorative environmental designs, the experience of water has also been successfully connected to several building functions, such as irrigation, plumbing, wastewater treatment, stormwater protection, and insulation. The design potential of water has been described well by architect Charles Moore in his classic study of water and architecture. Yet, Moore notes how often the absence or distorted expression of water in modern architecture reflects a growing human estrangement from the natural world. He suggests:

> Water is a natural material, and . . . although controlled by gravity and natural laws, it can be coaxed, shaped, and transformed. We can try to achieve harmony with nature, we can try to ignore it, or we can try to master it—or we can find ourselves, at the end of the twentieth century, in a confused, ecological attempt to do all three at once. As we in our century have steadily removed ourselves from the ideals of nature . . . we have risked losing intimate contact with water. . . . Water, in all its variations, interpretations, and presentations, shares a simple, common origin. It has inherent, immutable properties that time cannot alter.[15]

However, buildings must also regulate the direct experience of nature and frequently exclude it from the interior environment. Take, for example, fire, which is typically suppressed because of the potential danger it poses. Yet the manipulated experience of fire within building interiors is a celebrated source of warmth, cooking, comfort, and protection, with its controlled use long viewed as a sign of civilization. Fire possesses great symbolic significance, and its experience in homes especially forms a highly satisfying, coveted element of organic design. Fireplaces allow this basic element of nature to penetrate a building's core and produce an experience of color, satisfaction, and movement. But, to be fully satisfying, fire must be revealed in ways that demonstrate its confident dominance and mastery.

Designing animal life into the built environment can be especially challenging. Technology, cost, and aesthetics often strongly discourage the presence of animals in building interiors. Modern health and safety factors, in particular, emphasize the maintenance of an antiseptic environment. Yet, when creatively designed into atriums, lobbies, and other public and private spaces, the pres-

Illustration 27. Ivy Covered Walls: The University of Michigan Law Quadrangle achieves a highly organic effect with its ivy-covered walls and integration into the vegetated landscape.

Illustration 28. Green Roofs: Green roofs can achieve low environmental impact objectives of improved stormwater management, insulation, and mitigation of heat island effects as well as offer vegetated environments that benefit people and wildlife.

ence of butterflies, fish, and even higher vertebrates (e.g., birds) can produce a visually exciting and satisfying contact with nature. Effective wildlife design can be emotionally and intellectually arresting, providing physical and mental restoration as well as a feeling of connection to the natural world.

The building facade itself can sometimes incorporate natural features. One common example is ivy and other vines climbing on exterior building walls (Illustration 27). A more unusual development in recent years has been the development of green roofs, which use vegetation to accomplish both biophilic and low environmental impact design objectives (Illustration 28). Low environmental impact goals include improved insulation, reduced stormwater runoff, lessened heating and cooling loads, diminished heat island effects, and reduced noise and air pollution. In addition, green roof design can also provide plant and animal habitat that enhances human relaxation, imagination, intellect, creativity, health, and productivity, especially in urban areas often lacking vegetation and open spaces.

The external landscape offers the greatest potential for designing the direct experience of nature. This can occur in constructed landscapes that include native plants and animals as well as food and cover for such wild species as fish, birds, and sometimes mammals. Ambitious designs can create habitats where wildlife flourishes and is highly accessible, including wetlands, vegetative corridors, and self-sustaining forest communities. Although the direct experience of nature in buildings and landscapes is frequently inhibited by the limitations of resources, knowledge, and technology, the greatest constraint is often a lack of imagination and the willingness to seek more compatible connections with nature in the built environment. With commitment, an experientially rich, sensuous, and deeply satisfying architecture can be created that puts us in touch with all of our visual, tactile, and other sensory attractions to the natural world.

Indirect Experience of Nature

Nature in buildings and landscapes can become so controlled and manipulated that it produces a radically altered state of nature requiring ongoing human management and intervention. Examples of such manipulated contact with the natural environment include planters decorating an interior lobby, fish in an aquarium tank, or formally designed fountains. Greatly transformed from their natural state, these features typically depend on continual human management and control to exist. But if these indirect expressions of nature are well designed, they can be deeply satisfying and beneficial (Illustration 29). Designing the indirect experience of nature often involves manipulating such environmental elements as vegetation, animal life, light, air, water, materials (e.g., stone, wood, cotton, hides, wool, leather), and even natural processes, such as aging, weathering, and climate. Categorizing these features as indirect experiences of nature can often reflect more a matter of judgment than an absolute statement of fact.

Illustration 29. Indirect Experience of Nature: An example of the indirect experience of nature, this university courtyard possesses many biophilic elements despite its monoculture of grass and its formal fountain requiring continuous human input.

Illustration 30. Inside Gardens: Commerzbank (*left*), an office tower in Frankfurt, Germany, designed by Norman Foster and Associates, has achieved exceptional energy efficiencies through its solar orientation, natural lighting, and double-wall construction. An innovative biophilic feature is its five "winter gardens" (*right*), with one located every thirteen floors.

An example of incorporation of the indirect experience of nature into a building's interior is Commerzbank in Frankfurt, Germany, which was designed by the firm Norman Foster and Associates (Illustration 30). An especially innovative organic design feature of this modern office building is its five "winter gardens," which are located every thirteenth floor and span three stories each within the sixty-five-story structure. These gardens are essentially interior parks that consist of plants linked to various geographic areas representing differing compass directions. The gardens have also been connected to the building's natural ventilation and lighting objectives and have reportedly helped to improve its energy performance.

The gardens allow employees to have an unusual indirect experience of nature within a tall, vertical structure—an important, innovative accomplishment because nearly all human contact with the natural environment takes place on the horizontal plane at ground level. The multiple three-story gardens dramatically alter this dynamic and have purportedly improved employee morale and productivity in the process. The gardens also diminish the typical hierarchical, status-differentiating effects of tall office towers, promoting instead a more

Illustration 31. (*top and bottom*) Natural Materials, Shapes, and Forms: These interior and exterior designs reflect the powerful effects achieved by using natural materials as well as mimicking and simulating natural shapes and forms.

Illustration 32. Prospect and Refuge: Views to a distant scene through an arch can provide a satisfying experience of refuge and prospect, as this Yale University scene demonstrates.

egalitarian contact among people, which more often characterizes parklike settings. However, Commerzbank's organic design features do not extend much beyond the gardens and the commanding views offered by the largely glass facade. Its modernist style and reliance on nonnative vegetation tenuously connects the structure to the surrounding area's culture and ecology. Although an impressive, ground-breaking accomplishment, Commerzbank still fails to meet the ideal of restorative environmental design.

Designing the indirect experience of nature often involves manipulating natural materials. The human affinity for natural materials is so deeply ingrained that artificial substitutes (e.g., imitation plastic)—no matter how striking the replication—often does not elicit much pleasure. Artificial materials typically seem fake; lacking strong evocative power, they rarely capture the subtle qualities of, for example, the grain of wood, the weathering of stone, or the sensory experience of once-living materials (such as the smell of leather or the feel of silk). It is difficult to imitate natural materials effectively because of their complexity: dynamic natural forms must adapt to myriad environmental influences over time in the struggle to survive, cope, and evolve. Natural materials communicate a logic that few imitations can replicate, despite human cleverness, ingenuity, and technology (Illustration 31).

The indirect experience of nature often reflects a response as much to a natural process as to a specific substance or organism. Some buildings, landscapes, and furnishings influence us deeply because they reveal the effects of weathering and historic transition, possessing what might be called the "patina of time."[16] This evidence of aging can be seen in old walls, moss-covered roofs, or corroded stone, all of which reveal the dynamic forces of time. Certain materials—stone, wood, tile, stucco—appeal to us because they reveal the texturing of shape and forms in response to aging and adaptation and sometimes even have other life forms attached, such as mosses, lichens, and vines.

What factors create a satisfying indirect experience of nature in buildings and forms? Drawing on the work of geographer Jay Appleton, Grant Hildebrand has emphasized the effects of six paired elements that reflect the inherent human affinity for nature often encountered in highly evocative building and landscape designs.[17] Hildebrand labels these complementary properties prospect and refuge, enticement and peril, and order and complexity. *Prospect* reflects the discernment of distant objects, a human tendency that has contributed evolutionarily to our ability to locate food, water, safety, and security. Prospect allows us to detect far-off movements, perceive distant objects and resources, and spy potential threats. In buildings and landscapes, it is often afforded through outstanding views, feelings of

Illustration 33. The ordered complexity of Mont St. Michel entices the visitor to explore and discover, while its perilous site implies uncertainty, risk, and thrill.

spaciousness, and light and brightness. *Refuge,* by contrast, reflects the complementary human desire for shelter and protection. Building and landscape designs that foster a sense of safety, comfort, warmth, and intimacy through the use of comfortable interior rooms, a fireplace, or a secluded garden often achieve a sense of refuge. As Hildebrand describes: "Refuge is spatial circumspection, darkness, and limited view; prospect is spatial openness, brightness, and extended view" (Illustration 32).[18]

Enticement, the first property of the second pairing, reflects the desire to explore, discover, and expand one's knowledge, a characteristic that has proven crucial to human adaptation and development. Buildings and landscapes can enhance our exploratory drive by providing opportunities for exercising imagination and creativity—for example, in response to natural detail and diversity that stimulate inquisitiveness, immersion, and interpretation. *Peril,* on the other hand, reflects the desire for mystery, challenge, and even risk that simultaneously attracts and repels. This effect can be achieved, for example, through the use of overhanging balconies, elevated passageways, obscured pathways, or heights that excite, challenge, and thrill as well as unsettle us. These design features encourage exploration and discovery but are often accompanied by the inclination to proceed with prudence and caution (Illustration 33).

In the final pairing, *complexity* reflects the human desire for detail, variety, and mystery, which throughout human evolution has enabled us to make difficult choices and to secure resources in response to the natural world (Illustration 34). *Order* is an equally basic inclination that reflects the desire for pattern, structure, and organization. Successful building and landscape designs frequently contain complexity and order in dynamic relation to each other, whereas designs that emphasize only one property often frustrate and disappoint. For example, complex designs that lack order frequently foster confusion, while exceedingly orderly designs that lack complexity can produce boredom. Hildebrand describes the value of this complementary relation: "Order and complexity are . . . necessary allies. Order without complexity is monotony, and is felt to be that in the deadly repetition of much speculative American [tract] housing of the late 1940's. . . . Complexity without order, however, is not more satisfying. Scenes . . . difficult to organize and interpret [are] not only rated low in preference; they [are] actually resented. The . . . American commercial strip is an example."[19]

The work of psychologists Rachel and Stephen Kaplan, which also draws on Jay Appleton's insights, also considers how building and landscape designs can incorporate the indirect experience of nature.[20] Kaplan and Kaplan use the terms *coherence, complexity, legibility,* and *mystery* to explain this design tendency. They suggest that people are attracted to buildings and landscapes that are rich in environmental complexity and mystery and that

Illustration 34. Order and Complexity: Widespread complexity characterizes this building's varied shapes and planes, yet the building is pleasing overall because its many naturalistic elements remain ordered.

offer frequent opportunities to wonder, imagine, explore, and discover. At the same time, they emphasize that successful designs frequently incorporate elements of coherence and legibility that avoid confusion and a feeling of chaos while also fostering a sense of orderliness and meaning.

Indirectly incorporating nature into building and landscape designs frequently results in satisfying and successful constructions. Some of the most sought after and costly structures possess many indirect elements of nature, as revealed by research conducted by psychologist Judith Heerwagen and ecologist Gordon Orians.[21] They report, for example, a decided preference (among randomly selected subjects) for building and landscape features that include distant vistas of nature, abundant opportunities for refuge and shelter, and facilitated movement and way finding. These and other design attributes that reflect the human affinity for nature are frequently preferred because they stimulate imagination and problem solving within safe environments, a condition instrumental for human evolution and development.

Symbolic Experience of Nature
The experience of nature in the built environment often occurs symbolically or vicariously, particularly within building interiors and facades. Building and landscape designs that involve contact with nature are frequently revealed through representation, allusion, and metaphorical expression. Moreover, such experience occurs far more often than generally recognized and significantly affects people's responses to and satisfaction derived from the built environment. Nature is represented symbolically through various guises—including decoration, ornamentation, pictorial expression, and shapes and forms that simulate and mimic nature—and in a wide diversity of building features—such as walls, doors, entryways, columns, trim, casements, fireplaces, furnishings, carpets, fabrics, art, and sometimes even an entire facade (Illustration 35).

The vicarious experience of nature in the built environment is revealed in obvious ways but often in highly subtle, obscure forms that may be difficult to recognize as reflections of the natural world. One example is an auditorium in my workplace. The room includes many simulations of nature in its floral-, leaf-, and fern-like patterns woven into the brick, wood, and ironwork and liberally employs natural materials, such as wood and stone. It also features sinuous organic curves that, on closer inspection, mimic shapes commonly encountered in nature—for example, in its arched ceiling, in the decorative ribs supporting the ceiling's vertical columns, and in the ordered complexity of the decorative brickwork and large spatial volumes of the high triangular room. Despite the room's practical inadequacies and lack of modern efficiencies, it is

Illustration 35. Representations of Nature: Scenes from nature sometimes appear in a building's facade, as with the Harold P. Washington Library in Chicago, designed by Hammond, Beeby and Babka, Architects. Roof top ornamentation by Kent Bloomer.

Illustration 36. (*above and opposite*) Naturalistic Symbols: Naturalistic symbols occur widely in the built environment, as revealed in the floral patterns, animal figures, and organic shapes of these building facades.

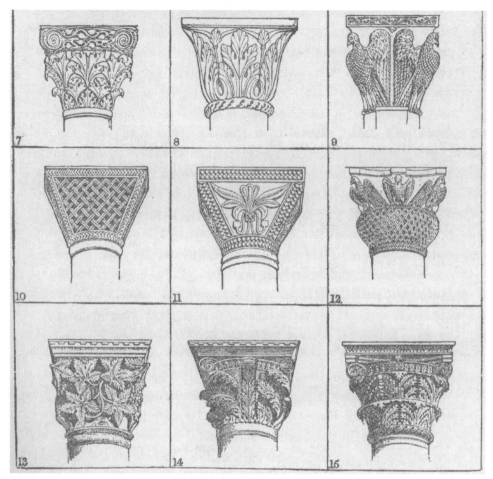

Illustration 37. Botanical Columns: Column capitals are often crowned with the shapes of plants, animals, and organic forms as depicted in John Ruskin's classic examination of Gothic architecture.

highly revered, especially among alumni who have become alarmed by the prospect of losing the room as the school prepares to build new facilities. Building designs that successfully draw on the human affinity for nature, even when indirectly and vicariously experienced, often exert a powerful hold on human emotion and imagination.

Many symbolic representations of nature in the built environment can be easily discerned. Such features include floral patterns in material adorning couches, carpets, curtains, and fabrics; animal figures carved into walls and mantels; organic forms etched along doorways and eaves; fern- and shell-like shapes carved atop capitals and columns; naturalistic designs woven into grills, walls, and fences; honeycomb- and egg-like forms embedded into arches, domes, and ceilings; environmental scenes painted in glass and carved into stone; and, on occasion, even the sound of water emanating from a fountain or the distant fragrance wafting from flowering

Illustration 38. Organic Shapes: The Ingalls hockey rink at Yale University in New Haven, Connecticut, designed by Eero Saarinen, has a distinctive organic shape that has been described as a pregnant whale and a fern.

shrubs (Illustration 36). These symbolic designs of nature occur throughout human history and across all cultures, though perhaps less so in modern, urban society. The ubiquity of these environmental simulations reflects a universal yearning often incorporated into building interiors and sometimes into exterior landscapes. In his classic work *The Grammar of Ornament,* Owen Jones describes a universal tendency for ornamentation that not only employs nature as model but, "whenever any style of ornament commands universal admiration, . . . will always be found to be in accordance with the laws which regulate the distribution of form in nature."[22]

Architectural historian George Hersey has also described the symbolic representation of nature in buildings and landscapes. He identifies an extraordinary diversity of these representations in the built environment, including shapes and patterns drawing on nearly all life forms, including cellular and microscopic organisms; invertebrate taxa, such as mollusks and insects; vegetation, such as ferns, flowers, and trees as well as their leaves; vertebrate creatures, including fish and fowl and, to a lesser extent, mammals; and even elements of human anatomy, not unusually the simulation or actual representation of reproductive organs. The extraordinarily widespread prevalence of these naturalistic representations prompted Hersey to suggest the following in the single case of plants:

One cannot hope to discuss the architectural use of plant ornament in a single chapter or even a single book. It is universal. . . . For example, among flowers and leaves, spiral phyllotaxis appears in the form of overlapping rows that radiate from a center to an outer rim. These and other comparable

Illustration 39. Gothic Architecture: Gothic architecture often includes organic forms that simulate the natural environment. Cesar Pelli's Ronald Reagan Airport, which is a reinterpretation of gothic architecture, simulates a forest canopy with its soaring vaulted roof.

arrangements show up over and over again in architectural ornament. . . . Probably the commonest botanical specimens in all of Western buildings are Corinthian capitals [see Illustration 37].[23]

The symbolic representation of natural forms and processes is often experienced intuitively—at times even unconsciously—in building design. For example, Yale University's hockey rink resembles an organic form, prompting many students to call it "the pregnant whale" (Illustration 38). Yet, from above, it more closely resembles the shape of a fern. Examining the motives of the rink's famous architect, Eero Saarinen, George Hersey suggests that Saarinen probably did not copy the shape of either a fern or a whale but, rather, that he unconsciously drew on instinctual affinities for organic forms. Hersey writes: "Saarinen was not . . . watching his fingers put forth leaves. [But,] with pencil and paper he was . . . mimicking structures found in nonhuman nature."[24] This intuitive tendency can be found in other well-known Saarinen designs, such as the striking birdlike form of the former Trans World Airlines terminal at New York's Kennedy Airport, which may help to explain the airport's notable appeal.

Nineteenth-century critic and designer John Ruskin praised the symbolic representation of nature in architecture, especially those found in Gothic design.[25] He commended the extraordinary range of simulated natural representations that occur in Gothic architecture's arches, columns, window ways, entry portals, doors, roofs, vaults, domes, ceilings, and facades. These designs reveal columns rising fanlike and sculpted, calling to mind ancient forests; elaborate capitals with an astonishing array of floral, leaf, and fernlike patterns; and an explosion of simulated organic forms drawing on qualities of light and shape mirroring the natural world (Illustration 39). As Ruskin describes:

> In that careful distinction of species, and richness of delicate and undisturbed organization, which characterize the Gothic design, there is the history of . . . thoughtful life, influenced by habitual tenderness, and devoted to subtle inquiry; and every discriminating and delicate touch of the chisel, as it rounds the petals or guides the branch, is a prophecy of the development of the entire body of the natural sciences. . . . Whatever is in architecture fair or beautiful is imitated from natural forms . . . a sympathy in the forms of noble building with what is most sublime in nature.[26]

These varied Gothic depictions of nature can be found in churches, cathedrals, palaces, and civic buildings throughout the world (Illustration 40). Kent Bloomer, a noted authority on the theory and practice of ornamentation, observes how often ornamentation in buildings reflects natural forms and functions and related cycles of environmental growth. He argues that much Gothic and other building ornamentation is a metaphorical language of conversation between the organic and inorganic, where through symbol and design nature is reclaimed in human artifice and fabrication. Bloomer comments on Ruskin's praise of the organic in Gothic architecture as follows:

> Ruskin's theories about the beauty, power, and distribution of ornaments were . . . rooted in the conviction that manifestations of nature revealed a sacred order capable of providing the most significant principles of architectural design. . . . Ruskin formulated principles of design that incorporated sculptural ornaments representing foliage [and other organic elements]. . . . An

Illustration 40. Yale University's Harkness tower in New Haven, Connecticut, designed by James Gamble Rogers, is an exceptionally beautiful illustration of the many organic qualities of Gothic architecture.

architect pursuing these principles was expected to select elements from the Gothic language of architecture and to gather figures from the panorama of living nature.[27]

Symbolic depictions of nature in building and landscape design are often disguised. Metaphorical representations of the natural world rely as much on instinctual affinities as on explicit depictions of environmental forms (Illustration 41). These architectural elements evoke sentiments that tap into our inherent responses to the patterns, movements, light, shape, and space encountered in nature. People prefer the textures, curvilinear forms, rounded and spherical surfaces, movements, and plasticity typically encountered in nature to the rigid, straight-line, abstract, and contrived geometries of artificially fabricated and designed forms and materials. Even the arresting effect of a constructed human artifact like a city skyline often owes its appeal to the varied, vertical shapes reminiscent of a complex forest as to any particular engineering marvel or technology. This effect is especially noticeable when the skyline is seen in juxtaposition to a prominent natural feature viewed from afar, such as a river or a mountain. Perhaps this helps to partially explain the pronounced effect of New York City's skyline as viewed against the Hudson or East River, and why—in addition to the horrific human tragedy of September 11, 2001—we lament the destruction of the lower Manhattan profile, particularly how the World Trade towers rose like gigantic living forms out of an organic-like skyline despite their having been little more than simple rectangular boxes (Illustration 42).

Similarly, on closer inspection, the irresistible qualities of such revered structures as Notre Dame Cathedral, the Taj Mahal, and New York City's Grand Central Station often reveal powerful organic qualities of light, color, material, texture, shape, and form that have been symbolically borrowed from the natural world. Inspired by nature, they grip the human imagination, communicating a subtle connection to the natural environment, even when the origin of our feelings remains obscure. Take Grand Central Station, for example (Illustration 43). A detailed examination reveals extensive natural materials of stone and marble; organic shapes carved into its elaborate metal work; a spaciousness in its central vault reminiscent of the outside world; sunlight descending from large rectangular windows; and even the simulation of an evening sky replete with constellations in an overarching ceiling.

Like other aspects of experience rooted in human genetics, these symbolic forms elusively reflect our affinity for nature. We take them for granted, often recognizing and appreciating their virtues when they are threatened or have been destroyed. This symbolic expression is an important aspect of the "pattern language" of timeless, celebrated creation that is described by architect Christopher Alexander in his seminal work on the subject.[28] Grant Hildebrand has

Illustration 41. (*above and opposite*) Metaphorical Representations of Nature: An affinity for nature in buildings often appears in disguised, or metaphorical, form. Both of these buildings draw on instinctual affinities for the natural world revealed in arches, pediments, tree-like shapes, and other naturalistic forms.

also explored how often building features symbolically evoke the human affinity for nature. Citing a single cathedral nave, he writes: "Complex natural surroundings . . . rich in quantity and variety of resources. . . . Each new image presents novel elements and relationships that also develop from and relate to what we have already seen; seemingly repeated elements and seemingly repeated intervals whose multitudinous minor variations make each iteration as different from any other, and as alike, as individuals of the same species."[29]

As Hildebrand intimates, many successful building designs evince an "organized variability" that is often encountered in nature. A basic architectural feature or decorative pattern mimicking some natural feature is initially established and then replicated in varied, albeit predictable, ways. When isolated or repeated exactly, these patterns often strike us as boring or monotonous, but when revealed in slightly altered and patterned ways, they frequently seem to constitute wholes that appear coherent, organized, and attractive. Many successful building designs reveal such compositions of varied connection and relationship. When this occurs in a dynamic, integrated fashion, the complexity rarely repels; rather, its aesthetic appeal rises from a combination of replication and variation experienced in an orderly, predictable pattern. This tendency in nature and in human design has been referred to as "biomimicry," also the title of a seminal book by Janine Benyus. As Judith Heerwagen writes:

Illustration 42. *Top:* The lower Manhattan skyline seen across the Hudson River suggests the vertical heterogeneity of an old-growth forest. *Bottom:* The destruction of the World Trade towers greatly diminished this effect, even though the towers were little more than rectangular boxes.

Illustration 43. New York City's Grand Central Station achieves its biophilic effect as a result of not only its spacious inner vault but also its subtle naturalistic elements, including the widespread use of natural materials and the organic shapes of its many features.

"Many of the world's most revered buildings contain biomimetic features. . . . They draw on design principles of natural forms. They have intricate fractal patterns in their spatial layouts and surface materials. They contain small, random variations in key elements rather than making exact replicates of forms, visual patterns, and spaces."[30]

Symbolically incorporating the shapes and forms of nature into the design of the built environment has also been called "biomorphic" architecture. Philosopher Yannick Joye defines biomorphic architecture as "designs whose shapes are similar to the formal grammar of living things." Examples of biomorphic architecture include both "stylized imitations" of living organisms (e.g., plants and animals) and more subtle simulations that reflect the "structural properties" encountered in the natural world (e.g., the replicated patterns and shapes of shells and leaves). Biomorphic design has been linked to the inherent human affinity for natural forms that—when successfully expressed—can enhance human physical and mental well-being.[31]

Architectural design that contains symbols of nature can often produce highly appealing and powerfully experienced places, drawing strength from an instinctual human emotional and intellectual proclivity for the natural world. Consider my recent encounter in the boardroom of a powerful institution. The room possessed an aura of power. When I looked about for the source of this effect, I noted high ceilings etched in floral relief and decorated moldings and pillars carved in fern- and leaf-like patterns. Looking down, I viewed a floor glowing with burnished wood, on which lay "oriental" rugs festooned with floral designs. Leather chairs circled the enormous burled wood table, floral patterns decorated the fabrics of the perimeter couches and hanging curtains, and an iron chandelier with curving branch-like arms hung from the ceiling. Natural light bathed the room, issuing from its oversized windows. I looked out one of the windows and saw a pleasing view of trees and shrubs, although another, far less satisfying window confronted only hard, artificial surfaces. This experience is only one example among many of how often we infuse the organic into interior and exterior settings to produce places of special power and meaning.

To be successful, symbolizing nature must avoid being merely decorative. It must also be integral to the building's design, woven into its context and structure, seamlessly moving from the human to the natural and back to the human again. We require far more understanding before being able to fully comprehend the complexities of symbolic design. However, we can conclude by returning to the nine values of biophilia discussed earlier, noting how often effective organic design gives rise to and affirms these values, underscoring the appropriateness of the designation "biophilic building design."[32]

Building and landscape design often reflects the utilitarian value of nature through material and physical security achieved by manipulating the experience of air, water, and other natural resources. This can occur in conventionally constructed buildings that protect people from the heat and cold of the external environment, or through more innovative technologies, such as wastewater treatment systems that use natural processes to purify wastes and sometimes even cultivate foods. However, a utilitarian value of nature in the built environment must be balanced, neither so excessive that it cuts off people from nature nor so weak that we feel vulnerable and unprotected. Pursuing a utilitarian value of nature also should not diminish or suppress other equally important biophilic values.

Negativistic and dominionistic values of nature in the built environment also emphasize the provision of shelter and protection from the elements, including wind, water, and geological forces. However, if expressed too excessively, these designs can dysfunctionally separate people from the natural environment, yielding structures that isolate us from nature's emotional richness and intellectual stimulation. Effective buildings and landscape designs must also foster the feelings of awe and wonder associated with perilous features of the natural world. Aesthetic, humanistic, and symbolic values of nature designed into the built environment can create beauty and a sense of connection as well as stimulate our interest, curiosity, and creativity. The incorporation of naturalistic, scientific, and moralistic values of nature into building and landscape design also fosters a sense of exploration, discovery, and inspiration. Some of our most cherished structures extol the human craving for an enduring and meaningful creation. By transforming the rigid geometry of material form into something seemingly timeless, we can achieve a sense of harmony and of participating in a larger and related world.

Vernacular Design

A critical aspect of restorative environmental design is buildings and constructed landscapes that connect to the places where they occur. This is referred to as vernacular design, defined in this book as the tailoring of the built environment to the particular physical and cultural places where people live and work. This meaning reflects the ordinary dictionary definition of the term *vernacular* as "native to . . . a particular country or region, . . . endemic, . . . relating to or characteristic of the style of architecture and decoration common in a particular region, culture, or period."[33] This definition underscores how vernacular design connects people and nature to a particular cultural and ecological setting.

As we have described, low environmental impact and organic design are essential elements of sustainability requiring considerable knowledge, ingenuity, and investments of energy, time, and technology to achieve. Yet, without vernacular connections to the culture and ecology of place, buildings and constructed landscapes are rarely sustained over the long term. Without a deep commitment and feeling of stewardship toward the places where the constructions occur, we generally do not devote the necessary physical, emotional, and intellectual resources needed to sustain these architectural accomplishments over time.

As described in chapter two, successful vernacular design evokes what both landscape architect Frederick Law Olmsted and Nobel Prize–winning biologist René Dubos called the "spirit of place."[34] When people are familiar with and meaningfully connected to the social traditions and natural settings of the places where they live, they become attached to that place's characteristic customs, traditions, and buildings and landscapes. The term *spirit* suggests that when this relationship among culture, environment, and architecture is pronounced, these places become alive for us, a part of our collective consciousness and identity. Building and landscape designs that affirm the spirit of a place reinforce our commitment to and stewardship for these places.

Effective vernacular design is the fusion of culture and ecology within a particular biogeographical context.[35] This accomplishment reflects the accumulated wisdom of a people and environment in adaptive relation to each other. Successful vernacular creation mirrors the iterative evolution of people in response to both natural and social forces. When this vernacular has been expressed effectively, both culture and nature become modified and even enriched by the exchange. Four critical elements of vernacular design can be identified, each of which is described in the following sections. These elements include the need to design

- In relation to the ecology of a place
- In relation to the cultural and social traditions of a place
- In manner that fuses culture and ecology, thus creating an emergent property within a biogeographical and historical context
- In ways that avoid "placelessness," in which a distinctive culture and ecology become so subverted that an area loses its special identity and spirit of place

Designing in Relation to the Ecology of Place

Effective vernacular design involves buildings and landscapes that are compatible with the ecology of their place at the site, ecosystem, and watershed levels. Achieving this compatibility requires knowledge of and sensitivity to various biophysical characteristics, including hydrology, soil, flora, fauna, atmosphere, and landscape features (e.g., wetlands and other distinctive ecosystems). Pioneering landscape architect Ian McHarg[36] used the phrase "designing with nature" to describe the appropriate matching of design and development with the physical, biological, and ecological properties of a geographic area, most particularly to its watersheds marking the interface of terrestrial and aquatic systems.

Designing with nature requires knowledge of physical parameters—such as water quantity and flow, surface and subsurface geology, and soil and aquatic chemistry—as well as an understanding of a broad matrix of biological variables—such as species composition, abundance, distribution, population dynamics, food and energy chains, prey-predator relations, and rare and imperiled, indigenous and nonindigenous, and keystone and ecologically important species. Vernacular design further requires knowledge of the ecological context of constructed buildings and landscapes, particularly ecosystem functions, structure, and dynamics. Comprehensive biophysical assessments and inventories ranging from the immediate building site to associated landscapes and watersheds must be conducted to obtain this information.

Following the principles of landscape ecology can help generate such knowledge and understanding across spatial and temporal levels. It can further help maintain and restore the functional integrity of affected ecosystems by identifying ways to minimize disruption and fragmentation of landscapes and watersheds through sensitive design and development. This can mean preventing the loss of or restoring ecologically important plant and animal species, maintaining critical hydrological and soil features, or sustaining biophysical factors and processes essential to maintaining ecological functions and systems. Landscape ecologists Wenche Dramstad and Richard Forman and landscape architect James Olson have developed useful design guidelines for sustaining ecological integrity. They urge avoidance of the following adverse ecological landscape-level effects of building design and development:

- "Fragmentation" (or breaking up) of large intact habitats into smaller dispersed patches
- "Dissection" (or splitting) of intact habitats into two or more patches
- "Perforation" (or creating "holes") within essentially intact habitats
- "Shrinkage" (or significantly decreasing the size) of one or more habitats
- "Attrition" (or fostering the disappearance) of one or more habitats[37]

Avoiding these disruptive ecological impacts can maintain landscape integrity and functioning by minimizing degradation and disruption to the land, water, and biota so characteristic of much contemporary construction and development. The authors suggest that a basic objective of landscape design is "reduc[ing] the landscape fragmentation and degradation so evident around us."[38] This requires land use and construction practices that avoid and minimize the disruption of essential nutrient, energy, and material flows of local habitats and ecosystems. Effective vernacular design must incorporate a view of the landscape as an integrated entity involving characteristic ecosystem patterns and processes that need to be sustained. The overall objective is to achieve "solutions . . . at the landscape level . . . that work with the larger pattern, understanding how it works, and designing in harmony with the structure of the natural system." Such solutions require the protection of important landscape features, including the following:

- Ecological "patches" containing important habitats, species sites, and ecosystems
- Edges, boundaries, or shapes within and among ecological patches that maintain and foster ecological richness and productivity
- Connections, corridors, and linkages between patches and habitats (e.g., riparian corridors) that facilitate the movement of energies, nutrients, and biotic elements across landscapes[39]

Effective vernacular design should also strive to restore and even enrich ecological functioning and productivity. People can add to as well as degrade natural systems. Like other "keystone species"—for example, an elephant on the savanna, an alligator in a water hole, a polyp on a coral reef, or a sea otter in a kelp bed—people alter the structure, diversity, and productivity of their natural systems. And, like these other keystone species, humans can diminish and potentially add value to their ecological systems. People are not some kind of "weed" species that inevitably degrades or destroys the health of the natural environment. Effective vernacular design suggests that people can instead help maintain, restore, and even enrich the productivity and vitality of their associated ecosystems.

Designing in Relation to Culture and History

Effective vernacular design requires consideration of the cultural and historical character of the places where buildings and other constructions occur. A rich literature exists on the cultural attributes of place (some briefly reviewed here and earlier, in chapter two).[40] The distinctive identity of a place is affirmed by designing in relation to a place's social and historical elements. Important features include regular, repeated events; familiar, valued surroundings; characteristic artifacts and designs; distinctive narrative and storytelling traditions; predictable customs and norms; and a feeling of community and shared relationship. Landscape historian John Brinckerhoff Jackson identified these cultural and historical attributes of place when he wrote: "Qualities I associate with a sense of place: a lively awareness of familiar surroundings, a ritual repetition, a sense of fellowship based on shared experience. It is the result of habit or custom reinforced by what might be called a sense of recurring events."[41]

These cultural and historical features foster an emotional and intellectual attachment to places. Buildings and landscapes that emerge as sites of loyalty and commitment reflect these qualities. These constructions reinforce people's sense of connection and relation to an area. The term *roots* aptly reflects this degree of psychological and biological association. The phrase *deep roots* intimates a condition of continuity and stability that describes an established historic and ecological relationship to land and place. The significance of having roots, especially its impact on human well-being, is often underestimated. As writer Simone Weil suggests:

> To be rooted is perhaps the most important and least recognized need of the human soul. It is one of the hardest to define. A human being has roots by virtue of his real, active, and natural participation in the life of the community, which preserves in living shape certain particular expectations of the future. This participation is a natural one in the sense that it is automatically brought about by place, conditions of birth, profession and social surroundings. Every human being needs to have multiple roots. It is necessary for him to draw well-nigh the whole of his moral, intellectual, and spiritual life by way of the environment of which he forms a part.[42]

The spirit of a place is a cultural and historical as much as a physical and biological condition. Reinforced by vernacular designs that encourage tradition and shared relationship, it reflects an attachment to an area, a feeling of belonging to both the culture and the land. The spirit of a place is revealed through a locality's distinctive buildings and landscapes—for example, the colonial architecture of New England, the adobe building style of the Middle East and the American Southwest, the white stone structures of the Mediterranean, the thatch roofs of the South Pacific, and more. These distinctive styles sustain an area's identity and become synonymous with its people, a vital thread affirming a characteristic and cherished way of life.

Building and landscape designs infused with the spirit of a place resonate with cultural meaning. They are experienced as positively charged "emotional spaces." More than inanimate wood, stone, glass, brick, or mortar, these structures become life-like placeholders of a distinctive personality and important symbols of a region's identity. They constitute, in effect, carriers of psychological significance that embody an area's singular and even spiritual character. As architect Tom Bender suggests: "A building, like a person, can have a soul . . . and can be part of the life of a community. It can be rooted in and convey the spirit of a strong culture and tradition. It can help restore to our surroundings a sense of sacredness and honoring of people, place, and diverse traditions. A building can demonstrate patterns which are sustainable and nurturing of the human spirit and of all life."[43]

Designing in Relation to Culture and Ecology

When reinforced through effective vernacular design, the spirit of a place is neither a cultural nor an ecological phenomenon but rather the integration and creative fusion of the two. The health and integrity of natural systems in human-dominated landscapes depend on positive connections between culture and nature. Likewise, an enduring culture requires a compatible combination of nature and human society. Nature and culture each become transformed through a process of mutual adjustment, with their successful integration resulting in what philosopher Mark Sagoff describes as harmonious places. Sagoff writes: "The concept of place combines the meaning we associate with nature and the utility we associate with environment. The result is an idea of surroundings that arise from harmony, partnership, and intimacy."[44]

The characteristic vernacular of a place is never the influence of culture or nature by itself but rather the effective combination of the two. This convergence of physical and human forces produces a distinctive vernacular tradition native to an area. This ongoing dialogue and exchange between the human and nonhuman builds an attachment to place. In time, this tradition becomes a source of meaning for its inhabitants, who defend and perpetuate place identity with loving allegiance. They become stewards of the land and of its culture revealed in characteristic buildings and landscapes. This congruence creates a distinctive and often healthier culture and ecology. Its successful result is what René Dubos called the "genius" of a place. He writes: "The genius of the place is made up of the physical, biological, social, and historical forces which together give its uniqueness to each locality or region. [People] always add something to nature, and thereby transform it, but [their] interventions are successful only to the extent that [they] respect the genius of the place."[45]

Vernacular design, thus, reflects an emergent state in which people are neither biologically determined nor culturally constructed creatures. Instead, human identity and design are the outgrowth of both learning and genetics. For this exchange to be successful, however, the interaction must occur within familiar, secure territorial boundaries. Effective vernacular design facilitates this subtle process of interaction, adaptation, and exchange of culture and nature within the context of a particular locality.

Unfortunately, most contemporary building design and construction ignores this interdependency of culture, nature, and place. Instead, many modern structures are the consequence of rapid large-scale development, resulting in the maladaptive transformation of both the natural and the cultural environment. Much contemporary architecture ignores the adaptive melding of culture and nature that characterizes good vernacular design, seeking instead to impose an abstract ideology and technology that typically results in the wholesale alteration of the human and natural landscape. Effective vernacular design can be achieved in a modern context of large-scale and short-term construction, but it requires sensitivity, knowledge, and forethought that meaningfully seeks to connect existing social conditions to the health and integrity of local ecological systems.

Designing to Avoid Placelessness
Unfortunately, contemporary architecture and land use practices often debase both culture and ecology and erode existing vernacular traditions. This phenomenon, sometimes referred to as *placelessness,* diminishes distinctive local and regional identities, often replacing them with uniformity and anonymity. Geographer Edward Relph describes placelessness in this way:

> If places are indeed a fundamental aspect of existence in the world, if they are sources of security and identity for individuals and for groups, then it is important that the means of experiencing, creating, and maintaining significant places are not lost. There are signs that these very means are disappearing and that "placelessness"—the weakening of distinct and diverse expe-

riences and identities of places—is now a dominant force. Such a trend marks a major shift in the geographical bases of existence from a deep association with places to rootlessness.[46]

Various contemporary trends have loosened people's sense of connection, affiliation, and attachment to the places where they work and reside. These trends include declining neighborhoods and communities, rapid social and geographic mobility, urban and suburban sprawl, loss of open space and environmental degradation, and an increasingly global and psychologically disconnected economy. The result has been a physical and mental separation of people from nature and culture. Mark Sagoff describes this phenomenon as one of "becoming strangers in our own land." As he suggests:

> Much of what we deplore about the human subversion of nature—and fear about the destruction of the environment—has to do with the loss of places we keep in shared memory and cherish with instinctive and collective loyalty. It has to do with the loss of . . . security when one relies upon the characteristic aspects of places and communities one knows well. What may worry us most is the prospect of becoming strangers in our own land.[47]

A sense of placelessness is often linked to large-scale development, short-term construction, and massive earth-transforming technology—practices that often reflect an indifference, if not disdain, for distinctive vernacular conditions. Such an approach to designing the built environment ignores the virtue of compatible connections among culture, nature, and history. Office towers, shopping malls, and housing developments are instead designed in abstract, universal ways that are disconnected from both local culture and ecology. These constructions strike us as anonymous and interchangeable, whether they occur in New York, Los Angeles, Brussels, Beijing, Buenos Aires, or Timbuktu. Rather than bearers of a distinctive regional or cultural identity, they resemble nightmares of anonymity that would more appropriately be labeled generic than contemporary architecture (Illustration 44). This design paradigm is formal and aloof, favoring the interests of professionals over the predilections of people residing within cherished cultural and ecological contexts.

Much contemporary architecture exists apart from history and environment. These constructions are ephemeral, tied to the latest aesthetic fad or cutting-edge technology, often abandoned when their modernist fashions become boring or obsolete. These buildings celebrate placelessness and typically do not foster loyalty among most people nor the commitment to renew and restore them over time. Ironically, the transience of

Illustration 44. (*above and opposite*) Nightmares of Anonymity: Modern office towers, public housing projects, shopping malls, and residential developments frequently use architectural styles distinguished by their oppressive monotony.

this type of design contrasts with its oft-touted economic and technical efficiencies. Even when this kind of design seeks to include vernacular elements, the attempt is often superficial, a kind of "commodified nostalgia" that mocks established and revered traditions.

Still, how important are these considerations of vernacular design? Is vernacular design an important aspect of restorative environmental design or just a romantic yearning for the past and a mainly negative response to the environmental and social excesses of much contemporary design? If contemporary architecture were to minimize its adverse impacts and foster a more positive connection between people and nature, would the deficiencies of vernacular design become marginal and even trivial? I think not. Sustainability is the commitment to retain, renew, and restore buildings and landscapes over time. Eliciting the motivation and resources necessary to maintain the built environment depends on people making cultural and ecological connections with the places where they live and work.

Restorative environmental design embraces more than building and developing new structures, no matter how environmentally benign or positively connected to the natural environment they are. Vernacular design reflects the additional ingredient of people living in knowing and respectful relation to their historical and ecological context who strive to preserve and protect the architectural and environmental integrity of their places. Lacking this familiarity and connection, people act carelessly toward both culture and nature, tending to look to consuming something new to satisfy their endless cravings in a continual process of excess and wastefulness. Loyalty and commitment to place remain the cornerstone of stewardship.

Low environmental impact and organic designs are necessary but not sufficient conditions for achieving restorative environmental design. Without a goodness of fit between culture, history, and ecology, design and development are inevitably transient and unsustainable. People who are deeply committed to their places and surroundings tend to be intolerant of activities that inflict damage on either the natural or built environments and take steps to counteract this harm. They exercise, as poet Gary Snyder suggests, a sense of "stewardship [that] means . . . find your place on the planet, dig in and take responsibility."[48] Vernacular design reflects the commitment to restore and renew a three-century-old building, once a butcher shop and today a computer store. Architectural forms recycled generation after generation are as much a part of sustainability as investing in the latest waste minimization technology or energy efficient system.

A narrow, shortsighted calculus has convinced many architects, developers, designers, planners, and politicians that they can ill afford the luxury of preserving the human and natural environments or meaningfully connecting constructions to the culture and ecology of place. This attitude is a prescription for failure. Communities and leaders paralyzed by the challenge of vernacular design perversely impede their regions' health and prosperity over time.

Conclusion

This chapter has proposed a concept of restorative environmental design that seeks to harmonize the natural and human built environments through implementing the three principles of low environmental impact, organic, and vernacular design. Not coincidentally, these three design objectives reflect the three concepts described in chapter two—ecosystem services, biophilia, and spirit of place—to explain how the human experience of natural systems nurtures and enhances people's physical and mental well-being. Figure 11 suggests that maintaining ecosystem services gives rise to the principle of low environmental impact design; that the maturation and development of biophilic values leads to the objective of organic design; and that engendering a spirit of place fosters the goal of vernacular design.

Restorative environmental design seeks to repair the relationship between nature and humanity in a world increasingly marred by environmental impoverishment and social and psychological alienation. Neither easy nor painless, this achievement will require considerable knowledge, motivation, and skill. Low environmental impact design has moved promisingly toward this goal. However, by becoming the dominant orientation of contemporary sustainable design, this approach by itself cannot restore our frayed relationship with the natural world. If left to function alone, it will yield structures that over time are often perceived as sterile, unappealing, and unworthy of preservation and protection. We will also need designs that foster a positive experiential connection to the natural world and affirm our enduring desire to connect with the culture and ecology of our places.

A personal anecdote may illustrate this difference. A few years ago, I visited several sustainably designed constructions located in the northwestern section of industrial Germany. One complex had incorporated the latest low environmental impact technology and was widely praised for its presumed contribution to the area's economic and social revitalization. The engineering was impressive, but the overall effect was disjointed and unsatisfying. Despite considerable achievements in energy efficiency, the use of less noxious materials, and reduced wastes, the complex felt aloof and alienating. Even its atrium, which incorporated water and vegetative features into the building, seemed more decorative than satisfying.

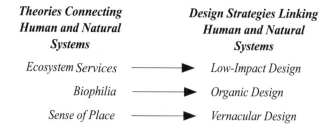

Figure 11. Theory Connecting Human and Natural Systems with the Principles of Restorative Environmental Design

In a nearby city, I encountered a very different project. This effort also included many low environmental impact design features, such as energy efficiency and less toxic products and materials. But, in addition, it elicited a positive affinity and connection to the natural environment and local culture. Interior spaces featured natural lighting and natural ventilation, the informed use of native vegetation, mediated connections between the inside and outside, and furnishings and decorative features that fostered both indirect and symbolic contact with nature. The surrounding landscape included a constructed lake and restored wetlands linked to the building's stormwater and irrigation systems that also provided aesthetic and naturalistic benefits for the employees and neighbors. The complex connected well to the local community because it was built in compatible relation to the cultural, historical, and ecological character of the region and nearby river.

At the risk of sounding naive, most intractable problems can be solved, as others have stressed before me, with an attitude of love or, in this case, "LOVE"—Low impact, Organic, Vernacular Environmental design. This acronym reminds us that the literal Latin translation of *biophilia* is "love of life." The values of biophilia, like the principles of restorative environmental design, require that we seek to harmonize nature with humanity if we are to achieve a just, secure, sustainable, fulfilling, and loving future.

The principles of LOVE call for a new way of thinking about building and landscape design, one that will require an altered design process that includes, at the least,

- Considering all biophilic values in building, landscape, and land use design and development
- Linking all material and resource flows that connect buildings and landscapes to larger biogeographical scales over time

- Incorporating diverse disciplinary understandings in the planning and design of the built environment, especially environmental, architectural, and engineering perspectives
- Connecting the constructed environment to diverse land use, transportation, and open space patterns and processes
- Ensuring long-term planning and analysis prior to development and then mandating measurable performance standards that account for environmental and human impacts of these designs
- Increasing people's awareness, appreciation, and understanding of the benefits of restorative environmental design
- Enhancing the capacity of buildings and landscapes to adapt to new knowledge and technologies of restorative environmental design over time[49]

These elements represent some of the basic procedural changes that achieving the promise of restorative environmental design will require. Clearly, the principles of LOVE and of a new ethic of sustainability will be needed to successfully resolve the modern environmental crisis. Chapter six explores the character of this ethical challenge.

6

Ethics of Sustainability

I believe that a code of ethics arises from the quality of our experience and our thinking. Since the time when we emerged from . . . the pre-human era we have had to tamper with our progress, consciously and purposely, with whatever wisdom we have been able to command. But evolution still operates. It is fortunate that we can't escape it. Esthetics in its many forms has evolved with us, affecting our judgments, shaping our way of life and our philosophy. . . . We have also nurtured an inherent concept of morals and of responsibility. We are toying with the qualities of generosity and tolerance, a sense of neighborliness in the Nature of which we are a part.

—Olaus Murie, "Ethics in Wildlife Management," *Journal of Wildlife Management* 18: 3 (July 1954: 291)

People's contact with natural systems greatly affects their physical and mental well-being as well as how the positive interaction between humans and nature can be maintained and restored in a world where the human experience of nature has become more and more degraded. Unfortunately, the appreciation of nature's role in human satisfaction and fulfillment has receded in modern society. This is seen even among some conservationists who equate sustainability with a narrow range of physical and material benefits related only to such practices as energy efficiency, pollution abatement, or habitat protection. The impaired human physical and material security that the degradation of natural systems causes is certainly a critical concern and an impediment to a sustainable future. However, this perspective of sustainability is too narrow and by itself fails to address other, equally important aspects of the contemporary environmental crisis. Most of all, it ignores many essential physical, emotional, intellectual, and spiritual benefits that people derive from their ongoing experience of healthy and diverse natural systems.

This distinction leads to the central question: What are we sustaining when we conserve and protect the natural environment? Of course we wish to avoid harm to human health and long-term impediments to material and economic prosperity. But these goals constitute the means, not the objective, of human existence. They may ensure a prosperous economy, but they do not guarantee or enhance human emotional, intellectual, or moral fulfillment. The quality of human life also depends on the positive experience of healthy natural systems. This too must be a basic objective of sustainability.

The human body, mind, and spirit evolved in a complex matrix of interactions with the natural world that to this day continues to affect our ability to think critically, to be creative, to discover, to show compassion, to care, and to realize a just and purposeful existence. As conventionally designed and developed, modern urban society has not only greatly diminished the material productivity of natural systems but also separated us from positive contact with nature as an irreplaceable source of our physical and psychological existence. Only by reconciling and harmonizing the natural and human built environments can we arrest and reverse these ominous trends and restore the biological basis for our well-being.

The recent focus on sustainable development is a welcome response to this challenge, but too often this objective has assumed a narrow, materialistic emphasis. Consider some definitions of sustainability. Among the most widely cited is the Brundtland Commission's definition: "[Meeting] the needs of those present without compromising the ability of future generations to meet their own needs." A more recent definition in the journal *Science* describes sustainability as "meeting fundamental human needs while preserving the life-support systems of planet Earth."[1] A definition central to the focus of this book is offered by the American Institute of Architects: "The ability of society to continue functioning into the future without being forced into decline through exhaustion or overloading of the key resources on which that system depends." Drawing on this definition, an extensively used book on sustainable design suggests that it seeks to "mov[e] away from extractive and disposable systems that are energy intensive, resource inefficient, and toxic toward cyclical, closed-loop systems."[2]

All of these definitions of sustainability and sustainable design certainly apply and deserve praise. Yet, they almost exclusively emphasize human physical and material dependence on and benefits derived from natural systems. According to these definitions, the primary objectives of sustainability are economic and resource efficiency, health, and pollution abatement. By contrast, these notions of sustainability express little or no consideration of how the experience of nature can also contribute to human emotional, intellectual, moral, and spiritual capacity and well-being. A sustainable society must have clean air, potable water, abundant resources, and the availability of basic ecosystem services. Yet meaningful, satisfying lives also depend on positive contact with nature as an integral aspect of ordinary human life. Narrow definitions of sustainability that stress only physical and material benefits fail to emphasize how a just and fulfilling existence also depends on maintaining an experiential connection with nature in an increasingly urban world.

Sustainable development fundamentally constitutes an issue of values and, thus, ultimately of ethics. It strikes at the heart of what we want from our association with the natural world and what we believe to be right and good in this relationship. Donald Kennedy, eminent scientist and past president of Stanford University, addresses this issue in the journal *Science*. He writes:

> We obtain value from our environment in various ways: We may use it for timber or for hunting, we may enjoy it for various nonuse values such as birdwatching, and we may extract pleasure from merely knowing that it's there. . . . Sustainability [requires] that the average welfare of the successor generation, with respect to the total of *all* these values, be as high or higher than that of the current generation. . . . Once we find agreement about what sustainability really means, we can ask what science [and technology] might contribute.[3]

Our ongoing reliance on nature certainly encompasses material and physical security aided by such practices as energy and resource efficiency, pollution control, and the preservation of ecosystem services. But, as Kennedy suggests, it also necessitates a respect for all values and benefits we derive from nature, a dependence that extends far beyond a narrow materialistic and economic calculus to embrace a broader conception of human self-interest. We need to recognize the widest range of values derived from our dependence on nature, one that also includes emotional connection, intellectual competence, the experience of beauty, a sound moral compass, and a world of enduring meaning and relation.

This matter of nature's values is ultimately an issue of ethics as well. It bears on what we view as good, just, and worthy, reflecting how our values of nature give rise to and sustain an ethic of justice and well-being. It fundamentally reflects on how we see ourselves fitting into the world. A concept of ethics that emphasizes only a narrow, utilitarian perspective of material and physical well-being derived from the natural environment will prove to be inadequate and, ultimately, counterproductive. On the other hand, an environmental ethic that advocates the intrinsic rights of nature independent of human interests and well-being will also prove to be misguided and, even worse, irrelevant. What we need—and what has been advanced in this book—is an environmental ethic in which the inherent human affinity for nature embraces a wide range of physical, emotional, intellectual, and spiritual needs, all originating in our biology and, thus, self-interest, even if greatly shaped by learning, culture, and experience.[4]

This biocultural environmental ethic is also utilitarian, but in a far broader sense than typically conceived. A utilitarian ethic advances the idea that an action is good or right when it contributes the greatest good to the greatest number for present and future generations.[5] From this perspective, a species, ecosystem, or environmental process is not so much a moral end as a means to a worthy human end, such as happiness, justice, or fulfillment. A utilitarian environmental ethic has been invoked to defend nature from injury that impairs or reduces people's material security and physical well-being or their just distribution. Seen in this way, species extinction, pollution, or resource depletion is morally reprehensible because it damages the utility of present and future generations who could exploit a biotic form or whose health might be impaired, such harms often being inflicted on the most vulnerable, such as children and the poor.

This ethical posture is better described as a narrow utilitarianism because its materialistic emphasis lacks an appreciation of other values of nature that are independent of human material interests, such as the love of nature or admiration of its beauty or being inspired by its spiritual qualities. These perceived limitations of a narrow utilitarian environmental ethic have prompted some to advocate a rights-based, or "biocentric," ethic that defends nature, especially its living forms, as moral ends in themselves, possessing an intrinsic right to exist independent of whether they advance human welfare.[6] From a biocentric perspective, nature is valuable because it engenders our affection, appreciation, love, and reverential devotion independent of its material utility.

The environmental ethic advanced here views both a narrow utilitarian ethic or a rights-based ethic as equally flawed and inadequate for generating an ethic of sustainable design and development. The narrow utilitarian ethic is correct but flawed for several reasons. First, much of the natural world will never yield material advantage to people, and most forms of pollution (with the possible exception of global climate change) affect relatively few people and can be remedied through technical and regulatory rather than ethical means. Second, an equally narrow utilitarian ethic can be advanced that argues for a species' extinction or for some form of pollution because it results in the greatest good for the greatest number of people now and in the foreseeable future. Third, the seeds of destruction are sown in any ethical calculus that favors a fraction of the natural world while intimating the expendability of the rest depending on compelling social and economic circumstances. Fourth, and most important, a narrow utilitarian ethic embraces only a partial, inadequate understanding of how much people benefit from their experience of nature for their physical, mental, and spiritual well-being.

The problem with a biocentric ethic, which extends moral standing to all of the natural world independent of human interests, is that it provides little practical guidance and convinces few. How does one choose between equally imperiled species or, more significantly, between human welfare and the well-being of nature? A biocentric position offers limited guidance in situations where an ethic is often most needed, not the choosing of good versus bad but between competing, equally virtuous goods. Moreover, by being indifferent to human needs and interests, a rights-based ethic convinces few to accept it and is, thus, politically untenable. Finally, a rights-based environmental ethic is largely unnecessary because the biocultural perspective advocated here embraces many of its most compelling arguments, such as sustaining nature because of its beauty, emotional appeal, and reverential qualities. The notion of biophilia considers these elements and more as instrumental to human physical, mental, and spiritual well-being.

This latter point returns us to the ethic of sustainability advanced in this book, which originates in a greatly expanded understanding and appreciation of human self-interest. This perspective is lodged somewhere between a narrow utilitarian ethic and an all-inclusive biocentric ethic. It marries a broad instrumentalism with varying aspects of a rights-based position. This ethic of sustainable design and development is utilitarian, but it also embraces an understanding of human welfare that views nature as an essential source not just for protecting the human body but for enhancing the human mind and spirit as well. It connects material and physical advantage to other, equally important benefits people derive from nature, including its aesthetic, emotional, intellectual, moral, and spiritual values. Biologist Edward O. Wilson advocated this form of environmental ethic in defending biological diversity, but it applies equally to an ethic of sustainable development. Wilson remarks:

> What humanity is now doing will impoverish our descendants for all time to come. Yet critics often respond "so what?" The most frequent argument is one of material wealth at risk. This argument is demonstrably true but contains a dangerous flaw—if judged by potential value, species can be priced, traded off against other sources of wealth, and when the price is right, discarded. . . . The . . . rights argument . . . like the materialist argument alone, is a dangerous play of cards. . . . The independent-rights argument, for all its directness and power, remains intuitive, aprioristic, and lacking in objective evidence. . . . A simplistic adjuration for the rights of [nature] . . . can be answered by a simplistic call for the rights of people. . . . In the end, deci-

sions concerning preservation and use of biodiversity will turn on our values and ways of moral reasoning. A sound ethic . . . will obviously take into account the immediate practical uses of species, but it must reach further and incorporate the very meaning of human existence. . . . A robust, richly textured, anthropocentric ethic can instead be made based on the hereditary needs of our species, for the diversity of life based on aesthetic, emotional, and spiritual grounds.[7]

Like Wilson's, the biocultural ethic of sustainability advocated here relates human material, emotional, intellectual, and spiritual well-being to human biology as well as to our species' capacity to exercise choice and free will in designing our world. The concept of biophilia offers this understanding of the convergence of human culture and biology. The biophilic values may be rooted in human genetics, but they are weak biologic tendencies that depend highly on learning and experience to adaptively mature. They reflect the richness of our reliance on nature for fitness and security and thus comprise a web of relational dependency so pronounced that an instrumental ethic for sustaining nature emerges from a profound realization of self-interest. Biophilia is the genetic substrate of an ancient evolutionary dependence on nature molded and shaped by human choice through learning and culture that can result in either adaptive or maladaptive expression. Each value is a thread of connection that forms an unrivaled basis for an ethic of sustainability. People see in their diverse connections to nature a moral rationale for sustaining the integrity of the natural environment. René Dubos advanced a similar ethic of sustainable design and development when he suggested:

> Conservation of nature is based on human value systems that rather than being a luxury are a necessity for the preservation of mental health. Above and beyond the economic reasons for conservation there are aesthetic and moral ones which are even more compelling. We are shaped by the earth. The characteristics of our environment in which we develop condition our biological and mental health and the quality of our life. Were it only for selfish reasons, we must maintain variety and harmony in nature.[8]

The biophilic values are a garment cloaking the human species in the health, beauty, and integrity of the natural world. The critical challenge confronting us in the design and development of the human built environment is how to sustain satisfying contact with natural systems as an essential basis for human physical and moral security. Contemporary society is no more intrinsically destructive or incapable of living in compatible relation with a healthy environment than previous societies have been. The current scale of environmental destruction is a design flaw rather than an inevitable deficiency of modern life. With care, understanding, and a sound ethical compass, we can design and develop even our most populated cities to avoid environmental damage as well as provide people with nurturing opportunities to connect meaningfully with the natural world.

We will inevitably behave in self-destructive ways when we lack psychological and spiritual well-being just as surely as we do when we lack material security. Violence and destruction are just as much a consequence of moral impoverishment as they are of resource scarcity. We are physically and mentally conditioned by the quality of our relation to the natural world. A broad anthropocentric ethic for sustaining the earth affirms our unyielding ties to creation. We can draw emotional, intellectual, and spiritual sustenance and guidance from celebrating this commonality. Ecologist Aldo Leopold envisioned this ethic of sustainability when he suggested nearly a half century ago:

> There must be some force behind conservation, more universal than profit, less awkward than government, less ephemeral than sport, something that reaches into all times and places . . . something that brackets everything from rivers to raindrops, from whales to hummingbirds, from land-estates to window-boxes. . . . I can see only one such force: a respect for land as an organism . . . out of love for and obligation to that great biota. . . . By and large, our present problem is one of attitudes and implements. We are remodeling the Alhambra with a steam shovel, and we are proud of our yardage. We shall hardly relinquish the shovel, which after all has many good points, but we are in need of gentler and more objective criteria for its successful use.[9]

Sustainability will not be achieved until we alter our basic ethical perspective of the natural world. Important, progressive change has occurred, as reflected in the evolving principles of sustainability and sustainable design. But the prevailing approaches have been limited, narrow and, ultimately, inadequate. Relying only on the logic of economic materialism, technology, and regulation has not been enough to resolve our environmental problems or to achieve sustainable development. Only a basic shift in our values and ethics can mitigate the scale of the contemporary environmental crisis.[10] This will occur when we not only acknowledge the need to use nature's resources efficiently and prudently but also when we recognize how our modern lives continue to depend on the quality of our experience of nature, which is integral to our physical, psychological, and moral existence.

Narrative Epilogue

Throughout this book, we have discussed how—even in the modern age—people continue to rely on positive contact with healthy natural systems for their physical, mental, and spiritual well-being. We have also considered ways to minimize the adverse environmental impacts of modern building construction and practice as well as how to restore beneficial connections between nature and humanity, especially in the modern city. Yet we still do not fully understand the science and practicalities of designing compatible and even harmonious relations between people and nature in an increasingly artificial and built world.

In the book's introduction, we suggested that intuition and imagination may be also useful in exploring and possibly filling in these knowledge gaps. This more subjective approach forms the substance of storytelling, a narrative tradition used in this epilogue in a series of five fictional stories. Four of the stories focus on a hypothetical person during his childhood, adolescence, early adulthood, and middle age. The final story briefly considers the life of one of his children and then a later generation.

These stories engage themes addressed in the earlier, more empirical chapters, including the role of nature in human maturation and development, the importance of community and place, environmental degradation in the modern age, and how a new design paradigm design can help restore compatible relations between people and nature in the contemporary city. This storytelling is, by definition, fanciful and speculative. Still, as a complement to the earlier chapters, these stories can hopefully add to our understanding of how we may harmonize nature and humanity in our increasingly populated and constructed world.

ONE

Of Forests and the Sea—1955: Middle Childhood

I remember it as a mostly tumbledown world, geographic precision being of little concern to a six-year-old, when physics is more feeling than substance. All I knew was that my world had this peculiar pitch gradually leading down through outdoor furniture and then winding through paths and thickets eventually to the road. The path across the road passed through beach roses and poison ivy before entering spiky grass, where thousands of ticks lurked, waiting to pounce. You were almost at the beach here, although you still had many stones to cross. A few prickly plants grew in this world of high sand beyond the tides and waves; in the spring, they formed a carpet of yellow, pink, and blue flowers. Beyond the rocks and plants lay the beach, exquisite, soft, stretching on endlessly, a place where time passed so slowly it almost seemed to stop and bend backward.

A trip to the beach often included Mom, older siblings, occasional cousins, friends and their parents, and sometimes neighbors. It also wasn't unusual to meet someone on the beach you didn't know but who almost always became a friend. Even when by yourself, you never felt alone because there were so many things to do, and so many creatures in the sand, below the sand, in the water, in the air, just about everywhere. The place crawled with crabs, beetles, terns, minnows, fish, cormorants, and fishermen. Though I rarely brought much with me, I was never bored. The beach provided endless adventure and exploration with few specific objectives or destinations.

It was just a big pile of sand, unending brown stretching unchanged to the horizon and complementing a gray sea. Yet it always enthralled us. We passed hours like minutes, punctuated by forays into the cool waters to shed the irritating heat or, sometimes, excess energy. We built forts, castles, channels, and moats, chased after crabs, engaged in small but never unimportant acts. Why did this pile of sand so enchant us? Perhaps because we felt intensely alive. We molded wonders from raw creation, modifying the world around us but never fundamentally changing or diminishing it. We simply reorganized its "beachness," enlarging its properties and boundaries.

The beach was a special part of our neighborhood. Ours was a small village by the sea in the mid-1950s, but I have learned since then that people in the cities can be as numerous as flies living close to one another but still be mostly alone and apart. In our neighborhood, people always seemed aware of one another as if the place were alive. Don't get me wrong—not everyone liked everyone else, and we were certainly not some saintly group. We had plenty of rivalries, jealousies, petty quarrels, and worse. Yet most of us operated in a kind of shared mutuality, a respectful alliance and feeling of responsibility for the whole, especially for the young. Whether we liked it or not, everybody knew just about everybody else.

We were also aware, especially the kids, of our physical world, taking pride, and even a measure of identity, in our special blending of the human with the natural. The houses were covered in rarely painted cedar shingles, the gray textures seemingly merging with the land and the muted colors of the sea. For unknown reasons, most homeowners left the surrounding pine-oak forest and understory of bayberry and blueberry largely untouched rather than converting them to grass and ornamental shrubs. Still, nearly everyone had a lawn bordered by flowers and gardens that thrived in the humid air. These were mostly modest additions that soon blended back into the forest. The forest itself was simple, consisting mostly of two kinds of trees, pitch pine and scrub oak. The area was known historically as the pine barrens because few trees and plants survived in its mostly sandy, impoverished soil. Yet people seemed to like that simple pine-oak forest as if it defined what was normal and expected about our neighborhood. People were reluctant to get rid of the trees, perhaps captivated by the sounds of the prairie warblers and bobwhites in spring, of the screech owls and cicadas in summer, or by how the trees cushioned the biting winds and northeasters of fall and winter. I suspect the adults also responded to the wonder shown by the kids in response to the forest and sea—and perhaps by the kids they still carried around in themselves.

For us children, the forest and sea were our neighborhood, our place of unending exploration, adventure, and discovery, perhaps even the birthplace of our sense of beauty and respect for creation. We constructed places of wonder in its bushes and brambles, bush houses and games of challenge and competition at the frontiers of curiosity and creation. We also relished being apart from the adults there, though always close by, wild but within striking distance of security, engaging in various risks but not too removed from the comfort and shelter of our homes and backyards. The hazards were real to us—skunks, poison ivy, ticks, climbing too high or falling too far, venturing away and perhaps getting lost, coming too close to the choppy waters and being swept away. Like all children, we tested the boundaries of our world, probing and indulging our curiosities and inventiveness. Most of the adults accepted this craving for adventure but rarely endorsed it aloud, usually warning us instead of the dangers of disregarding our fears.

Still, this world of intimacy had its share of somber moments, even terrible ones, which I recall today with an almost paralyzing sadness. Above all else, I remember the death of my father and, soon after, nearly losing my own life as well. I don't wish to indulge my particular pathos, recognizing how often boys and girls lose their parents to premature death, whether by accident, illness, or more deliberate design, and yet learn to get on with the business of living. Still, his death when I was six years old lodged a sense of inexplicable loss in my gut like some deep black hole I continue to carry around inside of me as if it were a disaster waiting to happen.

I knew Dad was ill, but this hardly registered in my young brain as something that could end a life so central to my existence. No one explained the extent of his illness to me, probably assuming, as adults often do, that young people need to be shielded from the realities of pain and irreversible loss. So, one night when Dad became ill and was rushed to the hospital, it never occurred to me that I would never see him again. When it finally became clear, the intensity of the news was bewildering and I denied it, looking for some different, more plausible explanation.

Looking back, I believe the only thing that kept me from becoming entirely swallowed up by despondency was the forest—most particularly, the company of a wren. I had by then retreated to the forest because it was a good place to be alone. I also secretly hoped that I could wander about and perhaps find Dad again. One time while sitting in the woods, I retreated into a strange fantasy, imagining myself far off in some backcountry, a place of deep craters and broken ground and a peculiar dark purple and blue sky above. I followed a tortuous route, being called back only after a long while by a distant, distracting sound. The sound became louder and more insistent and, finally, impossible to ignore.

As my fantasy dissolved, out of the haze emerged a small wren.[1] The tiny bird perched on a low branch no more than a foot from my nose above a thick, dwarfish tree. Its shiny eyes stared at me intently, its small head crowned by a lighter curved stripe, speckled white spots on its brown body, the creature's smallness at odds with the intensity of its call and its seemingly angry eyes. The bird's song as much as its presence commanded my attention, forcing me to retreat from my sorrow. Its song rose in a loud, aggressive melody, hypnotic and forceful, an ebullient cry from a creature so small it would have fit in the palm of my hand.

Only the most optimistic would think the wren had actually been singing to me, imparting some brand of solace. But to my six-year-old brain—and, truthfully, to part of me today—I was convinced that it was. At the time, I did not doubt that the bird was communicating with me and, in fact, recognized me. Wrens were very much a part of our lives back then, thriving in the pine-oak forest at the margins of the wild and tame, each morning loudly advertising their presence, sounding at first light with their long lyrical cries, taking possession of the woods as if they owned it, the sound always shocking when you spied its tiny origin.

More importantly, wrens had occupied a special place in our family, and not long before, one had actually became an unofficial part of the household. This had occurred the previous spring while we were on vacation. A female wren had flown through the laundry room window mistakenly left ajar and proceeded to build a nest atop folded laundry at the bottom of a wicker basket. There she sat on her unhatched eggs upon our return. Most birds confronted by people under such circumstances would have panicked and abandoned their nest. But wrens, being very bold and nearly fearless, sometimes do not. Also, most people encountering a wild animal in their home would chase it away or worse. But my mother just accepted the bird's presence.

So, although initially agitated by the sight of my mother, the bird settled down, and Mom soon acted as if the creature on its nest in the laundry basket were really not so unusual an event. The two of them—and then all of us—soon settled into an accommodation, with the wren allowing Mom to go about her laundry business, the others of us staring, while it continued to warm and eventually hatch its eggs and then, along with her mate, feed the incessantly demanding chicks. The adult wrens would fly in and out of the window, bringing insects and other fare, and before long the chicks were jumping onto the windowsill and flying out. Soon enough, they disappeared back into the forest.

As I leaned against the tree that lonely, disturbing day staring in utter stillness at the wren, mesmerized by its melodious song and fierce countenance, I wondered whether this bird might be one of the chicks raised in the laundry basket, perhaps returning to help one of those humans who had opted for its life rather than its death. I also remember wondering whether pity could be a solely human possession. What was undeniably real to me was the bird's insistence on my full attention as it sang for what seemed like the longest time. I sat staring back, the creature inches from my face, its flute-like piccolo rising louder but never shrill, reaching a crescendo then tumbling back, one note falling on top of another before reaching bottom and rising again.

The song became unbearable, and I spoke to the bird. Rather than fleeing, the wren became tensely silent as it continued to pay me full and mindful attention. So, I poured my heart out—perhaps more inside my head than aloud—telling the bird of my sufferings and seeking some explanation and validation but, of course, receiving none. Yet I felt oddly relieved, more accepting of the tenuous relation between life and death, of connections that might dissolve my terrible loneliness, comforted by a broader encompassing world that included Dad and myself. This six-year-old even wondered whether the branch, the tree, the soil, the clouds on high, a single species of bird, and a little boy could be bound by some string of substance and time.

As I stayed there, I felt myself become another speck in the woods, attuned to its many details and happenings. An ever-widening circle of awareness and connection radiated out, starting with the wren. A vole entered and exited, then a catbird, soon a honeybee, a dragonfly, beetles and ants, scrub oaks and poison ivy, the wind and the sky—all alive and a part of me. Boundaries between life and nonlife dissolved. A garter snake appeared, and I felt fear and an impulse to flee. The wren spied the serpent and flew off, making me feel more alone and afraid. But I remained, and after a while, the snake basking in the warm sun became just another part of it all. For the first time since Dad's death, I felt alert and alive, preferring the company of even a snake to the loneliness of the black hole inside me.

I realized then how much I wanted to be with my family. Yet, even after returning to the land of humanity, I still visited that special spot in the woods where I had encountered my peculiar communion with the wren. The place became a halfway house for me between human creation and a broader one. I saw in the wren a parallel universe, autonomous yet familiar, a place where kinship could occur despite immense differences.

I have no desire to continue dwelling on my loss, although I must conclude with what happened next—my particular brush with mortality, an incident of terror that still makes me shudder to this day. Ironically, what occurred stemmed from the well-meaning intentions of those helping me at the time. Walking with me during the full moon following Dad's death, my uncle pointed out a vague face in the moon that I had never noticed before. He said Dad was looking down on me. The revelation never left me, and the next day I impatiently waited for darkness to see my father's face again in the moon and perhaps get closer to him.

I went to bed early, much to everybody's surprise. When it was completely dark, I climbed down the tree outside my window. I made my way to the beach as the full moon was rising above the horizon, orange and magnified by the heat rising from the ground. I stared for a long time before proceeding and then sought the rowboat beneath the pier, used to rescue people foolish enough to venture into the dangerous riptide just offshore. I reasoned with the unassailable logic of a six-year-old boy that if I could get close enough I could even talk to Dad.

But we lived where two sounds joined, a place known as the chop because of its almost continuously choppy waters. Indeed, if the tide and currents were just right, as often occurred during a full moon, the waves would become breaking surf, a place even small skiffs avoided. My little boat soon encountered the chop and gathered speed, unavoidably turning to the northeast despite my best efforts. The water passed quickly underneath the thin hull separating me from the sea. The boat soon slipped out of my control, and I was swept out to sea, helpless and afraid. In the distance, I could see and hear the bell of the green channel buoy, its eerie light blinking like some horrible eye. The wooden boat started to fill as seawater struck the sides and started to splash over. The boat swayed and bounced in the virulent surf, sending an awful terror through me. The boat slowly filled with water, becoming unbalanced, its rotation increasing with the swell as I paddled furiously to escape the vortex.

The boat twisted more and then suddenly flipped over. I was in the water, helplessly swept by the current, strangely wondering whether, if I drowned, would I join Dad in the sky. Despite my gathering panic, I remember thinking how warm the waters felt. I cried for help but no one heard, and even in my youth I sensed the hopelessness of it all. A peculiar calm replaced my terror as furious waves passed over me. It had been only seconds, but it felt like forever.

I then saw the blinking light of the buoy as I was carried rapidly toward it. I tried angling myself into its sweeping tide, hoping to intercept the great metal float. Some internal compass worked, and after much thrashing it appeared that I just might reach it. The buoy suddenly loomed much closer and larger than I had imagined. Hard and metallic, emerging out of the darkness, it had metal ladders joining a circular rail and walkway that encircled the structure. Sooner than expected, I was thrown against the hard metal surface, the air knocked out of me as I painfully crashed into its side. In blind panic, I somehow managed to grab onto a metal rung. Desperately holding fast, I clung to its side, rushing waters swirling past me, my life hanging by a thread of ebbing strength. Slowly, using all the power left in me, I pulled myself closer to the buoy. I felt a gentle eddy as the tumultuous waters swept past me on both sides. Exhausted, I lingered in relief before gathering some reserve and then slowly, painfully, climbing one rung after another until I reached the circular shelf, where I collapsed.

I lay there drained and thankful, eventually dropping into a consuming stupor and then sleep. I was soon awakened by the noise of a helicopter and not long after by a flotilla of boats. Mother, discovering my disappearance, had started a search that soon revealed the missing rowboat. The rest was my particular fifteen minutes of fame, followed by the more mundane business of growing up. Dad's death and my close call left some lingering wounds as well as much wisdom. If nothing else, I felt a deeper appreciation of the varied creation that surrounded me and of my rightful place within it. Even for a little boy, it bordered on a kind of serenity.

TWO

From Apple Orchards to Shopping Malls—1972: Late Adolescence

My world had become anonymous after having lived where every bird, bush, neighbor, and school chum felt like one extended family. Mom had not wanted to move following Dad's death but eventually could no longer deny the difficulty of a single woman in the late 1960s finding a job in a rural area that could support three kids and pay tuition for one about to go to college. And our house by the shore had become valuable, so—sacrifice being her second nature—Mom sold it. Shortly after, we moved to the suburbs of the medium-size city where Mom and Dad had lived during college, when she had studied nursing and Dad, law.

I was undeniably sad about leaving our village, but twelve-year-old boys are resilient and moving to the city seemed pretty exciting. Initially, I had no quarrel with our new town, although our neighborhood—despite its many houses—was distinguished mostly by the absence of distinction, with every house looking just about like the others and the parallel streets forming a maze worthy of the finest rodent. Still, the development had its charms, not the least being the large number of children my age and the many activities that ruled most of our days. I was also delighted that some wild places could be found not far away, despite passing through a jungle of lookalike houses squarely pegged on tiny lots and surrounded by a sea of grass and asphalt to get there.

Arriving at the nearby river was more than worth the effort. At first little more than a ten-foot creek and shallow enough to wade across, the river also had some deep holes where you could swim and where trout and ducks occasionally congregated. Partly because of its constant motion and many changing moods as it moved through new banks, vegetation, and all the critters there, to us kids the river had a personality like some living thing that adapted but somehow always remained the same. One moment the river was black; the next, with blinding sparkles reflecting off its surface. Sometimes it was barely audible as it slid over some smooth bottom; other times, it cascaded loudly over some ledge or forgotten dam where people had once struggled mightily to harness its fickle power. Apart from us few kids, however, the neighborhood seemed barely aware of the river on a daily basis, although I suppose most recognized its presence in less obvious ways. It certainly lent our ordinary housing development a special quality that most recognized with pride, and the homes closest to the river always sold the quickest and for the highest price. One time when a major road was proposed that would have covered a stretch of the river, the neighborhood rose like a mighty storm, howling and protesting, until the project was killed.

The world of people that surrounded this little island of wildness included our housing development, some big roads, and a nearby shopping strip astride one of the larger thoroughfares. This road was our great ribbon of commerce, the site of countless convenience stores, mini malls, fast food restaurants, gas stations, auto dealers, and more. You could find just about anything there—although never exactly what you wanted—and the employees never seemed to recognize you. Just beyond the main drag, a new interstate had been completed the year before, a road so large that it cut the landscape like a knife through butter, indifferent to most natural obstacles and more than willing to transform a hill or swamp. Few developments had yet been built along the interstate, but rumors flew fast about the greatest of shopping malls slated to be built next to the town's last remaining farm and one of its largest forests. Both the interstate and the farm were also near the high school I attended.

At the time, the high school consumed most of my thoughts, if for no other reason than that I felt like a misfit there. Its hugeness overwhelmed me. The red brick facade, large white columns, and huge clock tower seemed like a temple from the ancient world, a seat of power that dwarfed the lowly adolescents who occupied it. Yet, paradoxically, the building's interior was drab, with dreary halls and rooms lacking color, light, or anything resembling the magnificent exterior. The teachers were largely well meaning, a few instructing with insight and eloquence, but like the students, they seemed numbed by the size and sameness of the school, its lack of stimulation dominating not only the architecture but also the pedagogy. Confronted by the raging hormones of two thousand teenagers, various rules and a prevailing rigidity tried to cap this volatile stew.

One particular day, boiling with anger out of proportion to the provocation that had stirred it, I actually bolted from the school. This would be hardly worth mentioning except that it set into motion a sequence of events that just possibly altered the rest of my life. Escaping from school, I fled northward, away from my normal route home, into a woodland, where I hoped I would not be discovered and, presumably, punished. I wandered the forest, eventually becoming hopelessly lost despite my best efforts at following a deer trail and hoping I might stumble on some old road.

I was completely unprepared to encounter another person, especially a scowling old man and his dog. I had become so anxious by then and preoccupied with not shifting my direction yet again that I did not notice them at first until, looking up, I was shocked by the sight of a man and his dog staring balefully at me not a hundred feet ahead. I can still see the man's stern look, the border collie beside him motionless yet with its upper lip curling back over canines with a predatory gleam. Their body language clearly communicated that my presence was neither welcome nor legitimate. After watching me squirm for a while, the old man announced that I was trespassing and demanded to know why I was there. I offered clumsy, unconvincing excuses replete with promises that I would never return and pleas that he not turn me in. A heavy silence followed, until finally he scolded me about how, if he had been hunting, I might have been shot and then added various other complaints about the state of youth in a world gone awry. Then, having settled all territorial and social issues, the old farmer congratulated me on fleeing the sterile halls of academia and heading into the real world of fields and forests. Most shocking of all, he invited me to join him and his dog on their walk.

Gratefully accepting, I felt like a man saved from the gallows who now was, miraculously, being asked to do what he wanted most. We walked for a long time, the old man's angry scowl soon being replaced by an animated, nonstop recitation about the land, its animals, plants, soils, and history. His knowledge was extraordinary; his intimacy with the land, undeniable. His name was Mortimer Richmond, although it would always be for me Mr. Richmond or, as he was more generally known, Farmer Richmond, no matter how close we became. He was then seventy-five years old, born and raised on his farm, the sixth generation since his ancestors had settled there in the early nineteenth century. His arthritis caused him to sway, but I soon learned he possessed more stamina than the sixteen-year-old at his side. By the time we arrived at his farmhouse, I was exhausted yet he showed little sign of fatigue.

To say Farmer Richmond loved the land obscured a deeper, more complicated relationship. He was more like a part of it, an intimate participant of its many rhythms and processes. While he obviously felt affection for it, he embraced the land with a wider breadth of emotions, including an occasional adversarial stance. His knowledge of the farm was legion, reaching far beyond matters of mere utility. He delighted in the land's beauty, its secrets, the opportunities it presented for mystery and challenge, and he deeply respected and feared its power. He never grew tired of deciphering the many complexities of its creatures, both great and small. He took pride in feeling in charge, but more as steward than as a conqueror. He was a participant who intervened rather than took away and who sought to add richness to what he saw as his extended family. Farmer Richmond regarded himself as chief trafficker in the flow of materials and nutrients that passed through the land like a fountain of living energy. He took possession of the land, but always with a sense of duty and a gentleness and respect for its independent birthright.

Perhaps I make Mortimer Richmond sound like some modern druid, a kind of pagan exercising an indiscriminate love for the natural and nonhuman. That would, however, be misleading. In fact, he reveled in manipulating the land and rarely hesitated to, for example, slaughter some animal, wild or domestic, although I never saw him do so wantonly or cruelly. He absolutely delighted in hunting, over the years having harvested just about anything legal and edible, including several creatures no longer on the list of game animals. I was initially appalled at this killing, but over time I recognized that it represented for him another entryway through which he became an active, intimate participant with the land rather than an outsider. He never killed unless he consumed his prey, consciously making the creature part of himself and, paradoxically, never hunting unless he had a reasonable chance of failing. The hunt was always serious and conducted with skill, was never seen as amusement or sport, and was practiced with restraint and never wastefully. I truly believe that for Mortimer Richmond, hunting was sacramental, another way he irrevocably tied himself to the land and its creatures.

This mentality revealed itself in his relation not only to deer and ducks but also to domesticated animals, plants, and even the inert properties of soil and water. He rarely hesitated to use, manage, or consume creatures, and he worked at manipulating the land to increase its productivity. But, beyond the objectives of security and abundance, he sought a shared, caring relationship with the land and all its life. He saw himself as a colleague more than a controller and sought full membership in the grace of what he called the "land community." Most of all, he sought to impart a more lush, diverse, and resilient world than the one he had inherited.

I owe to Mortimer Richmond much of my abiding interest, knowledge, and emotional attachment to the natural world. At the time, I was not above exploiting his knowledge for my own purposes with surprising effect. My biology skills increased, particularly the ability to use my ears and other senses rather than just my eyes to see and identify all that surrounded me. Farmer Richmond taught me to discern the slightest anomaly in the landscape, to locate my visual prey by recognizing the variation in the setting; in doing so, he helped me to experience so much more of interest and quality than I would otherwise have encountered. I drank deeply from this stimulation and understanding and emerged ravenous for previously unknown treasures, determined to experience as much as possible before I feared it would disappear in a tenuous world. Given my adolescent shallowness and his gruff ways, I sometimes wonder why we became such steadfast friends, why he took me under his wing at a particularly difficult time in his as well as my own life. Possibly he discerned a kindred spirit in this teenage boy's affinity for nature that perhaps reminded him of an earlier version of himself, albeit one needing cultivation and refinement.

He probably enjoyed my unabashed admiration, so at odds with the increasing hostility he encountered from his two children, a thirty-two-year-old son and thirty-year-old daughter. The children had fallen under the spell of an economic fortune being dangled before this historically poor family by a major shopping center developer who wanted to purchase the farm. Farmer Richmond had already rejected three progressively higher offers for the property. So, while he seemed the epicenter of knowledge and wisdom to me, Mortimer Richmond's children considered him a stubborn old man who was standing in the way of a wealth and status none of them had ever known or thought possible and now desperately wanted.

The farm had originally been 350 acres, but when I met Farmer Richmond, it had been reduced to about 200 acres. He had sold lots to people who had thought they wanted a rural setting but who, once they moved there, typically objected to the pungent smell of cow manure in summer, brush burning in spring, and gunfire in the fall. Selling the lots helped financially, but the farm continued to struggle, bringing in little more than a subsistence income. Farmer Richmond raised dairy cows, but regulations, huge new industrial farms, and a growing distrust of local agriculture had marginalized his cattle operation. He had shifted to more profitable crops like apples and established a roadside stand, but sales were seasonal and the apple business also succumbed to factory farming and the consumers' inclination for bright red, perfectly formed apples. The growing relationship between the agribusiness operators and big commercial shopping chains also did not help. Probably his worst mistake economically was refusing to bathe his soil and subject his animals to a vast array of chemicals, pesticides, growth hormones, antibiotics, and the like. He rejected the logic of the new ways of farming trumpeted as the triumph of science and technology over nature. He denied both the rhetoric and supposed corroboration, thereby confirming for all, most particularly his children, that he was an ornery primitive out of step with progress and the modern world.

Mortimer Richmond was thus perceived as an impediment to prosperity and the chance his children craved to escape the pejorative label "swamp Yankee." I am sure they loved and admired their father, having known a lifetime of his keen insight and intelligence, but they resented his stubborn desire to remain a dirt farmer. Their mother had been the family's glue; their father, more often larger than life and usually away in the fields and forests. So, following their mother's death, the family had grown apart, his children going to college and then moving to the city, the first generation in the family to have college educations and live apart from the land. They had become urban professionals—the son an accountant and the daughter a medical technician. They were proud of their education and the fact that they no longer worked with their hands, smug in knowing they now earned more than their father ever had as a farmer. They occasionally visited the farm but did not find its long, hard labors and economic uncertainty appealing. To them, the farm represented backwardness and oppression—and, now, an obstacle to unimaginable wealth and security.

This all became clear to me one early Saturday morning when I arrived at the farmhouse. Mr. Richmond had told me to come early so he could show me the rattlesnake den that had miraculously survived in the forest despite the area's extensive development and influx of humanity. He had never told anyone about it before and swore me to secrecy, fearing that if it were found out, there would be a chorus of demands for the snakes' elimination.

As I approached the house, I heard angry voices inside. Letting my curiosity get the better of me, I waited silently at the base of the stairs. Farmer Richmond's son was berating him, arguing that the farm was worth more money than he might earn in many lifetimes and that besides his father could use a portion of the sale to buy a bigger, better farm elsewhere. His daughter then scolded their father as being unfair and preventing them from a life of prosperity just so he could indulge his romantic fantasy of an obsolete way of life. She claimed that the world had changed and that it was now time for them to move on and enjoy a wealth none of their family had ever known before. Farmer Richmond responded angrily and, after some heated arguing, told his children to leave and never return until they accepted his right to determine the future of the land. Looking back, I wonder if that particularly painful moment had not provoked his children to justify their subsequent legal actions in conspiracy with the developer and town officials, which finally settled the issue. I later learned that the children actually owned the farm, their parents having transferred the title years before, ironically to avoid taxes that would have forced them to sell the farm.

All these Byzantine family and financial matters were irrelevant to me at the time. All I wanted was to romp in the woods with Farmer Richmond and help out on the farm. So, following his children's departure, I was delighted to set out with him in search of the incredible rattlesnake den. As always, he knew every hill, valley, stream, and wetland, never using a map or compass. He instead invoked memories of particular trees, stonewalls, creeks, and other cues that eventually led him to a nondescript spot in the woods that marked the serpents' den. I was excited but in truth scared at the prospect of confronting this creature that no one else knew remained in our suburban town, and I felt anxious around snakes despite my fascination for all wild things.

The entry to the den was at the base of a great rock tucked into a hollow almost out of sight. The hole was extremely small as we forced our way through to what Farmer Richmond promised would be a much larger cave. I was nearly paralyzed with fear as I peered into that dark hole. I probably would have fled if not for Farmer Richmond telling me he had also been terrified when he first discovered the den many years before until he had finally screwed up the courage to enter.

The cave did indeed get much larger once we entered. We then made our way to a narrow ledge where we could spy the creatures below. In the restricted light, we at first could only see the coiling mass vaguely. Because it was early spring, the cold-blooded creatures hardly moved. Still, as my eyes adjusted, I began to make out the snakes. I counted at least ten. They were oblivious to our presence at first, but soon our moving about alerted them. I also suppose the heat of our bodies, more than our sound, aroused their attention; I had read that a rattlesnake's ability to sense temperature allowed it to find a mouse six feet away even if blindfolded and without a sense of smell.

We squeezed into the corner of the overhanging ledge, peering down into the now-alerted, moving snakes. As minutes passed, it became apparent how little actual danger these creatures posed. A mounting confidence and false bravado took hold of me as we continued to observe the snakes in utter fascination. Looking back decades later, I recognize the moment as among the most intense of my life, totally absorbing and incredibly intimate. For that instant, the world stood utterly still and I was suspended in time and place. Many years later, I still vividly recall the sight and even the smell of the place, its shapes, the quality of the light and air, the memory of it all permanently seared into my mind. Few experiences have since offered the clarity, even peace and reverence, that I felt that day in the company of the snakes and Farmer Richmond.

For the rest of the year, I continued to roam the woods and leftover margins of our rapidly developing suburb. I had found a new sense of balance, and I carried it around inside me like some treasure. Somehow the experience seemed to have reconciled for me the solitary and the social, the civilized and the primitive, the wild and the tame. I had found my place in my town, and part of me now identified with it.

But this newly discovered calm soon disappeared before a mighty storm that descended. Following relentless, behind-the-scenes economic and political machinations, the powerful forces arrayed against Mortimer Richmond finally succeeded. Aided by a team of lawyers and officials, his children had managed to sell the property to the developers. When I first heard about it, I ran from school to the farmhouse, bursting in on Farmer Richmond and demanding to know if it was true. He confirmed the sale but, strangely, seemed less angry than tired, and determined to move on. His children had given him a golden parachute with a substantial share of the sale price. He then announced to my shock that he would be moving and purchasing a new farm in upstate New York, where a modest agricultural economy still persisted and farms were available at reasonable prices. In a bewildering few months, Mortimer Richmond departed the town of his ancestors, physically and spiritually uprooted and feeling a profound loss but relatively cheerful at the prospect of his new home and life. His children's betrayal, however, was unforgivable to him, and father and children never spoke again.

What crushed Farmer Richmond most was the developers' actions just two days following the sale. They descended on the farm with an army of bulldozers and proceeded to level more than fifty acres of forests, fields, and orchards. Soon after, the devastated landscape was transformed into a series of indistinguishable boxes and temples of merchandise decorated by an occasional prisoner shrub or tree. What had been a mosaic of apple blossoms in spring, golden grass in summer, bright leaves in fall, and lingering lavender in winter had become oppressive geometric edifices surrounded by asphalt, concrete, and an altogether suffocating homogeneity. The access road to the mall had also destroyed the rattlesnake den. I never saw or heard of one again, although perhaps a few clung to survival in some remote hollow on the water company's land.

After graduating from high school, I soon left town for college on the West Coast. The destruction of the farm had become my defining moment, closing the door on my particular childhood and home. Nonetheless, I had excelled in school, and—aided by some athletic success—I had been admitted to a prestigious university. My passion had become being financially successful and independent. Without realizing it, I had embarked on a path that some day would transform me into those I had come to loathe. Yet, despite many dead ends over the ensuing years, I would eventually return to the wisdom and spirit of Farmer Richmond and the beauty of the land. But that is another story for another time.

THREE

Geographic Sketches Here and There: 1985—Early Adulthood

My undergraduate and graduate business school years were wonderful times, probably the first and last period in my life when I indulged in a kind of immoderate narcissism. However, they left me grossly unprepared for the harsh reality that followed. My beginning job after graduate school in the mid-1980s was initially quite satisfying. I worked as a junior analyst with a large investment banking firm located in Los Angeles. The financial rewards were grossly out of proportion with anything I justifiably or legitimately deserved, yet I certainly did not turn my back on the compensation, and I indulged the fruits of my good fortune—

a large, expensive apartment high enough over the city's smog to see the ocean beyond, a Porsche, and other assorted material benefits. I regularly reminded myself of my mother's many years of sacrifice that helped me get to this point and how I could now make her life more comfortable and secure in return.

I also had little time to brood over matters of meaning and morality and life's direction. Like others at my stage of ambition and lack of seniority, I worked fifteen or more hours each day. I had unending analyses to complete, meetings to attend, reports to write, and deals to strike in a frenetic world of details and requisite posturing and privilege. Despite a lingering dis-ease, I set questions of purpose aside, although I felt a secret distaste for how I lived and what I represented. At an earlier time, I had believed that I would someday contribute something of lasting value to the world; now, I sensed that ideal slipping away in the falsehood I had become.

As at other times in my life when I had faced doubt and uncertainty, I took refuge in the natural world, retreating during my few days off to the national forests and mountains in and around Los Angeles. The great sprawling city itself possessed relatively little undeveloped land, much of its surface having been converted into hardscape and development by its large, rapacious population. The Los Angeles basin sat within a magnificent bowl of mountains, dissected by canyons and once-extensive wetlands, streams flowing to the sea in a climate so perfect you were almost always comfortable. But this beauty had been disfigured and degraded by the excesses of want and greed. The basin now was dominated by cement watercourses, plumes of polluted air, and a blanket of development so vast it defied the imagination that it could have been created in little more than a century. The sprawl was like a swarm of locusts undercutting the life blood of the good life it aspired to consume. The mutilation of its landscape gnawed at me, an evisceration so complete that it left only pockets of relatively undisturbed habitat.

The resulting elimination of the area's abundant wildlife was especially troubling. The basin had been an island of evolution, geographically separated by its great mountains, deserts, and ocean, and the recipient of periodic tectonic convulsions, which created a living stew of new, wondrous footholds on the ladder of life. But what constituted for many people the triumph of human ingenuity and technology had been for its indigenous creatures a usurpation of natural capital so complete it left few survivors in its path. The landscape and its native life had become anemic, reduced to a remnant of its former self.

Yet a few remaining pockets of the original lushness and wonder could be found. When I had time to escape from work but not enough time to travel to the more distant national forests, I would often seek them out. I would flee to one or another canyon, highland, wetland, desert margin, or chaparral secreted within the great megalopolis. This relief from the urban tumult was always restorative, although never relaxing. I would feel a kind of agitated tranquility, a fever of activity that produced an odd sense of peace. I drank deeply like some wanderer in the desert stumbling on an oasis. Eventually, I would slow down and let the accumulated tension drain from me like sap into a soft, forgiving ground.

I stumbled across places that held detail beyond my capacity to absorb, always elusive and somewhat mysterious. I realized that the more I explored, the more I would uncover in an endless process of discovery. I took solace in immersing myself, following paths across rocky hillsides, pushing through shrubs and meadows, fording springs, stumbling on flashes of brilliant color, exalting in the songbird and insect sounds and the cries of circling hawks, marveling at the irruption of life in a parched land. My senses sated, I would sometimes sit down or gaze up at the sky in hazy contentment. Unfortunately, my normal work reality rarely afforded much time for indulging such vestiges of interest.

Still, I particularly recall one time when work had become especially intense and I had been at the office day and night for almost five weeks. I was finally given the next morning off. I awoke early, bent on visiting one of my favorite canyons on the other side of town. A narrow crevice sliced into a mountain by some earthquake, the canyon had easy access from a nearby street.

Entering the canyon, I was enthralled by the expanding early morning light and emerging details of the surrounding landscape. I walked up the steep path for perhaps thirty minutes before being startled by an anxious whisper nearby. There beside the trail sat a young woman crouched behind a large rock, earnestly motioning me to kneel and be quiet. She then silently pointed up in the direction of the canyon wall. At first I saw nothing, but then, gradually, the vague outline of first one and then two animals became distinguishable. Incredibly, a mountain lion was lying prone on a narrow shelf in the cliff's side, feeding on a deer. Cougars were known in other parts of California, particularly because of well-publicized, rare attacks usually on joggers. But I had never heard of one being seen in densely populated Los Angeles, although I later learned of other, occasional sightings.

We remained still, staring at this improbable scene for what seemed like hours but really was no more than minutes. We absorbed it all like a sponge, knowing we probably would never see something like it again. We later speculated how a creature so large could have made its way through the great megalopolis, let alone find, kill, and feed on prey in this ocean of humanity. We felt a mix of anxiety, wonder, and reverence as we marveled at this rare privilege of ancient creation. The creature finally rose and—with a defiant snarl that seemed to acknowledge its awareness of our presence—reluctantly abandoned its hard-earned prey and skulked off into the mountain canyon. We never knew what became of this animal who disappeared into the gathering sounds of the awakening city.

We sat stunned and hardly uttered a word, sensing that speech would surely break the magic of the moment. We reveled in our shared admiration of this creature and its ability to survive in a modern, urban world. Our impossible moment together turned out to be one of those rare times when people sharing a unique experience become close friends instead of strangers lacking a common past.

The woman's name was Nicole, and she was an architect. She had also been raised in the East and educated in the West and had moved to Los Angeles seeking fame and fortune. She loved architecture and had many original ideas about designing in ways that prevented environmental damage and brought people into closer connection to nature. She had a position in a firm she originally had thought was committed to this new environmental ideal, but she soon learned that the realities of the marketplace dictated otherwise. Both she and the firm were often forced to compromise and subordinate much beyond the profit motive. Most of the firm's projects were lowest-cost designs of large office towers, mega-malls, and residential complexes that essentially ignored issues of energy efficiency, minimal resource use, waste avoidance, or restored contact with nature. The prevailing logic rejected most environmental considerations, trumpeting a perspective of people as separate from natural systems and processes.

Nicole also loved the remnants of undisturbed nature that managed to survive within the great metropolitan basin. So we became good friends and for the next several months visited various areas of wildness within the human sea, until I learned I was being transferred to my firm's office in Osaka, Japan.

I soon departed for Japan, where I plunged into an entirely new world of work, culture, and a loneliness I had never known before. I had studied Japanese in college but now quickly learned how little I knew and understood of this complex society. I settled in, working impossibly long hours. On my few days off, I visited various natural and cultural areas across that long, lovely archipelago. Japan's population of some 130 million people lived in an area about the size of California.[1] Yet the country was surprisingly diverse and, in many places, relatively unpopulated, physically ranging from the boreal forests of Hokkaido to the subtropics of Okinawa, as far as from the Canadian Maritimes to the Caribbean Sea. Most of the Japanese people lived along or near the coast, where staples of rice and fish were traditionally found. This left most of the mountainous two-thirds of the country sparsely populated and often culturally diverse. The combination of mountains, islands, and latitudinal distance had produced an extraordinarily diverse plant and animal life.

Despite my travels throughout the country, I felt largely disconnected from anything familiar, much of the time fighting off loneliness and ennui bordering on depression. Part of my problem was the city of Osaka, which was remarkably unattractive and largely estranged from the country's traditional culture or ecology. Its development featured an obsession with concrete and steel that seemed almost cancerous, making even Los Angeles look good by comparison. Osaka's commercial center had destroyed nearly all remnants of the natural and historical, with its urban life an oppressive obsequiousness to the gospel of economic materialism and modernity. The city bordered the sea, but its waterfront had become mostly asphalt and artifice, with hardly a wetland intact. The architecture was a cubist horror, a numbing anonymity of geometric boxes. If buildings could talk, these would loudly proclaim the triumph of technology over the human body, mind, and spirit.

Ironically, traditional Japanese architecture included some of the world's most beautiful designs. Glimpses of this nobler tradition could still be seen but were becoming rare. Fortunately, a city existed not far away that retained this ancient architectural face, if for no other reason than its immense tourist popularity. It was the city of Kyoto, Japan's historic capital and site of many Buddhist temples and historic palaces. Kyoto had also fallen prey to economic technological efficiency, but amid its congestion and pollution one could still encounter architectural wonders in its ancient buildings and created landscapes, all in an exquisite setting of converging rivers and mountains.

I first visited Kyoto to see some of the traditional seats of Japanese power and religion. I became immersed that day in the grace of its architecture and gardens. The impact was cumulative rather than the effect of a single experience or construction; I felt a growing sense of an overall pattern that was more contextual than specific, interlocking and coherent. In the gathering dusk of that first day, I was absorbed by the resonating echoes of a bell, the swirling sand of a rock island, waves radiating from fish lightly breaking a pond surface, and an intensity of colors of blossoming azaleas, rhododendrons, and the deep green of varied mosses. Dew rose from ancient pines along with the sonorous songs of wood thrushes. All this and more captured me in a spiral of connected light, sound, feeling, thought, and spirit. I sensed a version of humanity in compatible relation to its natural surroundings, surely a stylized idealization of the real but beautiful and harmonious nonetheless no matter how much it borrowed from nature.

I visited Kyoto many times and soon met and came to know others who believed the future of Japan depended on restoring this blend of traditional culture and the natural environment along with the realities of a modern society. I became friends with one group of people who were aspiring developers. They trumpeted a vision of development they called the "middle path," which sought to combine historic Japanese architecture with contemporary technology in an urban setting. They planned to test the economic and aesthetic viability of their ideas in a large-scale residential and commercial development in a rundown part of Kyoto. They intended nothing less than to construct an entirely new neighborhood that joined traditional Japanese design with a restored environment that also included modern communications and business technologies. They had preliminary plans, had obtained half the necessary financing, and had purchased the land and started remediation of the contaminated site, where factories had once operated. I was soon swept along by their intelligence and optimism, although I remained skeptical of the project's long-run economic feasibility. Even so, I helped develop the business plan and brought the project to the attention of venture capitalists I knew through the investment bank.

My continued participation in the project, however, as well as my intention to remain in Japan, was soon called into question by two almost simultaneous events. First, I received a letter from Nicole, who informed me she was leaving her firm and moving back to Boston. She and some friends were starting their own design company dedicated to the principles of sustainability and environmental restoration. More incredibly, she asked if I would become their partner and chief financial officer.

At the time I was slavishly devoted to my conventional path of wealth and success gained by climbing the ladder in a multinational corporation committed to economic globalization. I was not about to give up such perceived gains despite the occasional disenchantment I felt about my lifestyle and larger purpose in life. But then, unexpectedly, I was assisted or, more accurately, pushed toward a decision. At the time, a collapse of investor confidence caused by huge borrowing, rampant speculation, and widespread corruption had led to a deep East Asian recession. Economic panic ensued, leading to many bankruptcies as developers were unable to pay back enormous debts. My firm, which had provided much of the capital for this expansion, also fell on hard times. Two months following Nicole's letter, which I still had not answered, I was called into my boss's office. He informed me that I had two choices given my lack of seniority: I could take a (hopefully) temporary leave of absence and remain in Japan, or I could return to the States to assume my former, lower-paying position. In shock, I simply blurted that the timing was perfect because I had just decided to leave the firm to take another position.

Four weeks later, in an almost dream-like state, I found myself boarding a plane back to the States. I bid fond farewell to my Japanese friends who had secured the balance of the finances needed to complete their project's first phase. I had thrown my flimsy skills at an equally high-risk venture and tied myself to a woman I had known only briefly and under highly unusual circumstances. Yet I felt an incredible lightness upon boarding the plane, heading with excitement and anxiety into an uncertain future. I was emboldened by the chance to seek a life of hopefully more lasting significance and perhaps find what I hoped to be a truer self. Whimsically, I thought that the worst I might encounter was failure.

FOUR

Seals in the Neighborhood—2004: Middle Age

By 2004, I came to recognize that my life had not turned out the way I had dreamed. I didn't necessarily feel like a failure, having understood that most of my fantasies of success were unrealistic to begin with. I had accommodated myself and emerged largely content with the life I had achieved, despite its limitations and disappointments. Twenty years previously, I had abandoned a promising career in international finance, which I suppose would have made me a rich man. Instead, I had made the deliberate choice to embark on a risky venture that eventually flamed out. I actually believed until then that I had been living a kind of charmed life predestined for success. My eventual failure was at first a harsh lesson in reality.

After returning to the States from Japan, I joined with my business partner, Nicole, and her colleagues in establishing a sustainable design and development firm. Nicole possessed the architectural skills, our partners had the engineering expertise, and I provided the financial knowledge. Nicole was a gifted designer, her work distinguished by its ability to minimize environmental impacts while also capturing a wonderful aesthetic. I conferred economic muscle through my contacts in the financial world that initially generated significant capital, which we invested in several large-scale developments.

Many factors contributed to our eventual demise. Our economic strategy was naive, based on the belief that a good concept along with a measure of idealism would inevitably surmount all obstacles. Our problem, however, was not just the uncertainty of innovation, in which something new almost always costs more and is, by definition, unfamiliar and risky. More basically, we had collaborated with some large-scale developers who possessed a very short-term horizon and looked for immediate profits, wanting to sell their developments soon after they were built. Long-term paybacks in energy and resource efficiency, or improved employee productivity that diminished the short-term bottom line, were viewed as "blue sky" abstractions, if not outright silliness. Also, most of the developers invested little of their own resources, relying on financing from large banks and foreign sources who were mainly motivated by the fastest return possible on their dollar. Contributions to the health of the natural environment or local communities were either ignored or regarded as irrelevant.

We also encountered government regulations that rejected our plans as violations of conventional requirements for processing wastes, using permitted materials, or consuming energy. Originally intended to protect the public, these regulatory impediments had, over time, become rigid rules imposed by inflexible bureaucracies that preferred the dictates of standard operating procedures to dealing with something new and innovative.

In the end, our failure was largely self-inflicted, the product of overambition and a good deal of hubris. We struggled for more than five years before finally throwing in the towel. Nicole and I then parted, me heading back to the conventional world of finance while she went with an established architectural firm. My return to the world of ordinary finance, however, was in a much-reduced capacity. My abrupt departure from the large investment firm and subsequent business failure had left me with a tarnished reputation. Eventually, I landed a job as branch manager with a regional bank in a small coastal Massachusetts city. What I at first thought would be a short-term exile in time became a twenty-year career. But I did meet a wonderful woman, who eventually became my wife and the mother of our two wonderful children.

I thus harbored few regrets. As a middle-aged man, I had found myself a solid member of a small city's economic elite, albeit a town a little long in the tooth, economically and socially a vestige of its former self. My work at the bank was often routine but still interesting. For the most part, I was appreciated by my colleagues and by the city's civic community as I tried to match resources with the potential to both do some good and make a profit.

Much of the time, however, I operated on automatic pilot, cruising through more than creating my life. My existence was safe, predictable, and largely secondhand. Even when I helped make good works happen, my satisfaction was mostly transient and focused on the accomplishments of others. Still, I was relatively content, finding joy in my family, friends, and the environment where we live. My wife was loving and caring, my two boys a constant source of pleasure. We lived in a restored house with a terrific view of the water, belonged to several clubs, and frequently explored the bay and its never-ending sources of beauty, wonder, and discovery. However, I still carried around inside me the nagging feeling of an unrealized self.

I continued to take special satisfaction in my lifelong passion for the natural world, quietly raging at the prevailing assumptions that equated progress with nature's disfigurement. Few among my friends and associates seemed to notice how much natural capital had already been lost, and how efforts at revitalizing the city continued in the flawed logic that economic advancement required environmental debasement. Despite my outrage at this insidious destruction, I remained largely silent—and sometimes even a personal contributor to the prevailing paradigm through my various lending activities at the bank. I did almost nothing to stop the spreading pox, beyond an occasional feeble protest or superficial support for the local land trust. I sometimes proselytized to others, but this rarely resulted in any meaningful action.

My position at the bank had revealed to me how much of the region's environmental destruction had been spurred by external forces and financial interests. Most of the recent development of large shopping centers, corporate parks, and residential complexes, mainly in the suburbs, had been the work of multinational banks and corporations. The structures were almost always unattractive and flimsy, using resources excessively while generating enormous quantities of wastes and pollutants and destroying natural habitat. They also totally relied on vehicular transportation over mass transit or anything pedestrian friendly.

Meanwhile, like many others, I despaired over how little remained of the old downtown and waterfront, which consisted mainly of boarded-up stores, seedy bars, an old whaling museum, abandoned factories, ancient piers, and a legacy of industrial waste slowly leaching its chemical stew into the harbor. Despite the dereliction, the old city and waterfront still possessed considerable charm and enormous economic potential. The harbor continued to be a natural wonder of various historical and biological treasures. One could find in its shallow waters and along its estuarine flats and deeper channels a wealth of mollusks and crustaceans and a nursery for the bay's abundant fish populations. The marshes also attracted resident, migrating, and wintering wildlife and, most miraculously, the return of harbor and gray seals in recent winters since their extirpation centuries ago. I often fantasized how some smart developer of particular boldness and imagination could make a fortune and do much good by restoring the commercial and environmental qualities of the old downtown harbor. This restoration could celebrate the comingling of human and natural history, allowing each to feed upon the other, progressively enriching culture and nature until the two became more than they could ever be apart, a thing of wonder and beauty teeming with energy and connection.

Then, seemingly in answer to my fantasies, a rare opportunity presented itself, although I failed at first to recognize it. It started with a relatively modest proposal submitted to the bank by the whaling museum, which for years had struggled to attract enough visitors to cover its payroll and preserve its extraordinary collection of whaling artifacts. Plagued by obsolete exhibits, a decrepit building, the city's dubious image, and, ironically, contemporary sympathy for whales that identified whaling with the creature's historic demise, the museum had barely survived. The museum had recently hired a new executive director, who had concluded that only modernization and expansion could save the museum by appealing to a broader public interested in marine mammals and the sea. The museum thus proposed relocating to a renovated factory building beside the harbor and asked my bank to help finance the development. Their strongest selling point was that they had already secured two-thirds of the $60 million needed from Silas Pease, patriarch of the city's once-great whaling family. Yet, despite the pledge, the bank rejected the loan. I argued for its approval but was dismissed as biased and unrealistic.

Nonetheless, the fire of possibility settled in my brain, and I could not stop thinking about the project. I speculated that, with some significant refocusing, it could be an enormous commercial, civic, and environmental success that would help restore the city and its harbor. One evening, in a moment of epiphany, I decided that this was probably my last, best chance to accomplish something significant and fulfilling in my life. I proceeded to put thoughts to paper and over the next several days sketched a greatly revised plan. I decided that the original proposal had been fundamentally flawed by its limited focus on a single outcome, rendering it largely aloof from its deteriorated community. Investors would always remain skeptical about sinking substantial resources into an unattractive, economically depressed area no matter how interesting the museum's new exhibits, restaurants, or stores promised to be. Paradoxically, the project had to be much bolder and more ambitious to succeed, broadening its vision from a single building and institution to economically and ecologically restoring the entire downtown and embracing within it a spectrum of civic, commercial, and even residential uses. There would also need to be thematic coherence among these disparate elements, with the museum serving as a catalytic core for reconnecting people to the sea and its aquatic environment.

In my scheme, the museum as centerpiece would be the focus of education and entertainment, combining commerce, ecology, and culture. The marine world would be the museum's emphasis but extended to include estuaries, wetlands, watersheds, rivers, and shores in addition to the ocean. It would be a museum of science and technology and of natural history and environmental studies and would also include a theater, an art gallery, and anthropological displays, all bound together by the celebration of a single element vital to human life—water.

The museum would be the initial attraction, but the project would succeed or fail only by transitioning from the museum to radiating circles of commercial, civic, and residential enterprise. There would also need to be effective, easy vehicular access and parking, but cars and streets would be subordinated to the whole, with traffic held to the periphery rather than placed at the center of the project. A viable residential community would further border on and affirm the aquatic environment. Schools would be organized around the relation of people to the sea, cutting across all traditional disciplines. Learning would occur in the classroom but be complemented by experience in the marine environment, theory joining with practice, the abstract with the personal and tangible.

The project would retrofit existing buildings but also construct new ones, all connecting the terrestrial with the aquatic and restoring ties to a healthy environment. Attractive waterfront views would be essential, structures evoking a positive connection between people and the sea. The architecture would blur lines separating the built from the natural environment, with exterior walls becoming a permeable skin that let the outside world intrude. People would be reminded of the aquatic environment not just through museum exhibits and decorative displays but also by the sight of an actual working harbor embedded into the flow of everyday life. Commercial stores would front the waterfront; office, manufacturing, and residential space would be housed in retrofitted and new buildings lining the river and old canals. A linear park would parallel the waterways and be joined to pedestrian trails, outdoor recreational areas, and restored wetlands that eventually connected the city to the suburbs and, in time, the countryside.

All buildings would minimize energy and resource use as well as wastes and pollutants. Energy would be produced on-site by exploiting sunlight, wind, and structural features that would lessen dependence on mechanical heating and cooling systems. The long-term goal would be to produce as much energy as consumed and to make waste an obsolete concept, with all discarded materials treated as valuable seed stock for future uses or returned safely to the natural environment. Buildings would be linked, with the waste heat of some becoming the heating and cooling sources for others. All materials and products would be recycled, and stormwater collected and cleansed for flushing, cooling, and irrigating. Toxic chemicals would be prohibited in the paints, adhesives, glues, carpets, woods, and other furnishings and, whenever possible, obtained from biodegradable and sustainably produced sources. Roadways would be designed to minimize erosion and runoff, with streets constructed of porous materials that would allow rainwater to percolate back into the ground. Landscaping would use native vegetation enhancing the productivity of local ecosystems.

The days and evening that followed were a fever of speculation and activity—a wild dream that in the cold light of day often seemed impossible, if not delusional. The bank's conservative mind-set would certainly have viewed these ideas as fantastic and troublesome.

Thus, any thought of bringing the concept before the bank would have been tantamount to professional suicide. Still, possessed by my vision, I frantically continued to refine the plan. I remained emboldened by one important aspect of the original proposal I still counted on being possible: the $40 million commitment of the quixotic patriarch of the city's old whaling family. As a bank officer, I knew he could afford the financing. However, I also knew he was furious about the bank's rejection of the museum proposal and about their perceived lack of daring and imagination. He had even made threats about seeking other financing and moving his fortune to another bank. I assumed he was still interested in the project and might even be willing to extend his support to my much bolder, albeit more expensive scheme if I could somehow bring the refashioned proposal to his attention.

So, in a fever in which the hot fantasy of imagination often clashed with the cold reality of what seemed possible, I continued to craft my case for a massive civic, commercial, and residential complex within a network of rehabilitated open space and restored harbor. I finally completed the document and, before I could think much about it or lose my courage, I boldly sent the proposal to the old patriarch. I heard nothing for more than a week, fearing more every day that not only had I offended him with my audacity but that he would inform the bank and I would be immediately dismissed. It was thus quite a shock when he called a week later. In more a monologue than a conversation, he informed me how much he liked the proposal and the prospect of partnering with me. He said that we needed to meet as soon as possible to discuss the next steps, and he promised one-third, or $200 million, of the estimated development cost—contingent on my raising the balance elsewhere. Finally, given the enormous scale of the project, he said he expected me to resign immediately from the bank and completely devote myself to the project. Moreover, I had twelve months to raise the additional $400 million before his offer would expire.

I knew well how hopes of acquiring this amount of financial support could easily become the detritus of a failed dream. I discussed all this and more with my wife and a few close friends, but to my surprise and delight they all counseled me to take the chance. So, the following week, I announced my resignation to the bank. Suddenly, I was frighteningly on my own yet nonetheless thrilled. I spent the first weeks hiring staff, refining the business plan, developing drawings, interviewing consultants, and beginning the gigantic task of raising a mountain of capital. Some wonderful architects, engineers, and businesspeople joined me, and together we developed what we viewed as a compelling and convincing proposal.

Over the new few months, we scored many notable successes and encountered considerable skepticism. Then came a string of rejections, so many I began to fantasize that the old patriarch had set me up for ruin. We then cast a wider and wider net and developed ever more supporting documentation. However, after nine months and despite having raised some $90 million, we were well short of our goal.

Finally, after we had contacted an extraordinary number of potential investors and gotten an equally remarkable number of rejections, we received modest interest from Emerson Bates, the controller of a venture capital fund managed as part of one of the country's largest educational endowments. Bates had once been in charge of the entire endowment, but after expanding it beyond anyone's wildest dreams, he stepped away from general operations to concentrate on higher-risk investments that offered the potential for both significant financial return and major social benefit. Bates especially liked projects he described as bordering on the "is" of today and the "ought" of tomorrow.

Having concluded that our project possessed this potential, Bates requested that we meet with him and his colleagues. Two additional meetings followed, each in response to questions that forced us to revise our plans but that left the core concept intact. We then heard nothing for the next seven weeks, with our twelve-month deadline approaching and our doubts increasing about how much longer we could continue. Finally, a letter arrived from Bates informing us that they had decided to provide the balance of the funds needed. The next fifteen months brought a frenzy of finishing plans, formal submissions, political negotiations, regulatory approvals, and—most glorious of all—construction contracts.

When all was said and done, the project's greatest success turned out to be not the new museum or commercial district but the establishment of a neighborhood of apartments, condominiums, townhouses, and single-family homes. The public's imagination had been fired by living in a place that included a restored historic harbor, a riverside park, outdoor recreational areas, pedestrian trails, and wildlife reserves. Families especially liked the idea of their children being able to play in open spaces near home, and everyone became addicted to the new fleet of water transport that had spontaneously emerged and turned the river, harbor, canals, and bay into an aquatic highway connecting the business and residential districts with new restaurants, recreational and entertainment attractions, and stores along the waterfront.

Pundits and politicians alike took credit for the project's mix of public and private uses within the restored harbor and historic area. Everyone praised the relatively few cars and roadways, abundance of open space, and combination of contemporary and traditional design. All extolled the new feeling of community and the surprising number of people from the suburbs who had purchased residences. These new urbanites said they especially liked the greater opportunities for meeting neighbors, not having to drive their children long distances, and experiencing the many cultural and environmental amenities along the waterfront. The initial lack of filled office space had been worrisome at first, but the problem eventually disappeared, with commerce apparently following the presence of a viable neighborhood and an attractive healthy environment rather than the other way around.

My life continues to be consumed by the project, yet I am happy and at peace. I recognize that I have had the rarest of opportunities to engage life at its fullest by trying to accomplish something of lasting good. I am reminded of the wisdom of something I read in Dante:

"Upon your feet! This is no time to tire!"
My master cried. "The man who lies asleep
Will never waken fame, and his desire

"And all his life drift past him like a dream,
And the traces of his memory fade from time
Like someone in air, or ripples on a stream.

"Now, therefore, rise. Control your breath, and call
Upon the strength of soul that wins all battles
Unless it sinks in the gross body's fall.

"There is a longer ladder yet to climb:
This much is not enough. If you
Understand me,
Show that you mean to profit from
Your time."[1]

FIVE

Reminiscence of Childhood and the City—Later Generations: 2030 and 2055
I occasionally reflect as a middle-aged man on events in my life that seem to have influenced who I've become. I presume that experience matters, especially epiphanies from one's youth. So I will indulge in one such reminiscence, an event so extraordinary I am sure it contributed to who I am today.

It was highly unusual back in 2030, and is still far from common today, to encounter a large ungulate—let alone a huge carnivore—in or near a city. Even now, the memory unsettles my soul. I was eight then, living with my parents and sister in Denver. Our home was in an "urban village," a relatively unusual attempt in those days to re-create an old-fashioned neighborhood within the city's core. The "village" consisted of single-family homes, attached townhouses, and a few multistory apartment buildings, all stitched together by footpaths, small parks, playgrounds, vegetable gardens, a shopping center, a high school, and a lower school. The large streets and parking areas were at the rear of the complex, meaning one had to navigate the main living and shopping areas by electric cart, bike, or foot. You could see the Rocky Mountains from the complex like some great wall looming in the distance, although my parents said that in previous years the mountains had vanished into a curtain of polluted air.

You would think a city so populated would offer few places for children to play. But besides our backyards, the village also had a number of small parks and, even more significantly, paths that led from the village to the city's recently established greenway system. The greenways were trails that linked various parts of the city to one another, to the suburbs, and, eventually, to agricultural areas and distant wilderness areas. People loved moving about the greenways by bike, foot, and even horseback. One moment you would be close to home, another downtown, next by a shopping center, and then, with persistence, a national forest. The greenways became so popular that newly constructed or renovated homes along its borders were the most expensive in the city. The village kids were not supposed to venture far into the greenways, and most of the time we were content to play in our backyards and nearby parks. But, occasionally, we snuck off to the greenways, often to one in particular where we had constructed a hideout and tree house in a large cottonwood. We worked hard at making our fort more comfortable than our parents could ever imagine and where we planned great battles and trips to distant lands.

One of my great pleasures was meeting Dad once a week for lunch at his office, a fifteen-minute walk from home. I loved his building. Tall and narrow, it rose like a needle, tapering at the top; from a distance, it looked like a forest because of its pyramidal shape, triangular window designs, and trees actually growing on the rooftop. The glass sides had tens of thousands of photocells, which—along with the building's fuel cells—generated most of its electricity. The rooftop included trees, gardens, and a pond; various sitting areas; meeting places; and two restaurants. The gardens and pond were also connected to the building's heating and cooling system, and the rainwater collected in the pond was used for plumbing and irrigating the six interior gardens.

Located every tenth floor, the three-story interior gardens contained plants, aviaries, and butterfly gardens, each representing a different Colorado habitat with information about those habitats. Also connected to the building's heating and cooling system, the gardens were places where you could have lunch or just sit. Some of the upper floors on each of the building's four sides also had ledges; here, great nests could be found where peregrine falcons raised their young and hunted pigeons. I could watch the birds all day, particularly when the nests were full or when the adults dive-bombed the pigeons at awesome speeds. The nests helped the once-endangered birds, who returned the favor by scaring away songbirds that otherwise would have crashed into the building's glass sides.

We often ate lunch at the office building, but sometimes we ventured to a nearby wetlands. Depending on the season, we saw yellow-headed blackbirds, black-necked stilts, avocets, turtles, frogs, fish, dragonflies, cattails, lilies, and more. I particularly recall one time toward the end of winter when we were huddled behind an interpretive display eating our sandwiches while trying to keep warm. Suddenly, we were startled by a loud splash. The critter didn't see us because we had been concealed. But when we looked up, we saw the retreating shape of a sleek gray animal sliding into the water, its sinuous body protruding before disappearing below the surface. My first thought was the Loch Ness monster, but then Dad exclaimed after a moment's reflection, "I'll be darned. It's an otter!" We saw the animal one more time before it disappeared for good, its cute whiskered face holding a small fish sticking out from both sides of its mouth.

Practically unknown in the city at the time, otters were thought to avoid swimming under bridges or entering less than pristine waters. But wetland and creek restoration had been going on for some time. The improvement in water quality coupled with a growth in otter populations had led some younger otters to venture into the great metropolis. We were incredibly proud of our discovery, although we soon learned that similar sightings had been occurring elsewhere in the city. And it wasn't long before a permanent otter population became part of the Denver scene. People were excited at first, but soon some began to complain about the otters decimating fish populations. It took some time before people learned to live with the otters while still managing to protect their property.

But my best wildlife experience of all occurred along the greenways. For me as a kid, the best part about the greenways was the very cold winter days when elk came thundering down from the mountains like a living avalanche, bursting into and through the city on their way to the warmer prairies and wet meadows on the east side of town. Before the greenways, the elk were not able to travel to their historic winter range because of fencing, degraded habitat, and historic overhunting. By the early twenty-first century, however, elk numbers had greatly increased in response to a decline in ranching, an increase in wildlife protection, and ecotourism. All of this would not have brought elk back into the city if not for the greenways, which provided the migratory corridors that were needed to connect the mountains to the plains. The greenways were, in effect, like restoring some great connective tissue that restitched all those open spaces.

Yet, following the greenways' completion, very few elk used the corridors at first. But then, when it seemed the elk population had reached some critical threshold or experienced a harsh enough winter, the small numbers became a stream, as if some great spigot had been turned on and out gushed tens of thousands of elk. The first few days, you would see only a lone animal or a small group, but soon a huge mass would appear and advance almost as one across the city. When this occurred, thousands of people turned out to gape, some cheering despite police, fire, and wildlife officials trying to keep them quiet and at a distance. An elk or even a person might occasionally be hurt, but more often the animals passed without incident, parading before the kids glowing, the adults ogling, the television commentators commenting, the merchants hawking, and the scientists studying. It quickly became the stuff of legend and a cause for annual celebration as well as a source of great pride for the city.

But I will always remember one event above all others. One winter, Dad had heard that elk would likely be passing through the city and had managed to obtain a permit allowing us to occupy a viewing blind in a preserve at the city's edge within dark, concealing pines. For four consecutive days, we arrived early in the bitterly cold mornings hoping to see elk, but nothing happened. Then, on the misty morning of the fifth day, we heard a snapping of twigs that sounded like heavy animals. Soon, barely discernible, ghost-like shapes appeared out of the cold fog, their numbers swelling until the ground nearly shook. Tawny browns and grays, bare heads and flaring spikes, massive hulks and some larger antlers left us in awe. In the weak light, they seemed like apparitions, ancient visages comingling with the present, coalescing and dissipating as they passed through our human-dominated landscape.

Then something far more improbable occurred. We had been watching the elk for perhaps an hour; most of the mature males had by then passed by, the mothers and new calves now following. Suddenly, something bolted from the pines opposite us that at first looked like a horse crossing the meadow at full gallop. The elk reacted as if a bomb had exploded, fleeing in every direction, yet one small yearling remained on the ground. The incident had taken seconds but seemed to unfold as if in slow motion. The creature that had streaked from the forest had been fast but hardly graceful and oddly lumbering, at first resembling a horse but lacking that animal's polish and grace. Besides, horses don't run down and pounce on elk. Even my unformed mind sensed I was in the presence of something wonderful and fearsome.

It was the greatest of all land predators, that enormous carnivore of arching back and unyielding determination. It was the great mythical bruin!

"Oh, my god!" Dad cried out. "A griz. But, it can't be!"

As far as anybody knew, with the exception of a few hardly believed biologists, grizzly bears were not found anywhere near Denver and only a small population had been rediscovered and augmented in the San Juan Mountains in the southwestern corner of the state. Occasional grizzly sightings had been reported in Rocky Mountain National Park, not far from Denver, but these were generally unconfirmed and dismissed. Yet this was no apparition. It was probably a young bear, hungry, recently awakened from a deep sleep, who had wandered the cold mountains, caught the scent of elk, and followed the great herd—a bear just young and dumb enough not to avoid its ancient archenemy: humans. Maybe it also sensed the diminishing threat from a once-lethal species that of late had embraced a new covenant of reverence for the wild, especially for its legendary lord of the mountains.

The young bear stood on its hind feet at Dad's yell, glaring in our direction. It rose perhaps six feet tall, its round, almost human-like face staring menacingly at us, while we gazed back too awed and frightened to flee. An electric arc of conflicting emotions passed between the bear and us like some great indigestible stew: fear, fascination, perhaps appreciation, and just possibly mutual respect. We certainly meant the creature no harm, yet Dad assumed an aggressive posture and yelled back at the bear, his first instinct being to protect his young. The bear in turn snorted and growled, his nose flaring. But he soon settled back on all fours and with great strength dragged his prey into the forest, quickly disappearing. Dad and I felt as though we had just experienced a massive hallucination. We soon told our tale to officials, who were skeptical at first. But following careful investigation and additional sightings, it soon became known that a small grizzly bear population had reestablished itself around Rocky Mountain National Park and adjacent wilderness areas.

My young boy's heart had been touched by something miraculous, something beyond amazing that would affect me for the rest of my life. If an eight-year-old can experience a transcendent moment, that was it—and I've carried it around inside me since then. I have reached back during moments of crisis and gathered strength from the memory of the bear. I can pluck the great bruin from the recesses of my mind like a constellation from the sky, retrieving some enduring meaning that somehow mutes whatever anxiety or uncertainty has befallen me.

Even now, as a middle-aged man in 2055, a day hardly passes without my recalling that singular instance of inspiration and joy. Just today, I awoke stressed by events at work and in the world. I read daily of wanton cruelties and needless destruction, circles of pain radiating from a world of indifference and greed. A pervasive loneliness and self-hatred sometimes seem to have afflicted humanity like a virus that imperils our species. At moments like this, I remember the great bear and gather my dogs for a walk up the mountain near where I live.

When I do this, the city is soon left behind as I follow a path lined with willows along a dry creek bed. Cries of cactus wrens and circling raptors appear to be carried by the wind. I move quickly, driven by the goal of reaching the summit until a mosaic of sensations slows me down. The dogs help, reveling in their curiosities, circling about and encased in a world of smell more than sight, drawn by a multiplicity of plants, rocks, and other signs of life. I begin to open myself to a world of endless detail. At first, I intellectualize, identifying various birds, flowers, and more. I count and classify, drawing pleasure from my growing familiarity and seeming control. But then I soon give way to an intense appreciation of wonder, beauty, and discovery. A monarch butterfly alights on a nearby rock, and I marvel at its orange and black patterns so in harmony that they defy the narrow interpretation of a mere evolutionary fitness. I am stunned by the miracle of this creature, so flimsy that it seems weightless but able to travel enormous distances. I am awed by its supposedly inconsequential brain, which guides it to distant lands despite weather and terrain.

I finally reach the summit and look back at the city spread across the plain, admiring its immensity and creation. I look up at the clouds and imagine the shape of my childhood bear. I travel with him across the sky, carried by winds connecting me to a world greater than myself. The great bruin never leaves me, has always been a part of my consciousness. We remain fellow travelers in the grandeur of our lives. And then I am stripped of my self-absorption and self-pity, carried along by this miracle of creation.

I return to my home and office no smarter or skillful but renewed and revived. I have drawn sustenance from the bear and the butterfly, been emboldened by their accomplishment. I have become the bear, rising on its hind legs, startled, apprehensive, yet irrevocably tied to those humans who stare back with anxiety but also with reverence and devotion.

Notes

Chapter One: Introduction

1. See, for example, L. White Jr., "The historical roots of our ecological crisis," *Science* 155 (March 10, 1967): 1203–7; R. Nash, *The Rights of Nature: A History of Environmental Ethics* (Madison: University of Wisconsin Press, 1989); J. Passmore, *Man's Responsibility for Nature: Ecological Problems and Western Traditions* (New York: Scribner's, 1974); H. Watanabe, "The conception of nature in Japanese culture," *Science* 183 (1973).

2. See, for example, United Nations Department of Economic and Social Affairs, Population Division, *Concise History of World Population* (London: Oxford-Blackwell, 1997).

3. See, for example, C. Kibert, "The promises and limits of sustainability," in C. Kibert, ed., *Reshaping the Built Environment: Ecology, Ethics, and Environment,* 9–38 (Washington, DC: Island Press, 1999); BuildingGreen, *Environmental Building News: The Leading Newsletter on Environmentally Responsible Design and Construction* (Brattleboro, VT; http://www.BuildingGreen.com).

4. S. Kellert, *The Value of Life: Biological Diversity and Human Society* (Washington, DC: Island Press, 1996); S. Kellert, *Kinship to Mastery: Biophilia in Human Evolution and Development* (Washington, DC: Island Press, 1997).

5. Various studies indicate considerable public support for environmental conservation and protection. See, for example, W. Kempton, J. Boster, and J. Hartley, *Environmental Values in American Culture* (Washington, DC: Island Press, 1996); R. Dunlap and R. Scarce, "The polls—poll trends: Environmental problems and protection," *Public Opinion Quarterly* 55 (1991): 713–34; R. Mitchell and R. Carson, *Using Surveys to Value Public Goods: The Contingent Valuation Method* (Washington,

219

DC: Resources for the Future, 1989); R. Inglehart, "Public support for environmental protection: Objective problems and subjective values in forty-three societies," *PS: Political Science and Politics* 28 (1995): 57–72; E. Ladd and K. Bowman, *Attitudes toward the Environment: Twenty-five Years after Earth Day* (Washington, DC: AEI Press, 1995).

6. These trends have been documented in various publications. See, for example, publications of the World Resources Institute, United Nations Environmental Programme, and Worldwatch Institute as well as the recently published J. Speth, *Red Sky Morning: America and the Crisis of the Global Environment* (New Haven, CT: Yale University Press, 2004).

7. E. O. Wilson, *Biophilia: The Human Bond with Other Species* (Cambridge, MA: Harvard University Press, 1984); S. Kellert and E. O. Wilson, eds., *The Biophilia Hypothesis* (Washington, DC: Island Press, 1993); Kellert, *The Value of Life*; Kellert, *Kinship to Mastery.*

8. See, for example, S. Kellert, "Experiencing nature: Affective, cognitive, and evaluative development in children," in P. Kahn Jr. and S. Kellert, eds., *Children and Nature: Psychological, Sociocultural and Evolutionary Investigations,* 117–52 (Cambridge, MA: MIT Press, 2002); P. Kahn Jr., *The Human Relationship with Nature: Development and Culture* (Cambridge, MA: MIT Press, 1999).

9. See, for example, R. Pyle, "Eden in a vacant lot: Special places, species, and kids in the neighborhood of life," in Kahn and Kellert, eds., *Children and Nature,* 305–28.

10. Dubos, *Wooing of the Earth,* 68.

Chapter Two: Science and Theory of
Connecting Human and Natural Systems

1. See, for example, R. Ulrich, "Biophilia, biophobia, and natural landscapes," in S. Kellert and E. O. Wilson, eds., *The Biophilia Hypothesis* (Washington, DC: Island Press, 1993); S. Kellert, *Kinship to Mastery: Biophilia in Human Evolution and Development* (Washington, DC: Island Press, 1997).

2. *American Heritage College Dictionary* (Boston: Houghton Mifflin, 1993), 1274.

3. J. F. Wohlwill, "The concept of nature: A psychologist's view," in I. Altman and J. Wohlwill, eds., *Behavior and the Natural Environment* (New York: Plenum, 1983), 7. Also see for contrasting definitions and conceptions of nature: J. D. Proctor, "Resolving multiple visions of nature, science, and religion," *Zygon* 39 (2004): 637–53.

4. E. O. Wilson, "Biophilia and the conservation ethic," in Kellert and Wilson, eds., *The Biophilia Hypothesis.*

5. C. Cooper-Marcus and M. Barnes, eds., *Healing Gardens: Therapeutic Landscapes in Healthcare Facilities* (New York: Wiley, 1999); P. J. Schmidt, *Back to Nature: The Arcadian Myth in Urban America* (Baltimore: Johns Hopkins University Press, 1990); C. J. Glacken, *Traces on the Rhodian Shore: Nature and Culture in Western Thought from Ancient Times to the End of the 18th Century* (Berkeley: University of California Press, 1967); K. Thomas, *Man and the Natural World* (New York: Pantheon, 1983); Y. Hongxun, *The Classical Gardens of China* (New York: Van Nostrand Reinhold, 1982); S. Kaplan and R. Kaplan, *The Experience of Nature* (New York: Cambridge University Press, 1989); P. Shepard, *Man in the Landscape: A Historic View of the Esthetics of Nature* (New York: Knopf, 1967); S. M. Warner, "The periodic rediscoveries of restorative gardens: 1100 to the present," in M. Francis, P. Lindsey, and J. Stone, eds., *The Healing Dimensions of People-plant Relations: Proceedings of a Research Symposium* (Davis: Center for Design Research, University of California, Davis, 1994).

6. See, for example, D. Relf, ed., *The Role of Horticulture in Human Well-being and Social Development* (Portland, OR: Timber Press, 1992); Cooper-Marcus and Barnes, eds., *Healing Gardens;* T. Hartig et al., "Restorative effects of the natural environment," *Environment and Behavior* 23 (1991): 3–26; T. Hartig, "Nature experience in transactional perspective," *Landscape and Urban Planning* 25 (1993): 17–36; Ulrich, "Biophilia, biophobia, and natural landscapes"; R. Ulrich, "Effects of gardens on health outcomes: Theory and research," in Cooper-Marcus and Barnes, eds., *Healing Gardens;* Kaplan and Kaplan, *The Experience of Nature;* C. Francis and R. Hester, eds., *The Meaning of Gardens* (Cambridge, MA: MIT Press, 1993); C. Francis and C. Cooper-Marcus, "Restorative places: Environment and emotional well being," in *Proceedings of the 23rd Annual Conference of the Environmental Design Research Association* (Oklahoma City, OK: Environmental Design Research Association, 1992); C. Marcus and C. Francis, eds., *People Places: Design Guidelines for Urban Open Space* (New York: Van Nostrand Reinhold, 1990); R. Young and R. Crandall, "Wilderness use and self-actualization," *Journal of Leisure Research* 16 (1984): 149–60.

7. See, for example, M. Gadgil, "Of life and artifacts," in Kellert and Wilson, eds., *The Biophilia Hypothesis,* 365–77; M. Gadgil and F. Berkes, "Traditional resource management systems," *Resource Management and Optimization* 8 (1991): 127–41; M. Chandrakanth and J. Romm, "Sacred forest, secular forest policies, and people's actions," *Natural Resources Journal* 41 (1991): 741–56; P. Ramakrishnan, "Conserving the sacred: From species to landscapes," *Nature and Resources* 32 (1996): 11–19; S. Sharma et al., "Conservation of natural resources through religion," *Society and Natural Resources* 12 (1999): 599–622.

8. See, for example, Glacken, *Traces on the Rhodian Shore;* Schmidt, *Back to Nature.* Also see P. Coates, *Nature: Western Attitudes since Ancient Times* (Berkeley: University of California Press, 1998); M. Oelschaeger, *The Idea of Wilderness* (New Haven, CT: Yale University Press, 1991).

9. See, for example, A. Fein, *Frederick Law Olmsted and the American Environmental Tradition* (New York: George Brazler, 1972); J. Todd, *Frederick Law Olmsted* (New York: Twayne, 1982).

10. C. Beverdige and P. Rocheleau, *Frederick Law Olmsted: Designing the American Landscape* (New York: Universe, 1998), 31. Also see F. L. Olmsted, "Introduction: Basic principles of city planning," in J. Nolen, ed., *City Planning: A Series of Papers Presenting the Essential Elements of a City Plan* (New York: Appleton, 1995); F. L. Olmsted, "The city beautiful," *The Builder* 101 (July 7, 1911); F. L. Olmsted, "The value and care of parks," in R. Nash, ed., *The American Environment: Readings in the History of Conservation* (Reading, MA: Addison-Wesley, 1968); C. Gilbert and F. L. Olmsted, *Report to the New Haven Improvement Commission* (New Haven, CT: New Haven Civic Improvement Committee, 1910).

11. R. Ulrich and R. Parsons, "Influences of passive experience with plants on individual well-being and health," in Relf, ed., *The Role of Horticulture,* 93–105; R. Ulrich, "Aesthetic and affective response to natural environment," in I. Altmann and J. F. Wohlwill, eds., *Human Behavior and Environment,* 85–125 (New York: Plenum, 1993); R. Ulrich, "Biophilia, biophobia, and natural landscapes," 73–137; T. Hartig et al., "Restorative effects of natural environment experiences," *Environment and Behavior* 23 (1991): 3–26; S. Kaplan, "The restorative benefits of nature: Toward an integrative framework," *Journal of Environmental Psychology* 12 (1995): 169–82; R. Parsons, "The potential influences of environmental perception on human health," *Journal of Environmental Psychology* 11 (1991): 1–23; R. Parsons et al., "The view from the road: Implications for stress recovery and immunization," *Journal of Environmental Psychology* 18 (1998): 113–40; M. Cooper-Marcus and M. Barnes, *Gardens in Healthcare Facilities: Uses, Therapeutic Benefits, and Design Recommendations* (Martinez, CA: Center for Health Design, 1995).

12. Ulrich, "Biophilia, biophobia, and natural landscapes," 73–137; S. Kaplan et al., "Rated preference and complexity for natural and urban visual material," *Perception and Psychophysics* 12 (1972):
354–56; R. Ulrich, "View through a window may influence recovery from surgery," *Science* 224
(1984): 420–21; R. Ulrich et al., "Stress recovery during exposure to natural and urban environments," *Journal of Environmental Psychology* 11 (1991): 201–30; R. Hull and A. Harvey, "Explaining
the emotion people experience in suburban parks," *Environment and Behavior* 21 (1989): 323–45;
E. Zube et al., ed., *Landscape Assessment: Values, Perceptions, and Resources* (Stroudsburg, PA: Dowden,
Hutchinson, and Ross, 1975); R. Kaplan, "Some psychological benefits of gardening," *Environment
and Behavior* 5 (1973): 142–52.

13. T. Hartig, M. Barnes, and C. Marcus, "Conclusions and prospects," in Cooper-Marcus and Barnes,
eds., *Healing Gardens*, 577.

14. Hartig et al., "Restorative effects of natural environment experiences"; T. Hartig et al.,
"Environmental influences on psychological restoration," *Scandinavian Journal of Psychology* 37
(1996): 378–93; T. Hartig and G. Evans, "Psychological foundations of nature experience," in T.
Garlking and R. Golledge, eds., *Behavior and Environment: Psychological and Geographical Approaches*,
427–57 (Amsterdam: Elsevier/North Holland, 1993).

15. See, for example, A. Ewert, *Outdoor Adventure Pursuits: Foundations, Models, and Theories* (Scottsdale,
AZ: Publishing Horizons, 1989); B. Driver et al., "Wilderness benefits: A state-of-the-knowledge
review," in R. C. Lucas, ed., *Proceedings of the National Wilderness Research Conference*, General
Technical Report INT-220 (Fort Collins, CO: USDA Forest Service, 1987); R. Knopf, "Human
behavior, cognition, and affect in the natural environment," in D. Stokols and I. Altman, eds.,
Handbook of Environmental Psychology (New York: Wiley, 1987).

16. See, for example, Ulrich, "Biophilia, biophobia, and natural landscapes"; J. Appleton, *The Experience
of Landscape* (London: Wiley, 1975); J. Heerwagen and G. Orians, "Humans, habitats, and aesthetics," in Kellert and Wilson, eds., *The Biophilia Hypothesis;* Y. Tuan, *Passing Strange and Wonderful:
Aesthetics, Nature, and Culture* (Washington, DC: Island Press, 1993); G. Hildebrand, *The Origins of
Psychological Pleasure* (Berkeley: University of California Press, 2000).

17. Kaplan and Kaplan, *The Experience of Nature;* S. Kaplan and R. Kaplan, *With People in Mind: Design
and Management of Everyday Nature* (Washington, DC: Island Press, 1998).

18. A sample of important studies includes Ewert, *Outdoor Adventure Pursuits;* B. Driver et al., "Wilderness ben-
efits"; annotated literature review in S. Kellert and V. Derr, *National Study of Outdoor Wilderness Experience*
(New Haven, CT: Yale University School of Forestry and Environmental Studies; Charleston, NH: Student
Conservation Association, 1998); A. Easley et al., *The Use of Wilderness for Personal Growth, Therapy, and
Education,* General Technical Report RM-193 (Fort Collins, CO: USDA Forest Service, 1990); R. Schreyer
et al., *The Role of Wilderness in Human Development,* General Technical Report SE-51 (Fort Collins, CO:
USDA Forest Service, 1988); L. Levitt, "Therapeutic value of wilderness," in *Wilderness Benchmark 1988:
Proceedings of the National Wilderness Colloquium,* General Technical Report SE-51 (Asheville, NC: USDA
Forest Service, 1989), 156–68; R. Ulrich, U. Dimberg, and B. Driver, "Psychophysiological indicators of
leisure benefits," in B. Driver, P. Brown, and G. Peterson, eds., *Benefits of Leisure* (State College, PA: Venture,
1991); Kaplan and Kaplan, *The Experience of Nature;* R. Kaplan and J. Talbot, "Psychological benefits of
a wilderness experience," in Altman and Wohlwill, eds., *Behavior and the Natural Environment;* B. Driver and
P. Brown, "Probable personal benefits of outdoor recreation," in *President's Commission on American Outdoors:
A Literature Review,* 63–67 (Washington, DC: Government Printing Office, 1976); B. Driver et al., eds.,
Nature and the Human Spirit (State College, PA: Venture, 1999).

19. Ewert, *Outdoor Adventure Pursuits.*

20. Kellert and Derr, *National Study of Outdoor Wilderness Experience.*

21. See, for example, K. Thomas, *Man and the Natural World* (New York: Pantheon, 1983); G. Carson, *Men, Beasts, and Gods: A History of Cruelty and Kindness to Animals* (New York: Scribner's, 1972).

22. See, for example, J. Serpell, *In the Company of Animals* (Oxford: Basil Blackwell, 1986); A. Katcher and A. Beck, eds., *New Perspectives on Our Lives with Companion Animals* (Philadelphia: University of Pennsylvania Press, 1983); A. Beck and A. Katcher, *Between Pets and People: The Importance of Animal Companionship* (West Lafayette, IN: Purdue University Press, 1996); R. Anderson et al., eds., *The Pet Connection* (Minneapolis: University of Minnesota Press, 1984); B. Fogle, ed., *Interrelations between People and Pets* (Springfield, IL: Thomas, 1981); B. Levinson, *Pets and Human Development* (Springfield, IL: Thomas, 1972); A. Rowan, ed., *Animals and People Sharing the World* (Hanover, NH: University Press of New England, 1989); A. Katcher and G. Wilkins, "Dialogue with animals: Its nature and culture," in Kellert and Wilson, eds., *The Biophilia Hypothesis.*

23. P. Messent, "Social facilitation of contact with other people by pet dogs," in Katcher and Beck, eds., *New Perspectives on Our Lives with Companion Animals,* 354.

24. Serpell, *In the Company of Animals,* 31.

25. See, for example, B. Levinson, *Pet-Oriented Child Psychotherapy* (Springfield, IL: Thomas, 1969); Levinson, *Pets and Human Development;* R. Corson and E. Corson, "The socializing role of pet animals in nursing homes," in L. Levi, ed., *Society, Stress, and Disease* (London: Oxford University Press, 1977); E. Friedmann et al., "Animal companions and one-year survival of patients discharged from a coronary care unit," *Public Health Reports* 95 (1980): 307–12; L. Hart et al., "Socializing effects of service dogs for people with disabilities," *Anthrozoos* 1 (1987): 41–44; J. Siegel, "Stressful life events and use of physician services among the elderly: The moderating role of pet ownership," *Journal of Personality and Social Psychology* 58 (1990): 1081–86; Serpell, *In the Company of Animals;* Fogle, ed., *Interrelations between Pets and People;* A. Fine, ed., *The Handbook of Animal Assisted Therapy: Theoretical Foundations and Guidelines for Practice* (New York: Academic Press, 2000); E. Friedmann, "Animal-human bond: Health and wellness," in Katcher and Beck, eds., *New Perspectives on Our Lives with Companion Animals;* R. Draper et al., "Defining the role of pet animals in psychotherapy," *Journal of Developmental Psychology* 15 (1990): 169–72; D. Allen, "Effects of dogs on human health," *Journal of the American Veterinary Medicine Association* 210 (1997): 1136–39; A. Katcher, "Interactions between people and their pets: Form and function," in Fogle, ed., *Interrelations between Pets and People;* A. Katcher, "Animal assisted therapy and the study of human-animal relationships," in A. Fine, *The Handbook of Animal Assisted Therapy;* A. Katcher and A. Beck, "Animal companions: More companion than animals," in R. Robinson and L. Tiger, eds., *Man and Beast Revisited* (Washington, DC: Smithsonian Institution Press, 1991); A. Katcher and G. Wilkins, "Animal-assisted therapy in the treatment of disruptive behavior disorders," in A. Lundberg, ed., *The Environment and Mental Health* (Mahwah, NJ: Erlbaum, 1998); A. Katcher, "Animals in therapeutic education: Guides into the liminal state," in Kahn and Kellert, eds., *Children and Nature;* A. Cochrane and K. Callen, *Dolphins and Their Power to Heal* (London: Bloomsbury, 1992); Siegel, "Stressful life events"; D. Moore, "Animal-facilitated therapy: A review," *Children's Environment Quarterly* 1, no. 3 (1984): 37–40.

26. A. Katcher et al., "Looking, talking and blood pressure: The physiological consequences of interaction with the living environment," in Katcher and Beck, eds., *New Perspectives on Our Lives with Companion Animals;* Friedmann et al., "Animal companions and one-year survival." Also see these related studies: E. Friedmann et al., "Pet ownership, social support, and one-year survival after acute

myocardial infarction in the cardiac arrhythmia suppression trial," *American Journal of Cardiology* 76 (1995): 1213–17; W. Anderson et al., "Pet ownership and risk factors for cardiovascular disease," *Medical Journal of Australia* 157 (1992): 298–301.

27. Katcher and Wilkins, "Dialogue with animals."

28. Serpell, *In the Company of Animals,* 114–16.

29. See, for example, K. Szasz, *Petishism: Pets and Their People in the Western World* (New York: Holt, Rinehart, & Winston, 1983); P. Shepard, "On animal friends," in Kellert and Wilson, eds., *The Biophilia Hypothesis;* Y. Tuan, *Dominance and Affection: The Making of Pets* (New Haven, CT: Yale University Press, 1984); A. Felthous and S. Kellert, "Children cruelty to animals and later aggression against people: A review," *American Journal of Psychiatry* 144 (1987): 710–17; S. Kellert and A. Felthous, "Childhood cruelty toward animals among criminals and non-criminals," *Human Relations* 38 (1985): 1113–29; L. DeVinner, J. Dickert, and R. Lockwood, "Care of pets within child abusing families," *International Journal for the Study of Animal Problems* 4 (1983): 321–36.

30. See statistics, for example, provided by the U.S. Pet Food Institute (http://www.petfoodinstitute.org) and the Humane Society of the United States (http://www.hsus.org).

31. See, for example, C. Levi-Strauss, *The Savage Mind* (Chicago: University of Chicago Press, 1966); F. Zeuner, *A History of Domesticated Animals* (New York: Harper & Row, 1963); Serpell, *In the Company of Animals;* Kellert, *Kinship to Mastery.*

32. See, for example, Ulrich, "View through a window"; R. Ulrich, "Effects of hospital environments on patient well being," in *Research Report 9* (Trondheim, Norway: Department of Psychiatry and Behavioral Medicine, 1986); R. Ulrich and O. Lunden, "Effects of nature and abstract pictures on patients recovering from open heart surgery" (paper presented at the International Congress of Behavioral Medicine, Uppsula, Sweden, 1990); Ulrich et al., "Stress recovery during exposure to natural and urban environments"; S. Kaplan and C. Peterson, "Health and environment: A psychological analysis," *Landscape and Urban Planning* 26 (1993): 17–23; Ulrich, "Biophilia, biophobia, and natural landscapes"; R. Ulrich, "Effects of interior design on wellness: Theory and recent scientific research," *Journal of Healthcare Design* 3 (1992): 97–109; R. Ulrich and R. Parsons, "Influences of passive experiences with plants on individual well-being and health," in Relf, ed., *The Role of Horticulture;* C. Baird and P. Bell, "Place attachment, isolation, and the power of a window in a hospital environment," *Psychological Reports* 76 (1995): 847–50; Parsons et al., "The view from the road"; R. Parsons, "The potential influences of environmental perception on human health," *Journal of Environmental Psychology* 11 (1991): 1–23; A. Taylor, "The therapeutic value of nature," *Journal of Operational Psychiatry* 12 (1976): 64–74; S. Verderber and D. Reuman, "Windows, views, and health status in hospital therapeutic environments," *Journal of Architectural Planning and Research* 4 (1987): 120–33; A. E. Van den Berg et al., "Health benefits of viewing nature" (in preparation); K. Korpela and T. Hartig, "Restorative qualities of favorite places," *Journal of Environmental Psychology* 16 (1996): 221–33; H. Frumkin, "Beyond toxicity: Human health and the natural environment," *American Journal of Preventive Medicine* 20 (2001): 234–39; Relf, ed., *The Role of Horticulture;* R. Clay, "Green is good for you," *Monitor on Psychology* 32 (2001); D. Hollander et al., "Health, environment and quality of life," *Landscape and Urban Planning* 89 (2002): 1–10; P. Grahm, "Green structures: The importance for health of nature areas and parks," *European Regional Planning* 56 (1994): 89–112; Hartig et al., "Environmental influences on psychological restoration"; Hartig et al., "Restorative effects of the natural environment"; C. Lewis, *Green Nature/Human Nature: The Meaning of Plants in Our Lives* (Urbana: University of Illinois Press, 1996); R. Parsons and T. Hartig,

"Environmental physiology," in J. Caccioppo et al., *Handbook of Psychophysiology* (New York: Cambridge University Press, 1999); B. Cimprich, "Development of an intervention to restore attention in cancer patients," *Cancer Nursing* 16 (1993): 83–92; R. Hull and S. Michael, "Nature-based recreation, mood change, and stress reduction," *Leisure Science* 17 (1995): 1–14; P. Mooney and P. Nicell, "The importance of exterior environment for Alzheimer residents," *Healthcare Management Forum* 5 (1992): 23–29; A. Taylor et al., "Coping with ADD: The surprising connection to green places," *Environment and Behavior* 33 (2001): 54–77; R. Nakamura and E. Fujii, "A comparative study of the characteristics of the electroencephalogram when observing a hedge and a concrete block fence," *Journal of the Japanese Institute of Landscape Architects* 55 (1992): 139–44; B. O'Connor et al., "Window view, social exposure and nursing home adaptation," *Canadian Journal of Aging* 10 (1991): 216–23; M. Francis, P. Lindsey, and J. Stone, eds., *The Healing Dimensions of People-plant Interactions;* A. Olds, "Nature as healer," in J. Weiser and T. Yeomans, eds., *Readings in Psychosynthesis: Theory, Process, and Practice* (Toronto: Ontario Institute for Studies in Education, 1985).

33. Cooper-Marcus and Barnes, *Gardens in Healthcare Facilities;* Cooper-Marcus and Barnes, eds., *Healing Gardens.*

34. See, for example, R. Ulrich, "Visual landscapes and psychological well-being," *Landscape Research* 4 (1979): 17–23; R. Ulrich, "Natural versus urban scenes," *Environment and Behavior* 12 (1981): 523–56; Ulrich, "Aesthetic and affective response to natural environment"; R. Ulrich, "Human responses to vegetation and landscapes," *Landscape and Urban Planning* 12 (1986): 29–44; R. Ulrich, "How design impacts wellness," *Healthcare Forum Journal* 20 (1992): 20–25; Ulrich et al., "Stress recovery during exposure to natural and urban environments"; Ulrich, "Biophilia, biophobia, and natural landscapes"; Parsons et al., "The view from the road"; plus all other references cited in note 32.

35. Ulrich, "View through a window"; Ulrich, "Biophilia, biophobia, and natural landscapes."

36. Ulrich, "Biophilia, biophobia, and natural landscapes," 107.

37. Ulrich and Lunden, "Effects of nature and abstract pictures."

38. Ulrich, "Effects of hospital environments on patient well being."

39. Katcher et al., "Comparison of contemplation and hypnosis."

40. See, for example, T. Godish, *Sick Buildings: Definitions, Diagnosis, and Mitigation* (Boca Raton, FL: Lewis, 1994); M. Baechler and D. Hadley, *Sick Building Syndrome: Sources, Health Effects, Mitigation* (New York: Noyes, 1992); M. Marcoin, B. Seifert, and T. Lindball, *Indoor Air Quality* (New York: Elsevier, 1995); R. Spiegel and D. Meadows, *Green Building Materials: A Guide to Product Selection and Specification* (New York: Wiley, 1999).

41. See, for example, J. Heerwagen and B. Hase, "Building biophilia: Connecting people to nature," *Environmental Design + Construction* (March 2001): 30–34; J. Heerwagen, "Green buildings, organizational success, and occupant productivity," *Building Research and Information* 28 (2000): 353–67; M. Boubekri et al., "Impact of window size and sunlight penetration on office workers' mood and satisfaction," *Environment and Behavior* 23 (1991): 474–93; W. Browning and J. Romm, "Greening and the bottom line," in K. Whitter and T. Cohn, eds., *Proceedings of the 2nd Intl. Green Buildings Conference,* Special Publication 888 (Gaithersburg, MD: National Institute of Standards and Technology, 1998); W. Fisk and A. Rosenfeld, "Estimates of improved productivity and health from better indoor environments," *Indoor Air* 7 (1997): 158–72; J. Heerwagen, "Affective functioning, light hunger, and room brightness preferences," *Environment and Behavior* 22 (1990): 608–35; J. Heerwagen, "The psychological aspects of windows and window design," *Environmental Design Research Association* 21 (1990): 269–80; J. Heerwagen et al., "Do energy efficient, green

buildings spell profits?" *Energy and Environmental Management* 3 (1997): 29–34; J. Heerwagen et al., "Environmental design, work and well being," *American Association of Occupational Health Nurses Journal* 43 (1995): 458–68; J. Heerwagen, "Windowscapes: The role of nature," in *Proceedings Second International Daylighting Conference* (Long Beach, CA, November 1986); J. Heerwagen and G. Orians, "Adaptations to windowlessness: A study of the use of visual décor in windowed and window-less offices," *Environment and Behavior* 18 (1986): 623–30; R. Kaplan, "Urban forestry and the workplace," in P. Gobster, ed., *Managing Urban and High Use Recreation Settings,* General Technical Report NC-163 (Chicago: USDA Forest Service, 1995); P. Leather et al., "Windows in the work-place: Sunlight, view, and occupational stress," *Environment and Behavior* 30 (1998): 739–62; N. Sensharma et al., "Relationship between the indoor environment and productivity: A literature review," *ASHRAE Transactions* 104 (1998); J. Veitch and G. Newsham, "Lighting quality and energy efficient effects on task performance," *Journal of the Illuminating Engineering Society* 27 (1998): 107–29; V. Lohr et al., "Interior plants may improve worker productivity and reduce stress in a windowless environment," *Journal of Environmental Horticulture* 14 (1996): 97–100; C. Tennessen and B. Cimprich, "Views to nature: Effects on attention," *Journal of Environmental Psychology* 15 (1995): 77–85; L. Larsen et al., "Plants in the workplace," *Environment and Behavior* 31 (1998): 261–81; R. Kaplan, "The role of nature in the context of the workplace," *Landscape and Urban Planning* 26 (1993): 193–201; J. Wise, "How nature nurtures: Buildings as habitats and their ben-efits to people," *Heating/Piping/Air Conditioning* (February 1997): 48–51, 78; Boubekri et al., "Impact of window size and sunlight penetration"; J. Stewart-Pollack, "The need for nature: How nature determines our needs for and responses to environments," *Isdesign,* September-October, 1996; E. Moore, "A prison environment's effect on health care service demands," *Journal of Environmental Systems* 11 (1982): 17–34; R. Kuller and C. Lindsten, "Health and behavior of chil-dren in classrooms with and without windows," *Journal of Environmental Psychology* 12 (1992): 305–17; Rocky Mountain Institute et al., *Green Development* (New York: Wiley, 1998); Pacific Gas and Electric Company, *Daylighting in Schools: An Investigation into the Relationship between Daylighting and Human Performance* (Sacramento: California Public Utilities Commission, research by Heschong Mahone Group, 1999); G. Katts, *The Costs and Financial Benefits of Green Buildings* (Sacramento: California Sustainable Building Task Force, 2003).

42. J. Heerwagen, J. Wise, D. Lantrip, and M. Ivanovich, "A tale of two buildings: Biophilia and the benefits of green design," *US Green Buildings Council Conference* (November 1996); J. Heerwagen, "Do green buildings enhance the well being of workers? Yes," *Environmental Design + Construction* (July 2000): 24–34.

43. J. Corbett and M. Corbett, *Designing Sustainable Communities: Learning from Village Homes* (Washington, DC: Island Press, 2000); all following related quotes are from this source. Also see for related per-spectives: R. Kaplan, "Nature at the doorstep: Residential satisfaction and the nearby environment," *Journal of Architectural and Planning Research* 2 (1985): 115–27; J. Nasar, "Adult viewers' preferences in residential sciences: A study of the relationship of environmental attributes to preference," *Environment and Behavior* 15 (1984): 589–614; Hartig, "Nature experience in transactional per-spective"; J. Talbot and R. Kaplan, "The benefits of nearby nature for elderly apartment residents," *International Journal of Aging and Human Development* 33 (1991): 119–30.

44. J. Lacy, *An Examination of Market Appreciation for Clustered Housing with Permanently Protected Open Space* (Amherst: Center for Rural Massachusetts, University of Massachusetts, 1990). Also see for related information: Rocky Mountain Institute et al., *Green Development;* L. Anderson et al.,

"Influence of trees on residential property values in Athens, GA (USA): A survey based on actual sales prices," *Landscape and Urban Planning* 15 (1975): 539–66.

45. See, for example, F. Kuo, "Coping with poverty: Impacts of environment and attention in the inner city," *Environment and Behavior* 33 (2001): 5–34; W. Sullivan and F. Kuo, "Do trees strengthen urban communities, reduce domestic violence," in *Forestry Report R8-FR 56, USDA Forest Service* (Atlanta: Southern Regions, USDA Forest Service); F. Kuo et al., "Fertile ground for community: Inner-city neighborhood common spaces," *American Journal of Community Psychology* 26 (1998): 823–51; F. Kuo et al., "Transforming inner-city landscapes: Trees, sense of safety, and preference," *Environment and Behavior* 30 (1998); A. Taylor, F. Kuo, and W. Sullivan, "Growing up in the inner city: Green spaces as places to grow," *Environment and Behavior* 30 (1998): 3–27; R. Coley and F. Kuo, "Where does community grow? The social context created by nature in urban public housing," *Environment and Behavior* 29 (1997).

46. Taylor, Kuo, and Sullivan, "Growing up in the inner city: Green spaces as places to grow," 24.

47. Coley and Kuo, "Where does community grow?"

48. See, for example, R. Costanza, B. Norton, and B. Haskell, eds., *Ecosystem Health* (Washington, DC: Island Press, 1992); R. de Groot, *Functions of Nature* (Amsterdam: Wolters-Noordhoff, 1992); G. Likens and F. Bormann, *Biogeochemistry of a Forest Ecosystem* (New York: Springer-Verlag, 1995); National Research Council, *Restoration of Aquatic Ecosystems* (Washington, DC: National Academy Press, 1992).

49. See, for example, Kellert, *The Value of Life;* Kellert, *Kinship to Mastery.*

50. See, for example, E. Babbie, *The Practice of Social Research* (Belmont, CA: Wadsworth/Thomson, 2001).

51. For more discussion of ecosystem service, see G. Daily, *Nature's Services: Societal Dependence on Natural Ecosystems* (Washington, DC: Island Press, 1997); H. Mooney et al., *Functional Roles of Biodiversity* (Chichester, Eng.: Wiley, 1996); E-D. Schulze and H. Mooney, eds., *Biodiversity and Ecosystem Function* (Berlin: Springer-Verlag, 1993); Y. Baskin, *The Work of Nature: How the Diversity of Life Sustains Us* (Washington, DC: Island Press, 1997); de Groot, *Functions of Nature.*

52. See, for example, S. Kellert, "Values and perceptions of invertebrates," *Conservation Biology* 7 (1993): 845–55; D. Pimentel, *Insects, Science and Society* (New York: Academic Press, 1975); D. Pimentel et al., "Economics and environmental benefits of biodiversity," *BioScience* 47 (1997): 747–57; Kellert, *Kinship to Mastery.*

53. Pimentel et al., "Economics and environmental benefits of biodiversity"; R. Costanza et al., "The value of the world's ecosystem services and natural capital," *Ecological Economics* 25 (1998): 3–15; D. Pearce and D. Moran, *The Economic Value of Biodiversity* (London: Earthscan, 1994).

54. R. Dasmann, *Environmental Conservation* (New York: Wiley, 1972).

55. See, for example, Wilson, *Biophilia;* Kellert and Wilson, eds., *The Biophilia Hypothesis;* Kellert, *Kinship to Mastery;* P. Kahn, "Developmental psychology and the biophilia hypothesis," *Developmental Review* 17 (1999): 1–61.

56. See, for example, C. Lumsden and E. O. Wilson, *Genes, Mind, and Culture* (Cambridge, MA: Harvard University Press, 1981); C. Lumsden and E. O. Wilson, "The relation between biological and cultural evolution," *Journal of Social and Biological Structures* 8 (1985): 343–59; J. Barkow, L. Cosmides, and J. Tooby, eds., *The Adapted Mind: Evolutionary Psychology and the Generation of Culture* (New York: Oxford University Press, 1992).

57. For more detailed descriptions of the nine biophilic values, see Kellert, *The Value of Life;* Kellert, *Kinship to Mastery.*

58. See, for example, J. Diamond, "New Guineans and their natural world," in Kellert and Wilson, eds., *The Biophilia Hypothesis;* R. Nelson, "Searching for the lost arrow: Physical and spiritual ecology in the hunter's world," in Kellert and Wilson, eds., *The Biophilia Hypothesis;* L. Maffi, ed., *On Biocultural Diversity: Linking Language, Knowledge, and the Environment* (Washington, DC: Smithsonian Institution Press, 2001); G. Nabhan, *Cultures of Habitat: On Nature, Culture, and Story* (Washington, DC: Counterpoint, 1997).

59. See, for example, P. Shepard, *Thinking Animals: Animals and the Development of Human Intelligence* (New York: Viking, 1978); P. Shepard, *The Others: How Animals Made Us Human* (Washington, DC: Island Press, 1996); E. Lawrence, "The sacred pig, the filthy pig, and the bat out of hell: Animal symbolism as cognitive biophilia," in Kellert and Wilson, eds., *The Biophilia Hypothesis;* D. Abrams, *The Spell of the Sensuous: Perception and Language in a More-Than-Human World* (New York: Pantheon, 1996).

60. See, for example, Appleton, *The Experience of Landscape;* Heerwagen and Orians, "Humans, habitats, and aesthetics."

61. H. Rolston, *Philosophy Gone Wild* (Buffalo, NY: Prometheus Books, 1986), 88.

62. R. Dubos, Wooing of the Earth (London: Althone, 1980), 109; Fein, *Frederick Law Olmsted and the American Environmental Tradition;* Todd, *Frederick Law Olmsted;* Olmsted, "The city beautiful"; Beverdige and Rocheleau, *Frederick Law Olmsted: Designing the American Landscape;* Olmsted, "The value and care of parks."

63. J. Jackson, *A Sense of Place, a Sense of Time* (New Haven, CT: Yale University Press, 1994).

64. Dubos, *Wooing of the Earth,* 110.

65. M. Sagoff, "Settling America or the concept of place in environmental ethics," *Journal of Natural Resources and Environmental Law* 12 (1992): 351–418.

66. S. Weil, *The Need for Roots* (New York: Harper Colophon, 1971).

67. E. Relph, *Place and Placelessness* (London: Pion, 1976), 12.

68. W. Berry, "The Regional Motive," in *A Continuous Harmony: Essays Cultural and Agricultural* (New York: Harcourt, 1972), 68–69. Also see W. Berry, *The Unsettling of America* (New York: Avon, 1978); W. Berry, *Sex, Economy, Freedom, and Community* (New York: Pantheon, 1993); W. Berry, *The Gift of Good Land* (San Francisco: Northpoint, 1981).

69. Sagoff, "Settling America."

70. Kellert, *The Value of Life.*

71. A. Leopold, *The Sand County Almanac, with Other Essays on Conservation from Round River* (New York: Oxford University Press, 1996).

Chapter Three: Nature and Childhood Development

1. U. Bronfrenbrenner, *The Ecology of Human Development* (Cambridge, MA: Harvard University Press, 1979); R. Barker, *Ecological Psychology* (Stanford, CA: Stanford University Press, 1968).

2. H. Searles, *The Nonhuman Environment: In Normal Development and in Schizophrenia* (New York: International Universities Press, 1960), 3.

3. P. Kahn and S. Kellert, eds., *Children and Nature: Psychological, Sociocultural, and Evolutionary Investigations* (Cambridge, MA: MIT Press, 2002).

4. R. Pyle, "Eden in a vacant lot: Special places, species, and kids in the neighborhood of life," in Kahn and Kellert, eds., *Children and Nature,* 319, 306.

5. M. Bloom et al., *Taxonomy of Educational Objectives: The Classification of Educational Goals; Handbook 1, Cognitive Domain* (New York: Longman, 1956). Also see C. Maker, *Teaching Models of the Gifted* (Austin, TX: Pro-Ed., 1982).

6. See, for example, P. Shepard, *Thinking Animals: Animals and the Development of Human Intelligence* (New York: Viking, 1978); P. Shepard, *The Others: How Animals Made Us Human* (Washington, DC: Island Press, 1996); S. Kellert, *The Value of Life: Biological Diversity and Human Society* (Washington, DC: Island Press, 1996).

7. E. Lawrence, "The sacred bee, the filthy pig, and the bat out of hell: Animal symbolism as cognitive biophilia," in S. Kellert and E. O. Wilson, eds., *The Biophilia Hypothesis* (Washington, DC: Island Press, 1993).

8. See, for example, E. O. Wilson, "Biophilia and the conservation ethic," in Kellert and Wilson, eds., *The Biophilia Hypothesis;* R. Pyle, *The Thunder Tree: Lessons from an Urban Wildland* (Boston: Houghton Mifflin, 1993).

9. D. Krathwohl, R. Bloom, and B. Masia, *Taxonomy of Educational Objectives: The Classification of Educational Goals; Handbook 2, Affective Domain* (New York: Longman, 1964). Also see Maker, *Teaching Models of the Gifted.*

10. Kellert, *The Value of Life;* S. Schwartz, "Are there universal aspects in the structure and content of human values?" *Journal of Social Issues* 50 (1994): 19–45; J. Grube et al., "Inducing change in values, attitudes, and behavior: Belief system theory and the method of value self-confrontation," *Journal of Social Issues* 50 (1994): 153–73.

11. L. Iozzi, "What research says to the educator, environmental education and the affective domain," *Journal of Environmental Education* 20 (1989): 3–13. Also see A. Katcher, "Animals in therapeutic education: Guides into the liminal state," in Kahn and Kellert, eds., *Children and Nature.*

12. O. Myers and C. Saunders, "Animals as links toward developing caring relationships with the natural world," in Kahn and Kellert, eds., *Children and Nature.*

13. R. Sebba, "The landscapes of childhood: The reflections of childhood's environment in adult memories and in children's attitudes," *Environment and Behavior* 23 (1991): 395–422.

14. E. Cobb, *The Ecology of Imagination in Childhood* (New York: Columbia University Press, 1977), 32. Also see L. Chawla, "Childhood place attachments," in I. Altman and S. Low, eds., *Place Attachment* (New York: Plenum, 1992); L. Chawla, "Spots of time: Manifold ways of being in nature in childhood," in Kahn and Kellert, eds., *Children and Nature.*

15. W. Whitman, *Leaves of Grass* (London: Putnam, 1997).

16. R. Carson, *The Sense of Wonder* (New York: HarperCollins, 1998), 54, 56, 100.

17. Carson, *The Sense of Wonder,* 100.

18. Sebba, "The landscapes of childhood," 401.

19. Searles, *The Nonhuman Environment,* 117.

20. B. Bettelheim, *The Uses of Enchantment: The Meaning and Importance of Fairy Tales* (New York: Vintage Books, 1977); Shepard, *Thinking Animals.*

21. Pyle, *The Thunder Tree;* Pyle, "Eden in a vacant lot"; J. Mander, *In the Absence of the Sacred* (San Francisco: Sierra Club Books, 1991); D. Orr, "Political economy and the ecology of childhood," in Kahn and Kellert, eds., *Children and Nature;* G. Nabhan and S. Trimble, *The Geography of Childhood* (Boston: Beacon, 1994).

22. D. Thomas, *Quite Early One Morning* (New York: New Directions, 1965), 4.

23. Kellert, *The Value of Life;* Kellert, *Kinship to Mastery;* S. Verbeek and F. de Waal, "The primate relationship with nature: Biophilia as a general pattern," in Kahn and Kellert, eds., *Children and Nature.*

24. S. Kellert, "Attitudes toward animals: Age-related development among children," *Journal of Environmental Education* 16 (1985): 29–39; Kellert, *The Value of Life.*

25. D. Sobel, *Children's Special Places: Exploring the Role of Forts, Dens, and Bush Houses in Middle Childhood* (Tucson, AZ: Zephyr, 1993); R. Moore, *Childhood's Domain: Play and Space in Child Development* (London: Croom Helm, 1986); P. Kahn, *The Human Relationship with Nature: Development and Culture* (Cambridge, MA: MIT Press, 1999); R. Hart, *Children's Experience of Place* (New York: Knopf, 1979).

26. Sobel, *Children's Special Places,* 159.

27. E. Erikson, *Identity: Youth and Crisis* (New York: Norton, 1968).

28. Sobel, *Children's Special Places,* 70, 74.

29. W. Stegner, *Wolf Willow* (New York: Viking, 1962), 21.

30. L. Chawla, "Significant life experiences revisited," *Journal of Environmental Education* 29 (1998): 11–21; Chawla, "Spots of time."

31. Shepard, *Thinking Animals.*

32. Shepard, *The Others,* 76. Also see Bettelheim, *The Uses of Enchantment.*

33. A. Ewert, *Outdoor Adventure Pursuits: Foundations, Models, and Theories* (Scottsdale, AZ: Publishing Horizons, 1989); B. Driver et al., "Wilderness benefits: A state-of-the-knowledge review," in R. C. Lucas, ed., *Proceedings of the National Wilderness Research Conference,* General Technical Report INT-220 (Fort Collins, CO: USDA Forest Service, 1987); S. Kellert and V. Derr, *National Study of Outdoor Wilderness Experience* (New Haven, CT: Yale University School of Forestry and Environmental Studies, 1998).

34. R. Kaplan and S. Kaplan, "Adolescents and the natural environment: A time out?" in Kahn and Kellert, eds., *Children and Nature.*

35. Bloom et al., *Taxonomy of Educational Objectives: The Classification of Educational Goals; Handbook 1, Cognitive Domain;* Krathwohl et al., *Taxonomy of Educational Objectives: The Classification of Educational Goals; Handbook 2, Affective Domain;* J. Piaget, *The Child's Conception of the World* (Totowa, NJ: Littlefield Adams, 1969); Maker, *Teaching Models of the Gifted.*

36. Searles, *The Nonhuman Environment,* 27.

37. See, for example, Pyle, *The Thunder Tree;* Pyle, "Eden in a vacant lot"; Searles, *The Nonhuman Environment;* Sobel, *Children's Special Places;* M. Thomashaw, *Ecological Identity* (Cambridge, MA: MIT Press, 1995); M. Berg and E. Medich, "Children in four neighborhoods," *Environment and Behavior* 12 (1980): 320–48; L. Chawla, "Children's concern for the environment," *Children's Environments Quarterly* 5 (1988): 13–20; L. Chawla, ed., *Growing Up in an Urbanizing World* (Paris: UNESCO; London: Earthscan, 2001); Hart, *Children's Experience of Place;* Kahn, *The Human Relationship with Nature;* P. Kahn, "Developmental psychology and the biophilia hypothesis," *Developmental Review* 17 (1999): 1–61; P. Kahn, "Children's affiliations with nature: Structure, development, and the problem of environmental generational amnesia," in Kahn and Kellert, eds., *Children and Nature;* S. Kaplan and R. Kaplan, *The Experience of Nature* (New York: Cambridge University Press, 1989); R. Moore, *Childhood Domain* (London: Croom Helm, 1986); R. Moore and D. Young, "Childhood outdoors," in I. Altman and J. Wohlwill, eds., *Children and the Environment* (New York: Plenum, 1978); Nabhan and Trimble, *The Geography of Childhood;* S. Ratanapojnard, *Community-oriented Biodiversity Environmental Education* (PhD dissertation, Yale University, 2001); V. Derr, *Growing Up in the Hispano Homeland: The Interplay of Nature, Family, Culture, and Community in Shaping Children's Experiences and Sense of Place* (PhD dissertation, Yale University, 2001).

38. Pyle, "Eden in a vacant lot," 323.

39. Nabhan and Trimble, *The Geography of Childhood*, 7.

40. Sebba, "The landscapes of childhood."

41. See, for example, Pyle, *The Thunder Tree*; Pyle, "Eden in a vacant lot"; Chawla, ed., *Growing Up in an Urbanizing World*; Hart, *Children's Experience of Place*; Kahn, *The Human Relationship with Nature*; Kahn, "Children's affiliations with nature"; Nabhan and Trimble, *The Geography of Childhood*; Ratanapojnard, *Community-oriented Biodiversity Environmental Education*; Derr, *Growing Up in the Hispano Homeland*; Orr, "Political economy and the ecology of childhood"; J. Wargo, *Our Children's Toxic Legacy: How Science and Law Fail to Protect Us from Pesticides* (New Haven, CT: Yale University Press, 1996).

42. See, for example, J. Applegate, "Patterns of early desertion among New Jersey hunters," *Wildlife Society Bulletin* 17 (1991): 476–81; Carson, *The Sense of Wonder*; G. Nabhan and S. St. Antoine, "The loss of floral and faunal story: The extinction of experience," in Kellert and Wilson, eds., *The Biophilia Hypothesis*.

43. R. White, *Young Children's Relationship with Nature: Its Importance to Children's Development and the Earth's Future* (Kansas City, MO: White Hutchinson Leisure & Learning Group, 2004).

44. White, *Young Children's Relationship with Nature*, 12.

45. Orr, "Political economy and the ecology of childhood," 291.

46. Pyle, *The Thunder Tree*.

47. S. Wells, R. Pyle, and N. Collins, *The IUCN Invertebrate Red Data Book* (Gland, Switzerland: World Conservation Union [IUCN], 1983); E. O. Wilson, *The Diversity of Life* (Cambridge, MA: Harvard University Press, 1992).

48. Pyle, *The Thunder Tree*, 145, 147.

49. Pyle, "Eden in a vacant lot," 318–19.

50. Pyle, *The Thunder Tree*, 146.

51. See, for example, Kellert, *The Value of Life*; B. Birney, *A Comparative Study of Children's Perceptions and Knowledge of Wildlife as They Relate to Field Trip Experiences at the Los Angeles County Museum of Natural History and the Los Angeles Zoo* (Ann Arbor, MI: University Microfilms, 1986); J. Falk and L. Dierking, *The Museum Experience* (Washington, DC: Whaleback Books, 1992); G. Mitman, *Reel Nature: America's Romance with Wildlife on Film* (Cambridge, MA: Harvard University Press, 1999).

52. See, for example, citations in Kellert, *The Value of Life*, section on zoos.

53. Kellert and Derr, *National Study of Outdoor Wilderness Experience*.

54. Pyle, *The Thunder Tree*, 148.

55. See, for example, Moore, *Childhood's Domain*; R. Mabey, *The Unofficial Countryside* (London: Collins, 1973).

Chapter Four: Harmonizing the Natural and Human Built Environments

1. V. Scully, *Architecture: The Natural and the Manmade* (New York: St. Martin's, 1991), xi.

2. D. Hoffman, *Frank Lloyd Wright: Architecture and Nature* (New York: Dover, 1986), 156.

3. See, for example, C. Kibert, ed., *Reshaping the Built Environment: Ecology, Ethics, and Environment* (Washington, DC: Island Press, 1999); Rocky Mountain Institute et al., *Green Development* (New York: Wiley, 1998); S. Mendler and W. Odell, *The HOK Guidebook to Sustainable Development* (New York: Wiley, 2000); S. Van der Ryn and S. Cowan, *Ecological Design* (Washington, DC: Island Press, 1996);

K. Yeang, *Designing with Nature: The Ecological Basis for Architectural Design* (New York: McGraw-Hill, 1995); L. Zeiher, *The Ecology of Architecture: A Complete Guide to Creating the Environmentally Conscious Building* (New York: Watson-Guptill, 1996); J. Farmer, *Green Shift: Towards a Green Sensibility in Architecture* (Oxford: Butterworth-Heinemann, 1996); J. Kraushaar and R. Ristinen, *Energy and Problems of a Technical Society* (New York: Wiley, 1993); K. Daniels, *Low-Tech/Light-Tech/High-Tech: Building in the Information Age* (Basel, Switzerland: Birkhauser, 1998); K. Daniels, *Sustainable Building Design* (Munich: HL-Technik AF, 2001); D. Orr, *The Nature of Design: Ecology, Culture, and Human Intention* (New York: Oxford, 2002); P. Hawken, A. Lovins, and L. Lovins, *Natural Capitalism: Creating the Next Industrial Revolution* (Boston: Little Brown, 1999); D. Jones, *Architecture and the Environment: Bioclimatic Building Design* (New York: Overlook, 1998); J. Lyle, *Regenerative Design for Sustainable Development* (New York: Wiley, 1994); W. McDonough and M. Braungart, *Cradle to Cradle: Remaking the Way We Make Things* (New York: North Point, 2002); BuildingGreen, *Environmental Building News: The Leading Newsletter on Environmentally Responsible Design and Construction* (Brattleboro, VT; http://www.BuildingGreen.com).

4. W. Shutkin, *The Land That Could Be: Environmentalism and Democracy in the 21st Century* (Cambridge, MA: MIT Press, 2001).

5. See, for example, United Nations Department of Economic and Social Affairs, Population Division; N. Livi Bacci, *Concise History of World Population: An Introduction to Population Processes* (London: Blackwell-Oxford, 1997).

6. See, for example, E. O. Wilson, *The Diversity of Life* (Cambridge, MA: Harvard University Press, 1992); P. Vitousek et al., "Human appropriation of the products of photosynthesis," *BioScience* 36 (1991): 368–73.

7. J. Heerwagen, "Do green buildings enhance the well being of workers? Yes," *Environmental Design + Construction* (July/August 2000): 24.

8. D. Orr, "Architecture as pedagogy," in Kibert, ed., *Reshaping the Built Environment,* 212–13.

9. J. Wines, *The Art of Architecture in the Age of Ecology* (New York: Taschen, 2000).

10. W. McDoungh and M. Braungart, "The NEXT Industrial Revolution," *Atlantic Monthly,* October 1998; McDonough and Braungart, *Cradle to Cradle.*

11. Lyle, *Regenerative Design for Sustainable Development;* N. Todd and J. Todd, *From Eco-Cities to Living Machines: Principles of Ecological Design* (Berkeley, CA: North Atlantic Books, 1994); Van der Ryn and Cowan, *Ecological Design;* Rocky Mountain Institute et al., *Green Development.*

12. See, for example, B. Pfeiffer and G. Nordland, eds., *Frank Lloyd Wright in the Realm of Ideas* (Carbondale: Southern Illinois University Press, 1988); G. Hildebrand, *Pattern and Meaning in Frank Lloyd Wright's Houses* (Seattle: University of Washington Press, 1991); Hoffman, *Frank Lloyd Wright: Architecture and Nature.*

13. See, for example, R. Dubos, *Wooing of the Earth* (London: Althone, 1980); A. Fein, *Frederick Law Olmsted and the American Environmental Tradition* (New York: George Brazler, 1972); J. Todd, *Frederick Law Olmsted* (New York: Twayne, 1982); C. Beverdige and P. Rocheleau, *Frederick Law Olmsted: Designing the American Landscape* (New York: Universe, 1998).

14. See, for example, K. Yeang, *The Green Skyscraper: The Basis for Designing Sustainable Intensive Buildings* (Munich: Prestel Verlag, 1999); C. Slessor, *Eco-Tech: Sustainable Architecture and High Technology* (London: Thames & Hudson, 1997); K. Daniels, *The Technology of Ecological Building: Basic Principles and Measures, Examples and Ideas* (Basel, Switzerland: Birkhauser Verlag, 1997).

15. See, for example, D. Klem, "Collisions between birds and windows: Mortality and prevention," *Journal of Field Ornithology* 61 (1990): 120–28; B. Jaroslow, "A review of factors involved in bird-

tower kills, and mitigative procedures," in *National Workshop on Mitigating Losses of Fish and Wildlife Habitats* (Fort Collins, CO: U.S. Department of Agriculture, 1979); M. Phair, "Towers increase bird fatalities," *ENR* 243 (1999): 16; J. Ogden, "Collision course: The hazards of lighted structures and windows to migrating birds," in *Fatal Light Awareness Program* (World Wildlife Fund, Toronto, 1999).

16. C. Kibert, "The promises and limits of sustainability," in Kibert, ed., *Reshaping the Built Environment,* 32.

17. See, for example, R. Thomas, ed., *Environmental Design: An Introduction for Architects and Engineers* (London: Spon, 1996); D. Annick, C. Boonstra, and J. Mak, *Handbook of Sustainable Building* (London: James & James, 2001); S. Szokolay, *Introduction to Architectural Science: The Basis of Sustainable Design* (Oxford: Architectural Press, 2004); European Commission, *A Green Vitruvius: Principles and Practices of Sustainable Architectural Design* (London: James & James, 1999); Karushaar and Ristiner, *Energy and Problems of a Technical Society;* Daniels, *Low-Tech/Light-Tech/High-Tech;* Mendler and Odell, *The HOK Guidebook to Sustainable Development;* Kibert, ed., *Reshaping the Built Environment;* BuildingGreen, *Environmental Building News;* D. Jones, *Architecture and the Environment: Bioclimatic Building Design* (Woodstock, NY: Overlook, 1998); D. Watson and K. Labs, *Climatic Design: Energy-Efficient Building Principles and Practices* (New York: McGraw-Hill, 1983); National Audubon Society and Croxton Collaborative, Architects, *Audubon House: Building the Environmentally Responsible, Energy-efficient Office* (New York: Wiley, 1994).

18. See, for example, U.S. Green Building Council, *Leadership in Energy and Environmental Design (LEED) Reference Guide,* version 2.1 (Washington, DC: U.S. Green Building Council, 2003); American Society of Heating, Refrigerating, and Air-conditioning Engineers (http://www.ashrae.org); U.S. Department of Energy, DOE-2 (http://www.eere.energy.gov/buildings/tools_directory); International Standards Organization 14000 Series (http://www.ems-14000.com/).

19. C. Jencks, *The Architecture of the Jumping Universe* (London: Chichester, 1997), 99.

20. See, for example, R. Spiegel and D. Meadows, *Green Building Materials: A Guide to Product Selection and Specification* (New York: Wiley, 1999); European Commission, *A Green Vitruvius;* Mendler and Odell, *The HOK Guidebook to Sustainable Development;* Kibert, ed., *Reshaping the Built Environment;* BuildingGreen, *Environmental Building News;* U.S. Green Building Council, *Leadership in Energy and Environmental Design (LEED) Reference Guide;* Thomas, ed., *Environmental Design;* Annick, Boonstra, and Mak, *Handbook of Sustainable Building;* Szokolay, *Introduction to Architectural Science;* National Audubon Society and Croxton Collaborative, Architects, *Audubon House.*

21. See, for example, U.S. EPA Energy Star Program (http://www.energystar.gov); Forest Stewardship Council (http://www.fsc.org/fsc); Institute for Sustainable Forestry (http://www.isf-sw.org); U.S. Department of Energy, Building for Environmental and Economic Sustainability (http://www.eere.energy.gov/buildings/tools_directory); International Standards Organization 14000 Series (http://www.ems-14000.com/).

22. Spiegel and Meadows, *Green Building Materials.*

23. National Audubon Society and Croxton Collaborative, Architects, *Audubon House.*

24. U.S. Green Building Council, *Leadership in Energy and Environmental Design (LEED) Reference Guide;* American Society of Heating, Refrigerating, and Air-conditioning Engineers (http://www.ashrae.org); U.S. Department of Energy (http://www.eere.energy.gov/buildings/tools_directory); International Standards Organization 14000 Series (http://www.ems-14000.com/); U.S. EPA Energy Star Program (http://www.energystar.gov); Forest Stewardship Council (http://www.fsc.org/fsc); Institute for Sustainable Forestry (http://www.isf-sw.org);

U.S. Department of Energy, Building for Environmental and Economic Sustainability (http://www.eere.energy.gov/buildings/tools_directory).

25. Todd and Todd, *From Eco-Cities to Living Machines*, 77; J. Todd, E. Brown, and E. Wells, "Ecological design applied," *Ecological Engineering* 20 (2003): 421–40; J. Todd and B. Josephson, "The design of living technologies for waste treatment," *Ecological Engineering* 6 (1996): 109–36.

26. Kibert, "The promises and limits of sustainability."

27. McDonough and Braungart, *Cradle to Cradle.*

28. U.S. Green Building Council, *Leadership in Energy and Environmental Design (LEED) Reference Guide*; American Society of Heating, Refrigerating, and Air-conditioning Engineers (http://www.ashrae.org); U.S. Department of Energy (http://www.eere.energy.gov/buildings/tools_directory); International Standards Organization 14000 Series (http://www.ems-14000.com/); U.S. EPA Energy Star Program (http://www.energystar.gov); Forest Stewardship Council (http://www.fsc.org/fsc); Institute for Sustainable Forestry (http://www.isf-sw.org); U.S. Department of Energy, Building for Environmental and Economic Sustainability (http://www.eere.energy.gov/buildings/tools_directory).

29. In addition to the references cited in notes 18 and 21, see, for example, J. Thompson and K. Sorvig, *Sustainable Landscape Construction: A Guide to Green Building Outdoors* (Washington, DC: Island Press, 2000); W. Dramstad, J. Olson, and R. Forman, *Landscape Ecology Principles in Landscape Architecture and Land-Use Planning* (Washington, DC: Island Press, 1996); I. McHarg, *Design with Nature* (Garden City, NY: Doubleday, 1971); K. Yeang, *Designing with Nature: The Ecological Basis for Architectural Design* (New York: McGraw-Hill, 1995); R. Forman et al., *Road Ecology: Science and Solutions* (Washington, DC: Island Press, 2003); R. Forman, *Landscape Ecology* (New York: Wiley, 1986); J. Cairns et al., National Research Council, *Restoration of Aquatic Ecosystems* (Washington, DC: National Academy Press, 1992); N. Dunnett and N. Kingsbury, *Planting Green Roofs and Living Walls* (Portland, OR: Timber, 2004); T. Beatley, *Green Urbanism* (Washington, DC: Island Press, 2000); K. Benfield, J. Terris, and N. Vorsanger, *Solving Sprawl: Models of Smart Growth in Communities across America* (New York: Natural Resources Defense Council, 2001).

30. See, for example, U.S. Green Building Council, *Leadership in Energy and Environmental Design (LEED) Reference Guide;* Rocky Mountain Institute et al., *Green Development;* Mendler and Odell, *The HOK Guidebook to Sustainable Development;* City of New York, Department of Design and Construction, *High Performance Building Guidelines* (New York: City of New York, Department of Design and Construction, 2002); British Research Establishment Environmental Assessment Method (http://www.breeam.org); *Minnesota Sustainable Design Guide* (http://www.msdg.umn.edu).

Chapter Five: Biophilic Design

1. J. Heerwagen and B. Hase, "Building biophilia: Connecting people to nature," *Environmental Design + Construction* (March/April 2001): 30.

2. R. Pelli, personal communication, 2003.

3. G. Hildebrand, *The Origins of Architectural Pleasure* (Berkeley: University of California Press, 1999), 18.

4. See chapter four, note 12.

5. Quoted in A. Boulton, *Frank Lloyd Wright: An Illustrated Biography* (New York: Rizzoli International, 1993), 32, 49, 77.

6. Quoted in C. Bolon, R. Nelson, and L. Seidel, eds., *The Nature of Frank Lloyd Wright* (Chicago: University of Chicago Press, 1988), 76.

7. G. Hildebrand, *The Wright Space: Pattern and Meaning in Frank Lloyd Wright's Houses* (Seattle: University of Washington Press, 1991).

8. See, for example, N. Solomon, "New building systems mimic nature and return to a biocentric approach to design," *Architectural Record* (September 2, 2002): 174–82; S. Kellert, Kinship to Mastery: Biophilia in Human Evolution and Development *(Washington, DC: Island Press, 1997);* E. O. Wilson, *Biophilia: The Human Bond with Other Species* (Cambridge, MA: Harvard University Press, 1984); J. Todd and N. Todd, *From Eco-Cities to Living Machines: Principles of Ecological Design* (Berkeley, CA: North Atlantic Books, 1994); Hildebrand, *The Wright Space;* Hildebrand, *The Origins of Architectural Pleasure;* J. Appleton, *The Experience of Landscape* (London: Wiley, 1975); S. Kaplan, "Aesthetics, affect, and cognition: Environmental preference from an evolutionary perspective," *Environment and Behavior* 19 (1987): 3–32; S. Quill, *Ruskin's Venice* (Brookfield, VT: Ashgate, 2000); J. Ruskin, *The Seven Lamps of Architecture* (New York: Noonday, 1977); E. T. Cook and A. Wedderburn, eds., *The Works of John Ruskin* (London: Library Edition, 1912); J. Benyus, *Biomimicry: Innovation Inspired by Nature* (New York: William Morrow, 1997); G. Feuerstein, *Biomorphic Architecture: Human and Animal Forms in Architecture* (Stuttgart: Axel Menges, 2002); C. Jencks, *The Architecture of the Jumping Universe* (London: Chichester, 1997); S. Kaplan, R. Kaplan, and R. Ryan, *With People in Mind: Design and Management of Everyday Life* (Washington, DC: Island Press, 1998); S. Kellert and E. O. Wilson, eds., The Biophilia Hypothesis (Washington, DC: Island Press, 1993); J. Heerwagen and G. Orians, "Humans, habitats, and aesthetics," in Kellert and Wilson, eds., *The Biophilia Hypothesis;* R. Ulrich, "Biophilia, biophobia, and natural landscapes," in Kellert and Wilson, eds., *The Biophilia Hypothesis;* G. Hersey, *The Monumental Impulse: Architecture's Biological Roots* (Cambridge, MA: MIT Press, 1999); J. Barow, L. Cosmides, and J. Tooby, eds., *The Adapted Mind: Evolutionary Psychology and the Generation of Culture* (Oxford: Oxford University Press, 1992); E. Haeckel, *Art Forms in Nature* (New York: Dover, 1974); K. Bloomer, *The Nature of Ornament* (New York: Norton, 2000); D. Pearson, *Earth to Spirit: In Search of Natural Architecture* (San Francisco: Chronicle, 1995); D. Pearson, *New Organic Architecture: The Breaking Wave* (Berkeley: University of California Press, 2001); C. Day, *Places of the Soul: Architecture and Environmental Design as a Healing Art* (London: Thorsons, 1990); C. Day, *Building with the Heart* (Devon: Green Books, 1988); M. Wells, *Gentle Architecture* (New York: McGraw-Hill, 1982); C. Alexander et al., *A Pattern Language: Towns, Buildings, Construction* (New York: Oxford University Press, 1977); C. Alexander, *A Timeless Way of Building* (New York: Oxford University Press, 1979); A. Lawlor, *The Temple in the House: Finding the Sacred in Everyday Architecture* (New York: Putnam, 1994); V. Scully, *Architecture: The Natural and the Man-Made* (New York: St. Martin's, 1991); Heerwagen and Hase, "Building biophilia"; J. Heerwagen, "Do green buildings enhance the well being of workers? Yes," *Environmental Design + Construction* (July 2000): 24–34; J. Heerwagen, *Bio-Inspired Design: What Can We Learn from Nature?* (Seattle: J. Heerwagen Associates, 2003); J. Stewart-Pollack, *Perceptions of Relevance among Interior Design Professionals Concerning the Inherent Human Need for Nature in the Design of the Built Environment* (M.A. dissertation, Vermont College of Norwich University, October 1999); D. Ingber, "The architecture of life," *Scientific American* (January 1998): 48–57; J. Weiss, K. Williams, and J. Heerwagen, *Human-centered Design for Sustainable Facilities* (Seattle: J. Heerwagen Associates, 2002); J. Wise et al., *The Impact of Energy Efficiency Improvements on Students' Performance* (Richland, WA: Eco-Integrations Inc., June 7, 1999); J. Wise et al., *Protocol Development for Assessing the Ancillary Benefits of Green Buildings: A Case Study Using the MSQA Building,* NIST Special Publication 908

(Washington, DC: U.S. Department of Commerce, National Institute of Standards and Technology, 1996); R. Dubos, *Wooing of the Earth* (London: Althone, 1980); G. Katts, *The Costs and Financial Benefits of Green Buildings* (Sacramento: California Sustainable Building Task Force, 2003); C. Moore, *Water and Architecture* (New York: Harry Abrams, 1994); Rocky Mountain Institute et al., *Green Development* (New York: Wiley, 1998); D. Wann, *Deep Design* (Washington, DC: Island Press, 1996); D. Wann, *Bio-Logic: Designing with Nature to Protect the Environment* (Boulder, CO: Johnson Books, 1994); R. Crowthers, *Ecologic Architecture* (Boston: Butterworth, 1992); C. Marcus, *House as a Mirror of Self* (Berkeley, CA: Conari, 1995); S. Van der Ryn and S. Cowan, *Ecological Design* (Washington, DC: Island Press, 1996); A. Spirn, *The Granite Garden: Urban Nature and Human Design* (New York: Basic Books, 1984); J. Farmer, *Green Shift: Towards a Green Sensibility in Architecture* (Oxford: Butterworth-Heinemann, 1996); S. Brand, *How Buildings Learn* (New York: Penguin, 1994); Earth Pledge Foundation, *Sustainable Architecture White Papers: Essays on Design and Building for a Sustainable Future* (New York: Earth Pledge Foundation, 2001); W. McDonough and M. Braungart, *Cradle to Cradle: Remaking the Way We Make Things* (New York: North Point, 2002); D. Orr, *The Nature of Design; Ecology, Culture, and Human Intention* (New York: Oxford, 2002); D. Jones, *Architecture and the Environment: Bioclimatic Building Design* (New York: Overlook, 1998); BuildingGreen, *Environmental Building News: The Leading Newsletter on Environmentally Responsible Design and Construction* (Brattleboro, VT; http://www.BuildingGreen.com).

9. Pearson, *New Organic Architecture,* 8–9.

10. Feuersten, *Biomorphic Architecture,* 45, 73.

11. Rocky Mountain Institute et al., *Green Development,* 27.

12. Ulrich, "Biophilia, biophobia, and natural landscapes," 91.

13. Quoted in Hildebrand, *The Origins of Architectural Pleasure,* 29.

14. Hildebrand, *The Origins of Architectural Pleasure,* 71.

15. Moore, *Water and Architecture,* 48–49.

16. B. Coldham; D. Watson, personal communication, 2001.

17. Hildebrand, *The Origins of Architectural Pleasure.*

18. Hildebrand, *The Origins of Architectural Pleasure,* 22.

19. Hildebrand, *The Origins of Architectural Pleasure,* 102.

20. Kaplan and Kaplan, *The Experience of Nature;* Kaplan and Kaplan, *With People in Mind..*

21. Heerwagen and Orians, "Humans, habitats, and aesthetics."

22. O. Jones, *The Grammar of Ornament* (London: Studio Editions, 1986), 2.

23. Hersey, *The Monumental Impulse,* 26.

24. Hersey, *The Monumental Impulse,* 39.

25. See, for example, S. Quill, *Ruskin's Venice;* Ruskin, *The Seven Lamps of Architecture* (1977); Cook and Wedderburn, eds., *The Works of John Ruskin.*

26. J. Ruskin, *The Seven Lamps of Architecture* (1880; reprint, New York: Dover, 1989).

27. Bloomer, *The Nature of Ornament,* 138–39. This book contains many important insights on the universal practice of ornamentation and its functional relation to the human affinity for nature.

28. Alexander et al., *A Pattern Language;* Alexander, *The Timeless Way of Building.*

29. Hildebrand, *The Origins of Architectural Pleasure,* 103.

30. Heerwagen and Hase, "Building biophilia," 32. Also see Benyus, *Biomimicry.*

31. See, for example, Feuersten, *Biomorphic Architecture;* Y. Joye, *Positive Effects of Biomorphic Design on Human Wellbeing* (Netherlands: Ghent University, 2004).

32. S. Kellert, "Ecological challenge, humans values of nature, and sustainability in the built environment," in C. Kibert, ed., *Reshaping the Built Environment: Ecology, Ethics, and Environment* (Washington, DC: Island Press, 1999).

33. *The American Heritage Dictionary of the English Language,* 3rd ed. (Boston: Houghton Mifflin, 1992).

34. See note 62, chapter two.

35. Todd and Todd, *From Eco-Cities to Living Machines;* BuildingGreen, *Environmental Building News;* Rocky Mountain Institute et al., *Green Development;* Kibert, ed., *Reshaping the Built Environment;* C. Kuntsler, *The Geography of Nowhere* (New York: Touchstone, 1993); J. Corbett and M. Corbett, *Designing Sustainable Communities* (Washington, DC: Island Press, 1993); P. Calthorpe, *The Next American Metropolis: Ecology, Community, and the American Dream* (New York: Princeton Architectural Press, 1993); J. Todd, E. Brown, and E. Wells, "Ecological design applied," *Ecological Engineering* 20 (2003): 421–40; J. Todd and B. Josephson, "The design of living technologies for waste treatment," *Ecological Engineering* 6 (1996): 109–36; U.S. Environmental Protection Agency, *Our Built and Natural Environments: A Technical Review of the Interactions between Land Use, Transportation, and Environmental Quality,* EPA 231-R-01-002 (Washington, DC: U.S. Environmental Protection Agency, January 2001); Spirn, *The Granite Garden;* I. Altman and S. Low, *Place Attachment* (New York: Plenum, 1992); R. Pyle, *The Thunder Tree: Lessons from an Urban Wildland* (Boston: Houghton Mifflin, 1993); R. Platt, R. Rowntree, and P. Muick, eds., *The Ecological City: Preserving and Restoring Urban Biodiversity* (Amherst: University of Massachusetts Press, 1994); B. Brown, ed., *Eco-Revelatory Design: Nature Constructed/Nature Revealed* (Madison: University of Wisconsin Press, *Landscape Journal* Special Issue, 1988); R. Forman, *Landscape Ecology* (New York: Wiley, 1986); R. Forman et al., *Road Ecology: Science and Solutions* (Washington, DC: Island Press, 2003); R. Dramstad, J. Olson, and R. Forman, *Landscape Ecology Principles in Landscape Architecture and Land-Use Planning* (Washington, DC: Island Press, 1996); I. McHarg, *Design with Nature* (Garden City, NY: Doubleday, 1971); K. Yeang, *Designing with Nature: The Ecological Basis for Architectural Design* (New York: McGraw-Hill, 1995); J. Thompson and K. Sorvig, *Sustainable Landscape Construction: A Guide to Green Building Outdoors* (Washington, DC: Island Press, 2000); M. Leccese and K. McCormick, eds., *Charter of the New Urbanism* (New York: McGraw-Hill, 2000); K. Benfield, J. Terris, and N. Vorsanger, *Solving Sprawl: Models of Smart Growth in Communities across America* (New York: Natural Resources Defense Council, 2001); P. Katz, *The New Urbanism: Toward an Architecture of Community* (New York: McGraw-Hill, 1994); N. Dunnett and N. Kingsbury, *Planting Green Roofs and Living Walls* (Portland, OR: Timber, 2004); P. Hawken, A. Lovins, and L. Lovins, *Natural Capitalism: Creating the Next Industrial Revolution* (Boston: Little Brown, 1999); Van der Ryn and Cowan, *Ecological Design;* J. Lyle, *Regenerative Design for Sustainable Development* (New York: Wiley, 1994); S. Mendler and W. Odell, *The HOK Guidebook to Sustainable Development* (New York: Wiley, 2000); U.S. Green Building Council, *Leadership in Energy and Environmental Design (LEED) Reference Guide,* version 2.1 (Washington, DC: U.S. Green Building Council, 2003); M. Johnson, *Life on the Edge: Urban Waterfront Edges with Aquatic Habitats* (New York: Hudson River Foundation, 1991); M. Johnson, *The Opportunity to Design Post-Industrial Waterfronts in Relation to Their Ecological Context* (PhD dissertation, University of Pennsylvania, Department of City and Regional Planning, 1990).

36. McHarg, *Design with Nature.*

37. Dramstad, Olson, and Forman, *Landscape Ecology Principles.*

38. Dramstad, Olson, and Forman, *Landscape Ecology Principles,* 48.

39. Dramstad, Olson, and Forman, *Landscape Ecology Principles,* 15.

40. See, for example, chapter two, notes 63 to 68. Also see D. Canter, *The Psychology of Place* (New York: St. Martin's, 1977); Altman and Low, *Place Attachment;* V. Derr, "Voices from the mountains: Children's sense of place in three communities of northern New Mexico," *Journal of Environmental Psychology* 22 (2001): 125–37; J. Eyles, *Senses of Place* (Cheshire, Eng.: Silverbrook, 1985); D. Hayden, *The Power of Place* (Boston: MIT Press, 1997); P. Lindholdt, "Writing from a sense of place," *Journal of Environmental Education* 30 (1999): 4–12; G. Mesch and O. Manor, "Social ties, environmental perception, and local attachment," *Environment and Behavior* 30 (1998): 504–20; H. Proshansky, A. Fabian, and R. Kaminof, "Place identity: Physical world and socialization of the self," *Journal of Environmental Psychology* 3 (1983): 57–83; E. Relph, *Place and Placelessness* (London: Pion, 1976); G. Snyder, *A Place in Space* (Washington, DC: Counterpoint, 1995); D. Sobel, *Children's Special Places* (Tucson, AZ: Zephyr, 1993); R. Thayer, *LifePlace: Bioregional Thought and Practice* (Berkeley: University of California Press, 2003); Y. Tuan, *Topophilia* (New York: Columbia University Press, 1974); Y. Tuan, *Space and Place* (London: Arnold, 1977); C. Twigger-Ross and D. Uzzell, "Place and identity process," *Journal of Environmental Psychology* 16 (1996): 205–20; N. Ardoin, "Ecoregional education: Sense of place and environmentally responsible behavior at an ecoregional scale" (PhD dissertation prospectus, Yale University, School of Forestry and Environmental Studies, 2004).

41. J. Jackson, *A Sense of Place, a Sense of Time* (New Haven, CT: Yale University Press, 1994).

42. S. Weil, *The Need for Roots* (New York: Harper Colophon, 1971), 38.

43. T. Bender, *Building with the Breath of Life: Working with Chi Energy in Our Homes and Communities* (Manzanita, OR: Fire River Press, 2000); T. Bender, *Learning to Count What Really Counts: The Economics of Wholeness* (Manzanita, OR: Fire River Press, 2002); T. Bender, "Building with a soul," in J. and R. Swan, *Dialogues with the Living Earth: New Ideas on the Spirit of Place from Designers, Architects, and Innovators* (Wheaton, IL: Theosophical Publishing House, 1996); T. Bender, "Being at home with our surroundings," *Urban Ecologist* 3 (1994); T. Bender, *The Heart of Place* (Manzanita, OR: Fire River Press, 1993).

44. M. Sagoff, "Settling America or the concept of place in environmental ethics," *Journal of Energy, Natural Resources, and Environmental Law* 12 (1992): 351–418 (352).

45. Dubos, *Wooing of the Earth.*

46. Relph, *Place and Placelessness*, 6.

47. Sagoff, "Settling America," 353, 358.

48. Snyder, *A Place in Space.*

49. See, for example, Rocky Mountain Institute et al., *Green Development;* Mendler and Odell, *The HOK Guidebook to Sustainable Design.*

Chapter Six: Ethics of Sustainability

1. See, for example, World Conservation Union (IUCN)/United Nations Environmental Programme (UNEP)/World Wide Fund for Nature (WWF), *Caring for the Earth: A Strategy for Sustainable Living: Second World Conservation Strategy* (Gland, Switzerland: IUCN, UNEP, WWF, 1991); National Research Council/Board on Sustainable Development, *Our Common Journey: A Transition toward Sustainability* (Washington, DC: U.S. National Research Council, National Academy of Sciences, September 1999); G. Brundtland, "The scientific understanding of policy," *Science* 277 (1997): 5325; W. Clark and R. Munn, eds., *Sustainable Development of the Biosphere* (Cambridge, UK: Cambridge University Press, 1986); R. Kates et al., "Sustainability science," *Science* 292 (2001): 641–42.

2. S. Mendler and W. Odell, *The HOK Guidebook to Sustainable Development* (New York: Wiley, 2000), 1.

3. D. Kennedy, "Editorial: Sustainability and the commons," *Science* 32 (December 12, 2003): 1861.

4. See, for example, S. Kellert, "Values, ethics, and spiritual and scientific relations to nature," in S. Kellert and T. Farnham, eds., *The Good in Nature and Humanity: Connecting Science, Religion, and Spirituality with the Natural World* (Washington, DC: Island Press, 2002); S. Kellert, *A Biocultural Basis for an Ethic toward the Natural Environment* (plenary presentation, American Institute for Biological Sciences, Washington, DC, March 22, 2003); E. O. Wilson, "Biophilia and the conservation ethic," in S. Kellert and E. O. Wilson, eds., *The Biophilia Hypothesis* (Washington, DC: Island Press, 1993).

5. See, for example, L. Pojman, ed., *Environmental Ethics: Readings in Theory and Application* (Belmont, CA: Wadsworth/Thomson, 2001).

6. See, for example, P. Taylor, "Biocentric egalitarianism," *Environmental Ethics* 3 (1981); B. Devall and G. Sessions, *Deep Ecology* (Salt Lake City, UT: Peregrine Smith, 1985).

7. Wilson, "Biophilia and the conservation ethic," 37.

8. R. Dubos, *Wooing of the Earth* (London: Althone, 1980), 126.

9. A. Leopold, *A Sand County Almanac, with Other Essays on Conservation from Round River* (New York: Oxford University Press, 1966), 228, 241.

10. L. White, "The historical roots of our ecological crisis," *Science* 155 (1967): 1203–7.

Narrative Epilogue

One: Of Forests and the Sea

1. The section on wrens was assisted by reading E. Lawrence, *Hunting the Wren: Transformation of Bird to Symbol: A Study in Human-Animal Relationships* (Knoxville: University of Tennessee Press, 1997).

Three: Geographic Sketches Here and There

1. See statistics and references cited in S. Kellert, "Japanese perceptions of wildlife," *Conservation Biology* 5 (1991): 297–308.

Four: Seals in the Neighborhood

1. Dante, *Inferno,* canto 24, lines 46–57 (trans. and ed. T. Bergin; New York: Appleton-Century-Crofts, 1954).

Illustration Credits

Index

Island Press Board of Directors